HMONG
MEANS FREE

In the series

Asian American History and Culture,

edited by Sucheng Chan

A list of books in the series
appears at the back of this volume.

HMONG
MEANS FREE

LIFE IN LAOS AND AMERICA

Edited and with an Introduction
by Sucheng Chan

TEMPLE UNIVERSITY PRESS
Philadelphia

Temple University Press, Philadelphia 19122
Copyright © 1994 by Temple University. All rights reserved
Published 1994
Printed in the United States of America

Library of Congress Cataloging-in-Publication Data

Chan, Sucheng.
Hmong means free : Life in Laos and America/edited and with
an introduction by Sucheng Chan.
p. cm. — (Asian American history and culture series)
Includes bibliographical references.
ISBN 1-56639-162-8 — ISBN 1-56639-163-6 (pbk.)
1. Laos—History—20th century. 2. Vietnamese Conflict,
1961–1965—Personal narratives, Hmong. 3. Vietnamese
Conflict, 1961–1975—Laos. 4. Hmong (Asian people)—
History—20th century. 5. Hmong Americans—California—
Cultural assimilation. I. Series.
DS558.8.H56   1994
959.404′092′2—dc20   93-11650

Contents

Illustrations

Illustrations

Preface

The 1990 U.S. census of population counted some one hundred thousand Hmong in the United States, more than forty thousand of whom are in California. Minnesota and Wisconsin ranked next, with over sixteen thousand in each state. Many studies have been done of the Hmong since they entered the United States as refugees in the late 1970s, but few of these contain accounts of Hmong experiences told from their own perspectives. This book, the first collection devoted entirely to first-person Hmong narratives, was produced in collaboration with four of my Hmong students at the University of California, Santa Barbara.

Since Southeast Asian Studies was one of my areas of specialization in graduate school, I have been more interested than have most of my Asian American Studies colleagues in the refugees who have arrived from Vietnam, Laos, and Cambodia since Communist governments came to power in those countries in 1975. As their numbers increased, I realized it was important to document their traumatic experiences during the war, during their flight, and after their arrival in the United States. But since I do not know the Vietnamese, Cambodian, Lao, or Hmong languages, I had to find indirect ways to record their stories.

During the 1979–80 academic year, I offered a course called "The Vietnamese Experience in America" at the University of California, Berkeley. To my knowledge, that was the first time such a course (in contrast to courses on Vietnam per se) had ever been given in the United States. Since there was virtually nothing available to assign as readings, I told the students in that class that much of the course work would consist of writing. In addition to writing assignments on various topics, the students wrote their autobiographies as a way of beginning to chronicle their people's survival and adaptation. I have kept the essays from that class all these years. Selections from these autobiographies, plus others written by Vietnamese students I have taught in subsequent years at the Berkeley, Santa Cruz, San Diego, and Santa Barbara campuses of the University of California, will appear in two forthcoming books.

In contrast to the numerous Vietnamese American students I have known, no Hmong students attended any of my classes until 1989, when I began teaching at the University of California, Santa Barbara (UCSB). One day, soon after I had spent only half a lecture discussing why the Hmong have come to the United States, one of the two Hmong students in my large introductory Asian American history class told me that his siblings and cousins now all wished to attend UCSB because I had done something that no other faculty member had ever done: include the Hmong in my curriculum. Deeply touched by how much such a token inclusion had meant to my student and his family, I asked him and his friend if they would be willing to help me interview older Hmong for a study of their experiences in Laos, in the refugee camps of Thailand, and in the United States. They agreed to do so.

In time, four students—Thek Moua, Lee Fang, Vu Pao Tcha, and Maijue Xiong—became my collaborators. At first, I gave them a set of questions to ask their interviewees, but I learned very quickly that such a methodology would not work well. In Hmong culture, younger people are expected to show great respect for their elders, and since asking questions is construed as a sign of rudeness, my students felt hesitant to interrupt the interviewees when they were speaking. So we discarded the formal questions. Instead, I told my students simply to ask their elders to tell about their lives from the beginning to the present and discuss with the students whatever aspects of their lives they wished to focus on. With this change in approach, the potential *interviewees* became *narrators*.

Furthermore, rather than try to collect a representative sample—representative, that is, in a positivist social scientific sense—I asked my student collaborators to gather the life stories of selected members of their own families because I thought the latter might be more willing than others to talk freely with them in order to teach them something about their heritage. In addition, since in Hmong society members of three or more generations often live in the same household, I hoped that by asking members of different generations within the same families to recount their common experiences, generational as well as gender differences might emerge. Though no claim is made here that the life stories in this book are representative in a social scientific sense, there are enough similarities among the narratives (told by individuals who grew up in different localities) to indicate that the experiences recounted here are not unique and provide a fairly reliable picture of how the Hmong lived before and during the wars of the 1960s and 1970s. At the same time, because the narrators talked about many topics, this book offers multifaceted and nuanced portraits of Hmong life during that period.

In addition to the narratives of the students' family members, there are two life stories, in Chapter One, that are included in this volume because the narrators have played a central role in helping other Hmong families to settle in Santa Barbara County. Jou Yee Xiong, the head of the Xiong family in Goleta, was the first person whom my students and I interviewed. He was an important community leader in Laos and, to this day, he is considered a leader of the Hmong community that has been transposed to Santa Barbara County. Local Hmong say he is more knowledgeable about the history of his people than anyone else in the area. His son, Ka Pao Xiong, has played an even more important role: he has served as the key link between the Hmong residents and various social service agencies in Santa Barbara County. His account reveals how a few educated individuals like him managed to help a people—who, until quite recently, depended on slash-and-burn agriculture for survival—to learn to function in the highly technological society of the United States.

The students began taping the narratives during their visits home. Sometimes, unable to finish, they simply left a tape recorder behind and asked the relevant family member to keep talking into it. We discovered that the information recorded during these unmonitored sessions was sometimes qualitatively better than what was said in face-to-face situations. Though more repetitive, these segments contained more details and more personal sentiments. This is particularly true of the women narrators. I had asked the students to talk to their grandmothers or mothers alone, without the presence of the menfolk, if at all possible, because I had noticed during the first interviews (which I attended) that men often interrupted women as they talked. As a result of this strategy, two grandmothers quite freely expressed their bitterness toward their deceased husbands, thus highlighting some of the ways in which women were mistreated in Hmong society. The stories told by the other women in this book also indicate very clearly the crucial contributions that Hmong women make: it is they who perform most of the backbreaking work in subsistence as well as cash-crop farming in their homeland.

This book also includes four autobiographies written in English by my student collaborators, each of whom gave a title to his or her work. The rest of the life stories, in contrast, are neither verbatim oral history transcripts nor written autobiographies. Rather, they are best described as twice-mediated tales. The first round of mediation occurred when my students translated the taped narrations into English. The vocabulary they used reflects both the colloquial American English they have picked up (such as "you guys," which I changed to "you children" in the case of a mother speaking to her children) as well as some of the more technical concepts they have learned in college (such as a shaman's "altered state of consciousness," or "culture shock," which I left as written).

Sometimes it is quite obvious that they used words or terms that reflect concepts or practices that probably do not exist in Hmong society. For example, one student, in translating her mother's story, had written that her grandmother "dated" many men. I changed the word "dated" to "saw" because dating, as a social practice, is culturally specific to American society, though it has now been adopted by young people in cities around the world. In other words, although "courtship" is a near-universal phenomenon, "dating" originally was quite American.

These and other editorial changes I have made in my students' English translations represent the second round of filtering. I corrected grammatical and spelling errors, rearranged some sentences and paragraphs for greater coherence, and eliminated some place names and minute details that might have caused confusion. The few minor additions that I made for the sake of clarity are shown in square brackets. For example, because most Americans know so little about

Laos, I indicated in square brackets that Vientiane is that country's administrative capital, where major government offices are located. (Until 1975, Laos also had a royal capital—Luang Prabang—where the king and his family resided.) I even inserted brief explanations for certain facts about the United States. For example, I indicated that Isla Vista is contiguous to the campus of the University of California at Santa Barbara, because this bit of information is relevant to understanding why one of the first Hmong families to be resettled in the United States came to Isla Vista, given the pivotal role that some University of California, Santa Barbara, students played in the process.

Let me explain why I decided to edit my students' English translations. I have no doubt that, like most people speaking in their native language, the speech of the Hmong is *not* "broken." Therefore, it would be an insult to them to translate their stories into an English script that contains grammatical and spelling errors, under the misguided notion that such a rendering would be more "authentic." My students made errors because they had to learn English as a second language. They very much wanted me to "clean up" their translations and their own writings, so that they read as smoothly as possible. They know, and I know, that one distinct form that racism in America has taken is the singsong pidgin English that many writers have used to depict the speech of Asian immigrants. As young immigrants, they have been taunted repeatedly for looking different and for not speaking English like "real Americans." Such humiliation is something that I myself also experienced when I arrived in the United States at the age of fifteen. For these reason, we do not want to present the life stories in poor English.

I am cognizant of the argument made by practitioners of the "new ethnography" that an unequal power relationship exists between indigenous informants, or narrators, vis-à-vis the scholars who record them and inevitably tamper with the material they record. While the editorial changes I have made may be criticized as an imposition of my "academic agenda" upon the storytellers, a different interpretation. is also possible: what I have tried to do is to make it possible for the narrators to share the stories of their lives with non–Hmong readers. The five English-speaking narrators (the four students and Ka Pao Xiong) read over each of the edited stories, made changes in them, and approved them for publication. Thus the editing was done with the explicit consent of individuals who represented themselves as well as members of their families.

Though my methodology may involve more tampering than is acceptable to those scholars who believe in the pristine nature of the words uttered by women or indigenous narrators, this book is the best approximation of Hmong "voices" we have available at present. For those who understand Hmong and would like to hear what the narrators actually said, I have deposited the original cassette tapes in the special collections department of the university library at the University of California, Santa Barbara.

The life stories recounted in this volume are valuable because they describe not only the myriad hardships the Hmong have experienced in Laos—a country ravaged by decades of war and revolution—and in the miserable refugee camps in Thailand, but they also indicate how some Hmong feel about their lives in the United States today. These reflections reveal many emotions, even though in traditional Hmong culture individuals are not supposed to show their feelings in public at all. In short, these are stories not only of suffering, but also of strength, courage, determination, and dignity.

Since it is now widely recognized that an author's or an editor's "position" greatly influences his or her scholarly writings, I would like to state my convictions regarding American involvement in the wars in Vietnam, Laos, and Cambodia and my attitude toward refugees from those countries who have settled in the United States. Throughout the war, I was an antiwar activist. Along with other left-leaning young Americans, I disparaged those who collaborated with the United States—especially South Vietnam's political and military elite and the Hmong mercenary soldiers in Laos paid by the U.S. Central Intelligence Agency—because they seemed to represent forces of venality and corruption.

Since 1975, the intellectual and political lenses through which I view that war have not changed much, but as I became acquainted with the refugee students from those countries, I have added a new dimension to my thinking. Sympathizing with their suffering and admiring their courage, I decided it is important to relate to them as human beings, rather than as children of people who may have espoused ideologies or engaged in actions to which I was opposed.

I became mindful of the fact that the immense problems that their homelands have experienced since the war ended—problems that have led to the unprecedented exodus of refugees—resulted from the enormous destruction unleashed upon those nations by America's most sophisticated weaponry during that long, sad war, as well as from failings of the present leaders of Vietnam, Laos, and Cambodia and their policies.

Sobered by the recognition that cruelty and exploitation are not confined to any one political system, whenever I have tried to integrate the experiences of these refugees from Southeast Asia into the larger story of Asian Americans, I have chosen to emphasize the tragic commonalities that mark the human condition. Though I do want my students to understand the conflicting political causes espoused by succeeding generations of leaders in various Asian countries *and* by U.S. foreign policymakers during the Cold War, I try to examine this history in a way that does not make anyone in my classes feel guilty. As many generations of students have taught me, when some individuals in a class feel defensive, it becomes difficult for the class as a whole to learn from each other and from history. It is in this spirit of enhancing understanding and mutual respect that this book has been created.

Given the range of topics covered in the narratives, this anthology is suitable for assignment not only in Asian American Studies, Ethnic Studies, Women's Studies, and U.S. immigration history courses, but also in courses on the family taught within sociology, anthropology, or psychology departments. And, of course, since the narratives deal with events in Laos, this book would be appropriate as a text in courses on Southeast Asia and on the American involvement in the wars in Laos, Cambodia, and Vietnam. Students taking courses in these fields, with the exception of those enrolled in Southeast Asian Studies, are unlikely to know a great deal about Laos and about the Hmong, however. That is why I have written a lengthy introduction to place the life stories into their larger historical, political, and social contexts. However, there are topics I probably do not delve into in sufficient depth to satisfy those who are especially interested in cultural differences among new immigrants and refugees and between them and Euro-Americans. Readers who are more interested in the kinship system, religion, customs, or other aspects of

A Hmong family in their village in Laos. *Courtesy of Kazoua Lo.*

A Hmong family in front of their house in Laos. *Courtesy of Kazoua Lo.*

A Hmong family in their poppy fields in Laos. *Courtesy of Kazoua Lo.*

Hmong performing a ritual in Laos. *Courtesy of Kazoua Lo.*

the social organization of Hmong life than in their political history may refer to the extensive bibliography I have provided to facilitate further study. This bibliography lists most of the available English-language writings about the Hmong and a selection of the existing literature on Laos.

My student collaborators, Lee Fang, Thek Moua, Vu Pao Tcha, and Maijue Xiong, who have adapted to life in the United States and are doing well in college, represent the "success stories" in the Hmong American community. But the success they have achieved is only part of the picture, since a vast majority of the Hmong continue to live in poverty, without much hope for improving their lot. Thus, while these four students may appear to be further examples of Asian Americans who, for the past quarter-century, have been touted by journalists and scholars alike as the "model minority," their accomplishments are, in fact, the exception rather than the rule.

Maijue, Vu, Thek, Lee, and I have produced this book because we hope it will enable other Americans to better understand the Hmong. At the same time, we like to think that the life stories collected here will serve as a record of the legacy that young Hmong Americans, who may no longer know the language of their ancestors, are inheriting today as they struggle to find a place for themselves in the multiethnic and multicultural society that is America.

Santa Barbara   SUCHENG CHAN
May 1993

Acknowledgments

I thank the Academic Senate Committee on Research at the University of California, Santa Barbara, for two grants that paid my student collaborators a salary while they collected the life stories. The funds also paid for the three maps prepared by D. J. McLaren of the university's Instructional Resources office. Most of all, I thank the narrators who have shared with us their interesting and inspiring life stories. And, of course, without the hard work of Lee Fang, Thek Moua, Vu Pao Tcha, and Maijue Xiong—members of the first generation of college-educated Hmong Americans—this book would not have been possible. I also extend my appreciation to Professors Daniel S. Lev of the University of Washington and K. Scott Wong of Williams College, who offered helpful comments that improved the manuscript. Finally, I am grateful to Mary Capouya of Temple University Press for guiding the manuscript's transformation into a book.

Personal and Place Names

Hmong is a monosyllabic language that had no written script until Western missionaries devised one for it in the early 1950s. When translating the narratives in this book, my students sometimes transliterated personal and place names in the romanized Hmong script and sometimes according to their sounds in English. To enable those who do not know the Hmong language to pronounce the names in this book, they are written as they sound in English, rather than in the romanized Hmong script.

The full name of most Hmong men consists of three words. In Laos, a person's clan name is placed first. There are about twenty Hmong clans. The most common clan names found among the Hmong now living in the United States are Cha (spelled Tcha by the family whose stories are told in Chapter Four of this book), Fang, Her, Ly (also spelled Lee), Lo (also spelled Lor), Moua, Thao, Vang, Vue, Xiong, and Yang. A Hmong male usually has two given names: one given in childhood and another conferred on him when he is an adult. When written in English, each of these three words is capitalized. Some individuals, however, do not have or use an adult name. Thus, the famous Hmong general, Vang Pao, has only two words in his name—Vang, his clan name, and Pao, his given name. A married woman keeps her father's clan name and does not adopt her husband's, even though she becomes a formal member of the latter's clan. Most women do not receive an adult name and use only the one given them during childhood. A small number of well-known, French-educated Hmong, such as Touby Lyfong and Faydang Lobliayao, have joined together their fathers' entire names and used them as their last names, which they write in the Western order. (That is to say, Touby Lyfong's father's name was Ly Fong, while Faydang Lobliayao's father's name was Lo Blia Yao.) Since Western writers have referred to these two individuals by the idiosyncratic form of their names, that convention is followed in this book.

When reference is made to individuals while they were living in Laos, the Hmong name sequence is given, with clan name first. After their arrival in the United States, however, their names are shown in the Western order, with the clan name used as the last name. Other modifications also occur. For example, Maijue Xiong has joined her two given names together (as I have also done with my Chinese given name, Sucheng, which I do not hyphenate, as many Chinese do) to encourage people to call her by her full given name. Thek Moua and Lee Fang, on the other hand, use only one of their given names to make it easier for their non-Hmong friends to remember.

There is great inconsistency in how place names in Laos, Vietnam, and Thailand are transliterated in English. For those places that can be located in a standard atlas, I have followed the most commonly used form—for example, Long Cheng is written as two separate words, but Thakhek is a single word, as shown in most atlases. For places that cannot be found on even very large and detailed maps, I have written their names as single words. That many places mentioned by the narrators could not be located on a map is not surprising, given the Hmong's old habit of moving away from their villages when the fertility of the soil was depleted in the surrounding countryside. Entire families, or even clans, would pull up stakes and establish a new village some distance away, slashing and burning a new section of the jungle for cultivation. They did this every seven to ten years, or even more frequently if the soil was poor. Unless other families moved into the old villages, these settlements ceased to exist after the original residents moved out.

Laos is the name of the country that is today called the Lao People's Democratic Republic. *Laotian* refers to all persons who are citizens of Laos, regardless of the ethnic group they belong to (Laos has more than sixty ethnic groups). *Laotian* is also used as an adjective to describe events, places, or things related to Laos as a whole. *Lao,* without the *s,* on the other hand, is the name of the dominant ethnic group in Laos, as well as the name of their language. Since *Laotian* is an Anglicized word, an *s* is added when the word is plural; in contrast, for *Hmong, Lao,* and *Thai,* which are transliterated words, no *s* is added when more than one individual is being referred to. *Rai* is a unit of land measurement in Laos and is equivalent to one-sixth of an acre.

Pre-1975 Laos and Southeast Asia

HMONG
MEANS FREE

General Vang Pao lecturing his troops in Long Cheng, Laos. *Courtesy of Xang Mao Xiong.*

The Hmong Experience in Asia and the United States

The Hmong living in the United States today came from Laos, a small landlocked country in mainland Southeast Asia. Their ancestors originated in southwestern China, in the provinces of Yunnan, Guizhou, Sichuan, and Hunan. For several thousand years, the central Chinese government dominated by Han Chinese basically left the Hmong (called Miao by the Chinese) alone, as long as they paid their tributes to the Chinese. However, the last dynasty in China, the Qing (1644–1911), founded by Manchus, followed a different policy. Qing armies and officials oppressed the Hmong, who rose in rebellion. In the early nineteenth century, this political persecution, along with increasing population pressure, led some of the Hmong to migrate southward into mainland Southeast Asia, where they settled in the mountainous regions of northern Burma, Thailand, Laos, and Vietnam.

Today there are still more Hmong in China—estimates range from 2.8 to 5 million, depending on whether one counts only the Hmong or combines all their cognate groups[1]—than in Southeast Asia and the rest of the world combined. There has never been an accurate count of how many Hmong live in each of the Southeast Asian countries. Virtually all those who have settled in the United States, however, have come from Laos, where they may have numbered as many as three hundred thousand in the 1960s.[2] Perhaps half of that number remains in Laos today and little is known about how they are faring. The hundred thousand or so now in the United States were forced to come here as a result of their "American connection," as will be discussed later in this introduction.

Laos: Geography, History, and Ethnic Composition

Measuring approximately ninety-one thousand square miles, Laos shares borders with five countries: Thailand to its west, Burma to its northwest, China to its north, Vietnam to its east, and Cambodia to its south. The country's major means of transportation is the Mekong River, which flows along much of Laos's present western boundary with Thailand. The Laotian stretch of the Mekong is divided by rapids into three navigable segments. From the end of the seventeenth to the late nineteenth century, three kingdoms existed in the area that is now Laos: Luang Prabang in the north, Vientiane in the middle, and Champassak in the south. In addition, the principality of Xieng Khouang occupied the northeastern part of present-day Laos. The two major plateaus within Laos, both of which are approximately three thousand feet above sea level, are the Plain of Jars (so called by the French because of the numerous large stone burial jars found there) in Xieng Khouang and the Bolovens Plateau in the southern panhandle of the country. South of the Plain of Jars lies the Phou Bia Massif—a mountain range that rises to almost ten thousand feet. Xieng Khouang and the Phou Bia mountains, as we shall see, have both been important in the history of the Hmong in Laos.

The only country that can be reached easily from Laos is Thailand. Between Laos and Vietnam lies the Annamite Cordillera—a range of mountains traversable at only six passes. High mountains similarly hinder access to Burma and China. The impassable cataracts of the Mekong River near the town of Khone and the Dangrek Range make movement between Laos and Cambodia difficult.

The Laotian sense of national identity, based primarily on the history of its dominant ethnic group, the lowland Lao, was formed during the reign of Fa Ngum, who founded the kingdom of Lan Xang ("land of a million elephants") in 1353, with its capital at Luang Prabang. The Lao concept of kingship was underpinned by Theravada

Buddhism and supported by the *sangha,* the monastic order, thereby endowing the king with both temporal and spiritual powers. The Buddhist monks provided the only education that existed in Laos until very recent times; they imparted to Lao young men the moral precepts of the Buddha, which stressed making spiritual merit by doing worldly good.

Despite the physical barriers that divided it from its neighbors, the kingdom of Lan Xang was repeatedly invaded. In the late fifteenth century, Vietnamese armies marched through Xieng Khouang all the way to the capital at Luang Prabang and held that city for a time before they were repelled. During the sixteenth century, Siam (the old name for Thailand) and Burma invaded Lan Xang five times, causing the reigning monarch to move the capital to Vientiane. Toward the end of the seventeenth century, disputes over succession broke Lan Xang into the aforementioned three kingdoms. The eighteenth century saw Burma sack Luang Prabang in 1753 and again in 1771, and Siam attack Vientiane in 1778. In the early nineteenth century, the Siamese again invaded Vientiane and reduced it to ruins, while the Vietnamese claimed the provinces of Xieng Khouang and Khammouane. The Laotian kingdoms managed to survive by acknowledging the suzerainty of both Siam and Vietnam.[3] Toward the end of the nineteenth century, a new imperial power, France, appeared on the scene and eventually made Laos into one of its five Asian colonial possessions (six, if one counts a small territory France held in southern China).

More than sixty ethnic groups belonging to several linguistic families are found in Laos. The dominant political and cultural group, the Lao, belongs to the Tai-speaking peoples called the Lao Loum ("Lao of the lowlands"). The Lao people occupy the lowlands of the Mekong valley on both sides of the Thai–Laotian border, and those in Laos comprise a little less than half of the total Laotian population. They grow rice in wet paddies for their staple and sugarcane and tropical fruits as cash crops. In the highlands dwell the Lao Theung ("Lao of the mountain slopes"), who speak Mon-Khmer languages and occupy the lower elevations, and the Lao Soung ("Lao of the mountain tops"), who speak Tibeto-Burman languages and live at elevations above three thousand feet. The two major Lao Soung groups are the Hmong and the Iu Mien.

The word Hmong means "free." However, older generations of

3

Western scholars and the lowland Lao have referred to the Hmong as Meo, which means "savage"—a term that the Hmong find derisive and unacceptable. The Iu Mien have been called Yao or Man in the existing literature, while the Lao Theung have been called Kha, which means "slave"—another derogatory name.* The Hmong and other highlanders cultivate dry upland rice and corn as staples and the opium poppy as a cash crop.[4] When French colonialists arrived, they introduced coffee and cotton as cash crops, but it is opium, more than any other product, that has drawn Laos into the modern capitalist world economy.

Laos and the Hmong under French Colonial Rule

In the history of Western colonialism in Southeast Asia, the French were relative latecomers. The Portuguese set up trading posts in Southeast Asia in the late fifteenth century, the Spanish claimed the Philippines in the sixteenth, the Dutch colonized Indonesia in the seventeenth, the British established settlements in Malaya in the late eighteenth and early nineteenth, but the French did not make any real efforts to acquire colonies in that part of the world until the mid-nineteenth century, though some French Catholic missionaries and traders had begun coming to Siam and Vietnam by the latter part of the seventeenth century.[5]

In 1858, the French sent the first of several naval expeditions to Danang, a port on the eastern seaboard of Vietnam. At that point they were interested mainly in securing the right to trade and not territorial aggrandizement per se, but the Vietnamese, who had chafed for almost ten centuries under Chinese rule, fiercely resisted the French and drove their ships off. Three years later, however, the French returned and took Saigon. Located in the southern part of Vietnam, Saigon became the beachhead for the French conquest of the rest of what eventually became French Indochina.

Saigon lies just north of the mouths of the Mekong River in the rich alluvial lands of the Mekong Delta. The Vietnamese call this

---

*Thousands of Iu Mien have also settled in the United States as refugees. [*Ed.*]

part of their country Nam Bo, meaning "southern region," while the French called it Cochin China after they annexed it. Since part of the fertile delta lies in Cambodia (which by then had become a mere shadow of the resplendent civilization that had existed there during the heyday of the Angkor empire in the late twelfth and early thirteenth centuries), the French decided to gain control over Cambodia also. They established a protectorate there in 1863.

As a prelude to further colonization, the French sent an exploratory party up the Mekong River in 1866, with the mistaken notion that the waterway might provide a route into China. China was in fact the country that the French were most interested in, but because the British had so firmly established their economic, political, and military presence there after the two Opium Wars (1839–42 and 1856–60), the French had to try to find a backdoor to China. The explorers discovered that the Mekong River is not navigable at certain locations where rapids interrupt its course. Later, hoping that perhaps the Red River, which runs from southern China through northern Vietnam and drains into the Gulf of Tonkin, would provide the route into China that they sought, the French conquered northern Vietnam in 1882. The Vietnamese call that part of their country Bac Bo, meaning "northern region," while the French dubbed it Tonkin. In August of the following year, the French occupied the royal Vietnamese capital at Hue, located in central Vietnam—an area called Truong Bo, meaning "central region," by the Vietnamese and Annam by the French.

Having acquired all of Vietnam, the French now thought of themselves as heir to the Vietnamese claims in neighboring Laos. Since the Siamese had tried repeatedly in the late 1880s and early 1890s to consolidate their hold over the Laotian kingdoms, when the French, in the person of Auguste Pavie, appeared on the scene, the Laotian rulers were willing to consider placing themselves under French protection as a counterweight to domination by the Siamese. Pavie had gained the favor of the king of Luang Prabang after he saved the old monarch's life during a raid on the latter's capital in 1887.

During this period, the British also became involved in this part of the world when they conquered upper Burma. They wished to keep Siam (which lies between Burma and Laos) as a neutral buffer state and in 1892 told the French that they would not stand in the way, should the latter wish to take over Laotian territory east of the Mekong River, as long as the French did not encroach upon the valley of the Menam Chao Praya—the river that flows through the heartland of what is now central Thailand. Following this understanding, when French and Siamese troops clashed, France used the skirmishes as a pretext to demand that Siam cede all territories east of the Mekong River to France. In the face of France's superior military power, Siam acceded to this demand in the Franco–Siamese Treaty of 1893. In 1904 and 1907, Siam was also forced to cede the provinces of Sayaboury and Champassak, respectively, which lie west of the Mekong, to France.[6]

Within French Indochina—composed now of Tonkin, Annam, Cochin China, Cambodia, and Laos—the French considered landlocked Laos the least important colony. In contrast to the forty thousand or so French people who descended upon the three regions of Vietnam to govern the local population and to exploit the natural resources there, only a hundred French colonial servants were allotted for Laos. This handful of Frenchmen administered Laos with the aid of Vietnamese, whom they brought to Laos to serve in the lower echelons of the colonial bureaucracy and in the Garde Indigène, a local militia. Meanwhile, the Chinese, who had traded in Laos for centuries, were encouraged to continue handling the retail and wholesale trade of the colony.

Since the number of administrative personnel was minimal, the French relied on the existing Laotian political structure as much as possible to maintain law and order. For example, the king of Luang Prabang negotiated successfully with the French to retain his throne, and the kingdom of Luang Prabang was ruled indirectly—at least in theory. In fact, however, the French governor-general of Laos exercised full authority over the king. Members of the Luang Prabang royal family as well as those from Xieng Khouang and Champassak were allowed to retain their social status but had very little political power. The French controlled the royal houses mainly by reserving the right to approve who might succeed the king of Luang Prabang or any of the princes whenever one of them died. Naturally, they always chose compliant figureheads. Outside the kingdom of Luang Prabang, Laotians came under direct French rule.

The French made Vientiane the administrative capital of Laos and divided the country into fourteen provinces called *khoueng,* each of which was in turn carved into cantons called *muong.* The *muong* were divided into districts called *tasseng,* each of which was made up of villages called *ban.* Lao village chiefs served as intermediaries between the French colonial administrators and their Vietnamese assistants, on the one hand, and their own people, the Lao, as well as other ethnic groups, on the other hand.

The French made little effort to develop Laos economically, socially, or culturally. After discovering that their hopes of creating a river empire in the colony was but a pipe dream, the only resource they tried to exploit was the country's tin deposits. They built few roads and no railways in Laos, as they had elsewhere in French Indochina. In the six decades that the French ruled Laos, they did not establish a single high school in the colony. In 1940, a total of only seven thousand Laotian youngsters were attending primary school.[7] Those who desired and could afford a high school education had to go to Vietnam or France to get one. To make Laos pay for itself, the French found four ways to raise revenue: by levying a head tax on all males between the ages of eighteen and sixty; by taxing the sale of opium, alcohol, and salt; by requiring each adult male to perform unpaid *corvée* labor; and by establishing a government monopoly on opium. The first three means of raising revenues are described below, while the French colonial government's opium monopoly will be dealt with in the next section.

The head tax was onerous because it had to be paid in cash. At that time, Laos had a subsistence and barter economy. To pay their taxes in cash, people had to find ways to produce commodities that could be sold for money. In many instances, they had to pay more than the officially imposed amount because the tax collectors demanded additional money for their own pockets. The taxes on opium, alcohol, and salt were imposed on everyone, regardless of whether or not a person consumed any of the taxed items.[8] The *corvée* required each adult male to contribute fifteen to twenty days of work a year. Not only were the men not paid for such work but, as Jou Yee Xiong, one of the narrators in this book, recalls, they often had to walk long distances to the work sites and had to supply their own food. The laborers cleared jungles, removed rocks from rivers, built and repaired roads, served as porters and messengers, and performed other kinds of hard, common labor. It was possible to buy off one's *corvée* requirement by paying an additional tax. Fines, imposed for even minor infringements, further enriched the colonial coffers.

Though the receipts from these various forms of taxation and from fines covered only about 15 percent of the colonial budget,[9] they imposed great hardship on the people, some of whom resisted by rising up against the French in the late nineteenth and early twentieth centuries. Only a few studies of these uprisings have been made, but a number of historians believe that resentment over taxation and the *corvée* was the main cause of the insurrections, even though some of them were led by religious figures and were millenarian in character.[10] Most of the rebels were highlanders because the French, who administered some of the areas occupied by the hill tribes as military outposts, were especially harsh on them. The French practice of using Lao chieftains and a few educated Tai Dam (the Black Tai, another ethnic group) to collect taxes from the highlanders meant that the payment of taxes was not tempered by any bonds of kinship or ethnic solidarity.

The first large anti-French uprising was undertaken by Lao Theung groups in the Bolovens Plateau in southern Laos from 1901 to 1907. One of the defeated leaders of this revolt escaped; many years later he led a more widespread movement that lasted from 1924 to 1936.[11] In northern Laos, Tai-speaking groups revolted from 1914 to 1923 in Nam Tha Province, in 1916 in Houa Phan Province, and in 1918 in Phong Saly Province.[12] The Hmong in Xieng Khouang Province revolted in 1919 under the leadership of Chao Bat Chay. The revolt actually began in the adjacent area of Dien Bien Phu across the border in Vietnam. When troops under French command chased Chao Bat Chay and his followers across the mountains into Laos, the band gained adherents among the Hmong in Xieng Khouang Province by calling for the establishment of an independent Hmong kingdom. The insurrection ended in 1921 when someone betrayed Chao Bat Chay to the French.[13]

In an effort to prevent a recurrence of such acts of resistance, the French established an autonomous Hmong *tasseng* (district) at Nong Het, to the east of the Plain of Jars near the Laotian–Vietnamese border, and allowed the Hmong there to govern themselves. Hmong organize themselves socially into exogamous clans; the Nong Het region had been settled by three clans from China—the Lo, the Ly, and the Moua. The two dominant ones in the 1920s and 1930s were the Lo and Ly clans. Traditionally, the Lo clan was allied with the Luang Prabang royal family, while the Ly clan was allied with the Xieng Khouang royal family.

The head of each of these clans desired the *tasseng* chief's position once it was established because it was very lucrative: the incumbent served as the broker for the sale of all the opium grown in the mountains surrounding the Plain of Jars in Xieng Khouang Province. According to the rules of the opium monopoly that the French had established in 1899 for Indochina, the only place that was allowed to grow opium legally was Xieng Khouang Province, although contraband opium was cultivated elsewhere. Profits from the opium monopoly contributed from 15 to 40 percent of the colonial budget at any given time.

The Lo and Ly clans, which had shared power in Nong Het, got into a feud in 1922. In 1918, Ly Fong, a bright and ambitious member of the Ly clan, tried to advance himself socially by kidnapping and marrying the favorite daughter of Lo Blia Yao, the head of the Lo clan. Even though Ly Fong already had a wife and children, the Hmong practiced polygamy as well as bride kidnapping, and Ly Fong's action was nothing unusual. Lo Blia Yao not only acquiesced to the marriage but made his new son-in-law his secretary. Ly Fong's new wife gave birth to a son, Touby, and a daughter. In 1922 she committed suicide after her husband allegedly beat her. In anger and sorrow, her father fired Ly Fong and severed all ties between the Lo and Ly clans.

According to Gary Y. Lee, a Hmong anthropologist now living in Australia, Lo Blia Yao's eldest son, Song Tou, administered Nong Het, but the French became dissatisfied and dismissed him in 1938. When Ly Fong offered himself for the position, the French appointed him, but he died one year later. The French then held an election and Faydang, the second son of Lo Blia Yao, ran against Touby, the son of Ly Fong. The larger number of votes went to Touby, not only because he was more educated (he and his two half-brothers were the first Hmong to receive high school diplomas), but also, according to Lee, "because Faydang's father had alienated many Hmong in the past through his authoritarian leadership."[14]

Some Western scholars, however, have given a slightly different version of the story, stating that the French divided Nong Het into two subdistricts, with Song Tou as chief of one and Ly Fong's eldest son (from his first wife) as chief of the other. According to this version, when the French chose Ly Fong to succeed Song Tou, Faydang went to see a member of the Luang Prabang royal family and asked him to intercede on his behalf. The prince got the French to promise that upon Ly Fong's retirement or death, Faydang would be appointed to the post that his elder brother had held. However, when Ly Fong died, the French broke their promise to Faydang and, instead, made Touby his father's successor.[15]

The antagonism between the Lo and Ly clans eventually became entangled in national and international politics and has continued to the present day. Toward the end of World War II, as the Free French (the anti-Nazi French resistance movement) parachuted commandos into the Plain of Jars to prepare for the French recolonization of Laos after the end of hostilities, they were aided by Touby Lyfong and his men. Later, when Americans started arriving, Touby Lyfong joined their counterinsurgency efforts against the Laotian and North Vietnamese Communists. Although, in time, Touby's importance was eclipsed by a young Hmong military leader named Vang Pao (who commanded the secret Hmong army that the U.S. Central Intelligence Agency recruited, supported, and used in the U.S. war against Communism in North Vietnam and Laos), he remained the titular head of the pro-Western group of Hmong until 1975.

Meanwhile, Touby Lyfong's rival, Faydang Lobliayao, followed an opposite political path. He formed a Meo Resistance League in 1946[16] and joined the Lao Issara, a nationalist group formed to secure Laotian independence at the end of World War II. When the Lao Issara split into factions, Faydang aligned himself with the one led by Prince Souphanouvong, which in 1950 became known as the Pathet Lao. (Pathet Lao literally means "land of the Lao," but popular American usage has made the term synonymous with "Laotian Communists.") Souphanouvong joined forces with the Viet Minh, an organization working for Vietnamese independence under the leadership of the revolutionary, Ho Chi Minh. Faydang became an important leader within the Pathet Lao. The Pathet Lao and the secret Lao People's Party it founded in 1955 came to power in 1975, establishing the Lao

People's Democratic Republic. Until his death in 1986, Faydang was the highest-ranking Hmong, first within the Pathet Lao and, after 1975, in the government of the Lao People's Democratic Republic.

Regardless of which external power was acting as overlord, the Hmong have consistently played a significant role in the political life of Laos for a number of reasons. First, they lived in the strategic border region between North Vietnam and Laos—one of the most fiercely contested terrains during the successive phases of the Indochinese conflict. Second, they have been extraordinarily hardy soldiers, capable of operating effectively both as guerrillas in the jungles and mountains and as regular troops in positional warfare. Third, they grew the opium that helped finance the French colonial adventure from the 1890s to the 1950s, the Japanese occupation from 1941 to 1945, and the American involvement in Indochina in the 1960s and early 1970s.

Given the pivotal role of opium in this story, we need to understand what opium is: how it is grown, processed, and sold; its role in the economic life of the hill tribes people of northern Burma, Thailand, Laos, and Vietnam; how it has become a commodity in the international contraband drug traffic; why those who deal in narcotics value it so much; and how it has been used to finance political activities and influence the fate of nations.

Opium and the Hmong

In relying upon opium as a source of revenue, the French were simply following in the footsteps of the British—the paramount power in Asia in the nineteenth century. Opium, an effective analgesic, has been used medicinally in small quantities for thousands of years. Asia did not have a large population of opium addicts, however, until the British smuggled increasing quantities of the drug into China during the eighteenth and nineteenth centuries in an effort to reverse Great Britain's negative trade balance with China. Thus, widespread opium addiction was one of the scourges that came to Asia with Western imperialism.

As the number of addicts in China increased and opium addiction began to afflict people from all socioeconomic backgrounds, the Chinese central government made an attempt to stop its illegal importation. In the city of Canton in southern China, an imperial commissioner seized twenty thousand chests of opium in British warehouses and burned the whole supply. In response, Great Britain sent a naval squadron to punish the Chinese, who lost the first Opium War in 1842. China was forced to pay a huge indemnity in silver to the British, open five ports to trade, limit the amount of custom duty it could charge on foreign imports, allow Christian missionaries to proselytize, and cede the island of Hong Kong to Great Britain. China's defeat meant that the opium trade would continue to flourish. In 1860, China lost a second war over opium, this time to Great Britain and France, and had to make additional concessions to the Western powers. French and British troops occupied Canton for several years, while China was forced to legalize the importation of opium. Thereafter, the number of addicts increased even more rapidly.

During this period, the Chinese emigrating to various places in Southeast Asia introduced the opium-smoking habit to the local inhabitants. With a ready clientele, the French colonial governors of Indochina decided to cover some administrative costs by creating a government monopoly over the manufacture, sale, and use of opium. They made money by controlling the processing of raw opium into smoking opium and by opening several thousand opium dens and shops throughout French Indochina to induce an ever larger number of people to become addicts.

Raw opium is the resin from *Papaver somniferum,* a species of poppy. There are twenty-eight genera and some two hundred and fifty species of poppy, but only one produces opium.[17] The active ingredient in opium is morphine, an alkaloid first isolated in its pure form by a German chemist in 1805. In addition to being a potent pain killer, morphine also creates a sense of euphoria in those who use it. Repeated usage, however, leads to a chemical dependency or addiction.[18] In the remote mountains of Southeast Asia, where no modern health facilities existed, opium was usually the only drug available to treat a variety of ailments, and its use was widely accepted.

The Hmong had learned to cultivate the opium poppy before their migration from China; in Laos, they grew small amounts for their own use and for trade. As the life stories in this book show, opium was one of the three main crops that most Hmong families grew. (The other two were rice for their own consumption and corn for their domestic animals.) The laborious work of planting the poppy seeds, thinning the seedlings, weeding the field, and harvesting the opium crop was done mainly by women. The opium was either sold for cash or exchanged for items the Hmong did not produce themselves. The latter included iron to be made into tools, silver to be made into jewelry, kerosene for lamps, textiles, salt, and other basic necessities. (Aside from opium, domestic animals were the only other tradable or salable items that the Hmong produced.) After the French came and began to tax them, the Hmong relied on the sale of opium for cash to pay taxes.[19]

The opium poppy grows best in rich, alkaline soil, so opium farmers in the highlands of Southeast Asia often look for land near outcroppings of limestone. In Laos, the plants only thrive at three thousand feet or more above sea level. The mature plants like a southern or western exposure, which provides the right amount of sunlight. The Hmong sometimes plant corn in the poppy fields to help shade the young poppy seedlings. Being very delicate, the plants also need to be protected from strong wind. The hillsides on which they grow cannot be too steep, because the tiny seeds, as well as the growing seedlings, can be washed away easily during heavy rains.[20] The poppy is usually planted between August and October and is harvested four months later when the plant has grown to a height of about four feet.

The crop is ready for harvesting when the brightly colored petals fall off the bulbs, which turn first from green to yellow and then to brown. Late in the afternoon, Hmong women carefully make vertical incisions in each bulb, using an instrument made of a length of bamboo or wood to which blades have been attached. A milky liquid oozes out from these incisions during the cool of the night. This sap or latex must be collected before dawn because rising temperatures cause it to coagulate into a thick resin that is difficult to scrape off the plants. The opium latex begins to lose moisture from the moment it is exposed to the air. As it dries, it turns darker until it becomes brown. To remove impurities from this raw opium, the Hmong dissolve it in boiling water and then filter the solution through pieces of cloth. The clean opium is then wrapped up for shipment.

The Hmong sometimes took the opium supply to town for sale, but more often than not, Chinese and lowland Lao merchants came to their villages to buy the year's harvest. After the French appeared on the scene, the price of opium was based upon the morphine content of the crop from each locality. (The morphine content in different batches of opium varies greatly, depending on how many years a field has been planted to poppy, the characteristics of the soil, and the extent to which the opium has dried since harvesting.) As chemical analysis in a laboratory was required to determine the morphine content of a batch, the Hmong often had to wait for weeks to find out what price the French would offer them. Merchants from the lowlands soon learned to take advantage of this situation and to appropriate a large part of the profit from this stage of the transaction for themselves. They showed up before the results from the laboratory came back, set a price themselves, and advanced cash or credit to the Hmong. These merchants thereby earned the differential—a large one in good years—between the price the French eventually decided upon and what they themselves had offered the Hmong.

Opium cultivation is well suited to the remote highland environment for several reasons. First, the value of opium per acre is very high. Though it requires an extraordinary amount of manual work, this is available in the form of unpaid family labor, which means that the larger a Hmong family is, the more poppy its members can cultivate. Second, poppy becomes productive and can therefore generate an income the very first year it is planted—unlike many other kinds of cash crops. Third, its peak period of labor requirement does not coincide with that of rice and corn, so the labor input of those who cultivate all three crops can be spread out over the year. Fourth, the poppy does not deplete nutrients in the soil; a poppy field can therefore remain productive for up to ten years without the use of fertilizers, which are still unavailable in the highlands of Southeast Asia. Fifth, opium is not a perishable product that has to be marketed within a short period of time. As a matter of fact—unlike most agricultural products in the tropics—the longer it keeps and ages, the more valuable it becomes. Sixth, it is compact, easily packaged, and can be carried over steep mountain trails on the backs of pack mules and mountain ponies—the only available forms of nonhuman transportation in that part of the world. Finally, there has always been a ready market for it, given its addictive quality.[21]

Even though opium was cultivated legally by the Hmong in Xieng Khouang Province, most of the raw opium that was manufactured as smoking opium in French Indochina was imported from China, India, Persia (now called Iran), and Turkey. By controlling the processing that took place within Indochina, the colonial government received all the profits derived from the large markup in price between the raw and processed opium. The government's opium dens and shops brought additional revenues. The main beneficiaries of the opium trade, therefore, were the Chinese and Lao merchants and the French colonial government, and not the Hmong who grew only a small portion of the crop processed in Indochina.

A new player in the opium trade appeared on the scene at the end of World War II, when the 93rd Division of the Kuomintang (KMT, meaning Nationalist Chinese) army moved into northern Burma and Laos, ostensibly to accept the surrender of Japanese troops, but in reality, to seize the opium harvest there. When the Chinese Communists assumed power on the mainland in 1949, the 93rd KMT Division, which had returned to southwestern China after seizing the 1945–46 opium harvest, once again moved into northern Burma. These armed men found a way to support themselves by gaining control over the opium cultivated by the Shan people in upper Burma. Their commanders became wealthy and powerful local warlords. When the Burmese government offered them a chance to be repatriated to Taiwan, where the rump KMT government had set itself up, they declined. After repeated attempts to oust them, the Burmese government finally drove them out of Burma by bombing their headquarters in the late 1950s. By 1962, they had managed to reestablish a base in northern Thailand, where they have remained ever since.[22] For the last four decades, these ex-KMT soldiers and their leaders have controlled much of the opium grown in the so-called Golden Triangle—the area where Burma, Thailand, and Laos come together.

Opium has been used increasingly, not in its original state, but in the form of its derivative, the deadly drug, heroin. Heroin, the common name for diacetylmorphine, is made by chemically bonding morphine with acetic anhydride.[23] It is far more powerful and addictive than opium, or even morphine, because it is absorbed much more quickly into the bloodstream. Its narcotic effect does not last as long as opium's, and addicts crave another dosage within a few hours. Heroin thus debilitates its users at an alarming rate.

Not only are the profits from heroin trafficking greater, but as a contraband, it can also be smuggled across international borders more easily. Unlike opium, which exudes an unmistakable characteristic odor that makes it impossible to hide, heroin has no discernible odor and is an easily packaged and hidden white powder. Its value is thousands of times greater than a similar quantity of opium.

Though there was a heroin addiction problem in the United States before World War II, most American addicts were deprived of their drug during the war due to the disruption in transatlantic transportation, which cut off the supply of heroin from Marseilles, France— the world center of heroin manufacturing before the war. After the war ended, however, the mafia became involved in heroin trafficking, and heroin addiction in the United States increased.[24] Addiction became a serious social problem when thousands of American GIs, who had fought in Vietnam in the 1960s and become addicts there, returned home.

Not only have French colonialists, Japanese imperial troops, Nationalist Chinese soldiers, American counterinsurgency forces, and certain military and political leaders of various Southeast Asian countries been involved in and benefited from the opium trade, so also have the more moralistic Communists. According to anthropologist David Feingold, agents of the Viet Minh, who led the Communist revolution in Vietnam, brought cloth, salt, and other desired necessities to Laos and bartered or sold them for opium. Then they took the opium back to Vietnam and sold it to Chinese merchants. With the hard currency obtained from these Chinese merchants, they paid for modern weapons from the Soviet Union or the People's Republic of China. Likewise, the Pathet Lao, who controlled the mountainous provinces to the northeast of Xieng Khouang Province, also used the profits from opium to finance their revolutionary movement.[25] Thus, the hands of every nation and group that has vied for political power in Laos and Vietnam in the last century have been stained by opium. The Hmong, who did the actual hard work of growing the opium, have merely been pawns in this dangerous illicit trade and, through it, in international power politics.

The Japanese Occupation of Laos

Although the opium that the Hmong grew was traded in the world beyond their villages, the Hmong, as a people, did not get entangled in world politics until the 1940s, when the feuding Ly and Lo clans took opposing sides vis-à-vis the French colonial regime and the Japanese army that came to occupy French Indochina. Under Faydang Lobliayao's leadership, the Hmong also became involved in the movement for Laotian independence during that same period.

One of the "midwives" of the Laotian independence movement was Japan, which has played a paradoxical role in the national liberation movements of many Southeast Asian nations. On the one hand, it was Japan that pushed the emerging nationalist leaders in those countries to proclaim their independence in early 1945; on the other hand, Japan was itself an imperialist power. It began to station troops in French Indochina in 1940 after signing a treaty with the Vichy French government (the Nazi-collaborationist regime) to allow Japanese troops to move freely in Indochina while the French colonial administration remained in power. During this period, as Jou Yee Xiong, one of the narrators in this book, indicates, the major Hmong clans took different sides: the Lo clan supported the Japanese, while the Ly and Moua clans remained loyal to the French. Boua Neng Moua, another narrator here, recalls that he and some other Hmong were recruited into the French militia to guard their villages against the Japanese. The Japanese troops used Laos mainly as a staging ground for attacking the Nationalist Chinese regime north of the border.

Japan had also come to an understanding with Thailand,* the only country in Southeast Asia that was never colonized. With Japanese backing, in early 1941 Thailand successfully demanded the return of all territory on the west bank of the Mekong River that France had acquired from Siam in 1904 and 1907. To mollify the king of Luang Prabang, who was furious at the loss of this territory and threatened to abdicate, the French compensated him and gave the Luang Prabang royal house a little more power: they turned the royal advisory

---

*Siam changed its name to Thailand in 1939, reverted to Siam from 1945 to 1948, and once again to Thailand thereafter. [*Ed.*]

council into a council of ministers and named Prince Phetsarath as prime minister and viceroy.[26]

In an effort to counter Japanese influence, the French also tried, for the first time, to promote Lao nationalism. (Japanese propagandists envisioned uniting all the peoples of Asia into a single "co-prosperity sphere" under Japanese leadership and control.) In contrast to the preceding half-century of colonial rule, when the French had done virtually nothing for Laos, they now encouraged a veritable Laotian cultural renaissance, with the publication of the very first newspaper in the Lao language, the performance of traditional drama and music, and the construction of some seven thousand primary schools.[27] Since the war had cut off communications between the French colonial administration in Indochina and France proper, the opium monopoly provided one of the few dependable sources of revenue for the French colonial government. Therefore, French officials made special efforts to travel into the mountains to encourage the Hmomg and other hill tribes to increase their poppy acreage.[28]

In France, meanwhile, the Resistance forces under Charles de Gaulle set up a provisional government in liberated Paris in August 1944. Fearing that the Japanese might formally take over Indochina, de Gaulle ordered Free French commandos to be parachuted onto the Plain of Jars in December 1944 to set up resistance bases there with the help of those Hmong under the leadership of Touby Lyfong.[29] In March 1945, realizing that the tide of the war was turning decisively against them, the Japanese suddenly arrested and imprisoned all French residents in Indochina and, as de Gaulle had predicted, seized control of the government. They asked the leaders in each of the Southeast Asian countries they occupied to declare their independence.

In Laos, the king, instead of declaring independence, initially called on his people to rise up against the Japanese. But when the Japanese occupied the royal capital and took the crown prince hostage, the king acquiesced and declared Laos's independence in April 1945. Prince Phetsarath, meanwhile, removed many of the Vietnamese in the government bureaucracy and in the Garde Indigène and replaced them with Laotians.[30]

When the Allies decided at the Potsdam Conference to use British and Nationalist Chinese troops to accept the Japanese surrender in

Indochina, Japan immediately ordered its commander in Indochina to turn power over to the newly independent governments in Vietnam, Laos, and Cambodia. Though the United States was not eager to see the French recolonize Indochina, President Harry S. Truman assured de Gaulle that he would not oppose the French return. British and Chinese troops did not get to Indochina until several weeks after Japan's unconditional surrender, however, and this brief interlude proved crucial, for it gave the Viet Minh—the independence movement in neighboring Vietnam under the leadership of Ho Chi Minh—time to consolidate its control over northern Vietnam. Viet Minh forces also moved into Laos in an effort to gain control over the towns along the Mekong River. At this critical juncture, Hans Imfeld, a Swiss artillery officer acting on behalf of the Free French, arrived in Laos and went to see the king. He persuaded the monarch to repudiate his declaration of independence and to proclaim that the French protectorate over Laos was still in effect. The king's proclamation infuriated Prince Phetsarath, who had hoped the king would unify all of Laos—including the territory in southern Laos outside the kingdom of Luang Prabang—under the king's authority.[31]

Soon thereafter, Prince Phetsarath's younger half-brother, Prince Souphanouvong, who had been working as an engineer in Vietnam, returned to Laos and became president of the Committee for Independent Laos (Khana Lao Issara), which had been founded by a group of nationalists.[32] Phetsarath was honorary president and Oun Sananikone (scion of another Laotian aristocratic family), vice president. They intended to create an army, with Souphanouvong as the commander, and to name their government the Lao Issara. The king, however, refused to endorse the Lao Issara, whereupon the provisional people's assembly established by the Lao Issara voted to depose him.[33]

In early 1946, as French forces marched northward to retake all of Laos, Prince Phetsarath, in a conciliatory gesture, offered to reinstate the king as a constitutional monarch. The king accepted this offer in April, just one day before French forces reoccupied Vientiane. As the French entered the city, the Lao Issara leaders fled across the river to Thailand, where they soon set up a government-in-exile in Bangkok. Later that year, the French and the crown prince reached an agreement to treat Laos as a single political entity. A national assembly was elected and its members drew up a constitution to make Laos a constitutional monarchy. Laos became a member of the French Union in 1947. The French then negotiated successfully with Thailand to regain the territory on the west bank of the Mekong River that had been ceded to the Thai in 1941.[34]

In Bangkok, meanwhile, the key members of the Lao Issara government-in-exile fell to quarreling among themselves. Many of them especially did not like Prince Souphanouvong's close relationship with the Viet Minh. In 1949, unable to resolve the differences among its members, the Lao Issara dissolved itself. Some of its leaders returned to Laos. Souphanouvong also left Bangkok and took his guerrilla forces to Ho Chi Minh's headquarters in northern Vietnam. At a congress in August 1950 (attended by the Hmong leader Faydang Lobliayao), Souphanouvong's group transformed itself into a resistance movement called the Pathet Lao.[35] From then on, the Vietnamese and Laotian Communists saw their fate as a common one. Among the leaders who emerged within the Pathet Lao movement was Kaysone Phomvihane, one among a handful of Laotians who had joined the Indochinese Communist Party founded by Ho Chi Minh in 1930. He served as chairman of the ruling Lao People's Revolutionary Party until his death in November 1992.

The Pathet Lao was the only group in Laos that actively engaged in armed struggle against the French during the First Indochina War (1946–54). Approximately 60 percent of the Pathet Lao's forces came from ethnic minority groups, particularly the Lao Theung, whom the lowland Lao elite had so despised and mistreated. Although more Hmong sided with the French, a substantial minority under Faydang Lobliayao supported the Pathet Lao.

Laos and the First Indochina War

In contrast to the Lao Issara who fled to Thailand when France reimposed its rule over Laos, the Viet Minh in neighboring Vietnam waged a ferocious war, called the First Indochina War, against their former colonial masters. This war began in March 1946, when the French bombarded the port of Haiphong in northern Vietnam and forced Ho Chi Minh's newly established government to evacuate to the countryside. Over the next eight years, the Viet Minh, under their brilliant strategist, General Vo Nguyen Giap, fought a bitter guerrilla war against the French.

Though the First Indochina War was fought primarily on Vietnamese soil, some battles took place in Laos. Viet Minh forces, usually in coordination with Pathet Lao guerrillas, marched into Laos to divert French troops from the fighting in Vietnam, as well as to secure territory in Laos itself. In 1953 four Viet Minh divisions, numbering some forty thousand men, invaded Houa Phan Province (also called Sam Neua Province), where the Pathet Lao had set up its headquarters. The Vietnamese also attacked Thakkek in the southern panhandle of Laos. The following year, Viet Minh forces thrust toward the royal capital at Luang Prabang and the administrative capital at Vientiane, striking fear into the hearts of the French and lowland Lao troops.[36] The Pathet Lao supplied the Viet Minh with guides, provisions, and intelligence reports.[37] The French, for their part, organized the Hmong followers of Touby Lyfong into partisan guerrilla units called the Meo Maquis to aid their own efforts.[38] Partly to reduce the number of fronts on which they had to fight, and partly in response to American political pressure, the French granted Laos full independence in October 1953.

During the 1953 Vietnamese invasion of Laos, an important event occurred that eventually played a role in ending French colonialism in Indochina. As Viet Minh forces advanced on Luang Prabang, the commander-in-chief of all French forces in Indochina tried to persuade the king to evacuate the royal capital. But the latter looked him in the eye and said that he was not going to move: the Vietnamese who had tried to take Luang Prabang in 1479, he declared, had failed, and neither would they succeed this time. The French, therefore, had no choice but to move seven elite divisions to northern Laos to defend Luang Prabang, for they recognized the symbolic significance of holding on to Luang Prabang and Vientiane. In other words, their decision to defend northern Laos was a political, rather than a military one.[39] As it turned out, the Vietnamese withdrew before they reached Luang Prabang because the French succeeded in cutting their supply line and the rainy season had begun.[40]

The king's refusal to leave Luang Prabang forced the French to prepare for another potential invasion of northern Laos. In November 1953, they parachuted sixteen thousand of their best troops into Dien Bien Phu, a small bowl-like valley surrounded by mountains in the northwestern corner of Vietnam, very close to the Laotian–Vietnamese border. This valley lies in the traditional invasion route from Vietnam into Laos. The French thought they would be invincible there because the terrain was so rough that they doubted the Viet Minh, who had no aircraft for parachuting troops or supplies into the valley or its surrounding mountain ranges, could transport enough weapons to the area to attack them. They never imagined that the resourceful Viet Minh would dismantle their large artillery, and that agile members of various hill tribes, including the Hmong—many of whom the Viet Minh and the Pathet Lao had successfully won to their anticolonial cause—would carry these pieces, one by one, up the treacherously steep mountainsides, reassembling the components when they reached the summits. To the complete astonishment of the French—and, when the news got out, of people around the world—Viet Minh forces, numbering thirty-three battalions, unleashed such a volley of firepower on the French troops holed up below in Dien Bien Phu that the French had no option except to surrender. Their defeat on May 8, 1954, forced France to withdraw from Vietnam, ending their more than eighty years of colonial rule.[41]

The 1954 Geneva Conference, convened to work out the political settlements for both the Korean War (1950–53) and the First Indochina War, divided Vietnam supposedly temporarily in two at the 17th parallel, pending nationwide elections scheduled for July 1955. The Communist Viet Minh gained control over North Vietnam, while an anti-Communist regime aligned with the United States and the Western allies ruled South Vietnam. Cambodia, which had received its independence the year before, as had Laos, remained intact as a single entity. Laos was not divided per se, but the Pathet Lao were allowed to "regroup" their forces in the two provinces already under their control—Phong Saly and Houa Phan (also called Sam Neua Province).

One of the least known facts about the First Indochina War is that by the time it ended, the United States was paying almost 80 percent of French war costs.[42] Though the United States had little interest in the French colonies, Americans were drawn unwittingly and indirectly into the conflict there largely because of developments elsewhere in the world. In the years following World War II, the victors of that war divided themselves into two camps—a Communist one dominated by the USSR and a Western one dominated by the United States. These two blocs soon engaged in a Cold War. Events around the world bode ill for the so-called Free World: the erection of the Berlin Wall, symbolizing the division of Germany; the fall of the Eastern European countries under the Soviet sphere of influence; the Communist victory in China (referred to by many Americans as the "loss of China," even though China was never ours to lose); the Korean War, during which American troops fought Chinese Communists face to face for the first time; and the defeat of the French in Vietnam.

During the Cold War, many American political and military leaders thought in geopolitical terms. They imagined countries to stand like a row of dominoes on end, so that if one fell to Communism, the ones behind it might fall in short order, too. First enunciated by Dwight D. Eisenhower, the "domino theory" became a dominant conceptual framework in American foreign policy in the 1950s and 1960s. Policymakers felt that the United States should make vigorous efforts to "contain" Communism wherever it seemed to be spreading. Were it not for this containment policy—a cornerstone of U.S. foreign policy during the Cold War—it is doubtful that Americans would have become involved in the affairs of Laos, a country in which the United States had little interest.

American Intervention in Laos

At the time the French pulled out of Indochina, the official American presence in Laos was a lone foreign service officer, who did not even have a secretary to type the reports he sent to the U.S. State Department.[43] Yet within a few short years, the United States had become inextricably entangled in Laotian politics. How did this happen? Why did it happen? To answer these questions, it is necessary to examine developments in Laos between 1954 and 1975. Unfortunately, these were so complex, with so many players actively competing with each other in the political arena and so much conflict among the individuals who formulated U.S. policy toward Laos, that it is well-nigh impossible to summarize what happened in any cogent manner. The bare outline given here, which leaves out many details, is a gross oversimplification, but it will doubtless still sound confusing.[44]

Though the U.S. State Department did not even establish a country desk for Laos until 1955, the United States had begun sending economic aid directly to the Royal Lao Government (RLG) in 1951. Unlike economic aid, military aid was channeled entirely through the French until their defeat in 1954 and even afterwards. The 1954 Geneva accords allowed the French to keep fifteen hundred military advisors in Laos, though no more than five hundred were stationed in the country at any one time because French forces were deeply mired in another war, in Algeria. In order to maintain Laos's neutrality during the Cold War, the accords stipulated that no other foreign country could station troops in Laos. The United States was thereby prevented from setting up a Military Assistance Advisory Group (MAAG) in Laos. (MAAG is a common designation for American military advisors sent to other countries.) To circumvent this restriction, the United States created a Program Evaluation Office (PEO) in 1955, staffed by retired military officers or officers temporarily placed on reserve status, to administer the military aid program. Wearing civilian clothes, they soon began training men from the Laotian police and the Royal Lao Army (RLA).[45] Meanwhile, the United States Operations Mission (USOM) oversaw the disbursal of economic aid.

Both the State Department and the Pentagon believed the best way to prevent the spread of Communism into Laos was to build up the RLA. Accordingly, the United States agreed to pay all the salaries of the troops and officers in that army.[46] No one in the United States had an accurate idea of how many men were actually in the RLA, however, because the Laotians insisted that they be allowed to exercise full control over military pay.[47] Americans were willing to close their eyes to abuses in this military aid program and supported the RLA at the level that its commanders requested, because the occasional forays made by Pathet Lao guerrillas into the territory under RLG control reminded them of the ever-present dangers of Communism.

Frustrated by the conditions under which they had to operate, some Americans in Laos eventually turned for help to the Central Intelligence Agency (CIA), whose agents could operate covertly—

and hence without any restrictions—to manipulate the outcome of political struggles in Laotian national politics. J. Graham Parsons, the American ambassador to Laos from 1956 to 1958, got along well with the CIA chief in Laos but not with the head of PEO. Thus, not surprisingly, he began to rely more and more on the CIA to get the results that he favored.

In particular, Parsons did not like Prince Souvanna Phouma—the brother of Prince Phetsarath and the half-brother of Prince Souphanouvong—who had emerged as the key political figure in Laos after 1954. A genuine neutralist, Souvanna tried patiently between 1954 and 1957—through the rise and fall of several cabinets, including some headed by himself—to put together a coalition government that would include pro-American rightists, nonaligned centrists, and pro-Communist leftists. Parsons felt that Souvanna relied too much on his French advisors, on the one hand, and was too accommodating to the Pathet Lao, on the other. When Souvanna visited Hanoi and Beijing in 1956, Parsons became convinced that he was indeed a Communist sympathizer.

Souvanna finally succeeded in forming a coalition government in November 1957. The Pathet Lao returned the two northeastern provinces set aside for them by the Geneva accords to the central government, while Souphanouvong joined the new government as minister of planning and reconstruction. Another Pathet Lao leader, Phoumi Vongvichit, became the minister of religion and fine arts. A cease-fire ended the sporadic fighting between RLA and Pathet Lao troops. At that time, the latter numbered approximately six thousand. A clause in the agreement that led to the coalition government stipulated that fifteen hundred of the Pathet Lao soldiers would be integrated into the RLA, while the rest would be discharged and returned to civilian life.[48] The agreement also provided for a supplementary election in May 1958 to fill twenty-one new seats in the National Assembly.

The United States was unhappy with this new coalition government—called the Government of National Union—because its composition legitimized the Pathet Lao's existence. Key American decision makers in Laos increasingly felt that the only government that would be acceptable to them was, not a neutralist one, but one that was strongly pro-American. In the months preceding the May 1958 election, U.S. personnel in Laos launched Operation Booster

Shot, a campaign to win the hearts and minds of the Laotian electorate, so that they would vote for the non-Communist candidates. The United States spent more than $3 million on a wide variety of village assistance and community development projects.[49] Despite this expensive effort, the results of the election shocked American officials. Instead of the rightist candidates emerging victorious, the predominant party was the Neo Lao Haksat—the popular front that the Pathet Lao had established in 1956 to field political candidates. Its candidates won nine seats, while its ally, the Santiphab (Peace Party), won four out of the total twenty-one. Souphanouvong received the largest number of votes among all the candidates who ran.[50]

The Pentagon, the State Department, and the CIA all decided that something had to be done to reverse this political swing to the left in Laos. On the pretext that corruption was rampant in the U.S. aid program, the United States cut off aid to Souvanna's government in June. Since the amount of U.S. aid far exceeded the country's national budget, the withdrawal of aid created a grave economic crisis. Souvanna lost a vote of confidence and resigned in July 1958, bringing to an end to the neutralist coalition he had worked so hard to craft.

Even before Souvanna's government fell, the CIA had already set up a Committee for the Defense of National Interests (CDNI), consisting of a group of pro-American young politicians. The next cabinet was formed by Phoui Sananikone, who claimed that his government would also be neutralist but, nevertheless, announced that Communism would be his number-one enemy.[51] Four CDNI members joined Phoui Sananikone's cabinet, while the two Pathet Lao ministers from the preceding cabinet were ousted. Phoui Sananikone did not protest when the new PEO director stated that Americans would now play a more open and direct role in training Laotian troops, even though doing so violated the Geneva accords. The Laotian commander whom the Americans looked most favorably upon was Phoumi Nosavan—the most rightwing of all the military leaders that the Americans supported.

In May 1959, Phoui Sananikone demanded that the two remaining Pathet Lao battalions be integrated into the RLA immediately. One complied, but the second, with about five hundred men and their families and domestic animals, somehow managed to slip through the RLA cordon and make its way back to northeastern Laos. Meanwhile, Souphanouvong and three other Pathet Lao leaders were placed under house arrest. Two and a half months later, the government charged Souphanouvong with treason and sent him and fifteen Pathet Lao leaders, who had been rounded up in the interim, to prison. In one of the most remarkable incidents in modern Laotian history, these men eventually won over their prison guards, who helped them escape in May 1960.[52]

Though grossly outnumbered by the RLA, whose strength had risen by now to some twenty-nine thousand men, the Pathet Lao remnants, with assistance from North Vietnamese troops and political cadres, began attacking government outposts in Phong Saly and Sam Neua provinces as well as in the highlands of southern Laos in July 1959. Civil war seemed imminent. At the end of the year, when the term of the National Assembly expired, Prime Minister Phoui Sananikone submitted his pro forma resignation to the king, but before he could form another government, Phoumi Nosavan, the CIA's and PEO's protégé, who had risen to the rank of general, marched into Vientiane with his forces in late December 1959 and occupied key government buildings. Phoumi's coup was legitimated by rigged elections the following April. CIA agents aided Phoumi in this effort: they were seen distributing bags of money to village headmen just before the elections.[53] In the new government Prince Somsanith became prime minister while Phoumi Nosavan became minister of national defense.[54]

The Laotian Civil War and the Hmong Armée Clandestine

Phoumi Nosavan did not have long to savor his triumph, however. In August 1960, a young paratrooper captain named Kong Le, who had received training at the Ranger School set up by the United States in the Philippines, staged his own coup. He demanded that the country return to a policy of genuine neutrality, that all foreign military bases be abolished, that Laos accept aid from all countries without strings attached, and that corruption within the government be eliminated.[55] To preserve the peace, the king brought Souvanna Phouma back as prime minister. Kong Le handed over the administrative functions that he had assumed to Souvanna, though his troops remained in

Vientiane to patrol and defend the city. To mollify Phoumi Nosavan, the king asked him to become the deputy prime minister as well as minister of the interior. But Phoumi Nosavan did not go to Vientiane to assume these posts. Instead, after consulting his uncle, the prime minister of Thailand, he remained in Savannakhet, his power base in southern Laos. There, he formed a Counter Coup d'État Committee. The CIA began chartering planes from Air America, a private airline, to supply his troops.[56]

The new American ambassador, Winthrop Brown, was supportive of Souvanna Phouma's efforts to reopen negotiations with the Pathet Lao. News of Kong Le's coup reached Prince Souphanouvong while he was hiking back through the jungles to northeastern Laos after his escape from prison. His followers broadcast their conditions for negotiations: termination of the civil war, return to a policy of "real peace and neutrality," the release of all Pathet Lao soldiers who had been taken prisoner, and the establishment of diplomatic relations and acceptance of aid from all countries with no political or military strings attached.[57]

Though Souvanna very much wanted to reach a settlement with his half-brother, Souphanouvong, the American ambassador could find no support for Souvanna in Washington, D.C. The reason was that the former American ambassador to Laos, J. Graham Parsons, who had always disliked and distrusted Souvanna, was now assistant secretary of state in charge of the Far Eastern Bureau, which gave him supervision over U.S. policies toward Laos. Parsons was not about to support any efforts at negotiations with the Pathet Lao. To make matters worse for Souvanna, Thailand, which sided with General Phoumi Nosavan, imposed an economic blockade on Laos. Meanwhile, under the influence of the pro-American Hmong leader, Touby Lyfong, the garrison at Xieng Khouang, which had been loyal to Souvanna, suddenly switched sides and went over to General Phoumi. Out of desperation, Souvanna turned to the Soviet Union for aid. For the first time, Laos recognized the USSR, which immediately set up an embassy in Vientiane.[58] In early December, when General Phoumi's forces began marching toward Vientiane and the commander of the Vientiane Military Region rebelled against Souvanna on Phoumi's orders, Souvanna and some of his ministers fled to Phnom Penh, the capital of neighboring Cambodia.[59]

The following day, one of Souvanna's remaining ministers flew to

Hanoi, where he negotiated with the Russians to airlift supplies to Kong Le's troops if the latter would form an alliance with the Pathet Lao in a common fight against General Phoumi's forces. Kong Le's troops withdrew from Vientiane several days later, drove Phoumi's forces out of the Plain of Jars, established their own headquarters there, and linked up with Pathet Lao forces. Between December 15, 1960 and January 2, 1961, the Russians flew over a hundred and eighty missions over the Plain of Jars, dropping food, weapons, and ammunition to the now-combined forces of Kong Le and the Pathet Lao. At this point, North Vietnamese troops entered Laos in large numbers and, together with the Pathet Lao, occupied portions of six provinces in northern Laos. Souvanna Phouma returned to Laos in late February and set up a government at Khang Khay, a small village in the Plain of Jars. Alarmed by the Communists' military advances, the United States gave up any pretense at abiding by the 1954 Geneva accords: the American military advisors who had been wearing civilian clothing and working under the PEO's aegis donned army uniforms once again. The United States finally established a MAAG in Laos on April 19, 1961.[60]

It was during this period of turmoil that the CIA began systematically recruiting Hmong into a mercenary army. The CIA had first heard of the Hmong when Edward Lansdale, one of its agents in Laos, became acquainted with the Hmong and their fighting ability. In the summer of 1959, the first members of the U.S. Army Special Forces (popularly known as the Green Berets) were assigned to the PEO in Laos. Some one hundred Green Berets were smuggled into Laos from Thailand aboard Air America planes. Called the Laotian Training Advisory Group of the PEO, their main duty was to train the RLA. Teams composed of twelve men each were assigned to each of twelve RLA battalions in the field, but the RLA officer corps did not respond well to the presence of the Americans. Friction also arose between the Special Forces and the French military advisors still remaining in the country. The CIA took advantage of this impasse and requested that half-teams of six Green Berets each be sent to train the Hmong in northeastern Laos and some of the Lao Theung tribes in southern Laos. Under the tutelage of the Green Berets, these mountaineers soon proved to be superior fighters, compared to the lowland Lao soldiers of the RLA, and quickly gained the CIA's favor.[61]

The CIA itself established direct relations with the Hmong in late

1960. A CIA agent, identified only as "Colonel Billy,"[62] went into the jungles to look for Vang Pao, the Hmong military leader, who had been a soldier since his early teens. As an eighteen-year-old soldier without rank in the Lao Territorial Army, Vang Pao had led two raids against the North Vietnamese forces that had penetrated into northern Laos. His daredevil exploits came to the notice of a French commander, who encouraged him to go to officer training school in southern Laos. In early 1954, he led the Meo Maquis units, which the French, in their desperation, hoped to use to break the siege of Dien Bien Phu. But Vang Pao and his men did not get to Dien Bien Phu until the day after it had fallen. Following the French defeat, he transferred many of the Hmong in the Maquis into the RLA. Before Vang Pao's French mentor departed from Laos, he gave Vang Pao a lot of arms and ammunition to hide in different locations in the Plain of Jars, in case the Maquis needed to protect themselves.[63]

When Colonel Billy found Vang Pao in late 1960, he asked the latter if the Hmong would be willing to help stop the Communist advance into Laos. According to Colonel Billy's account, as told to Jane Hamilton-Merritt, Vang Pao replied: "For me, I can't live with Communism. I must either leave or fight. I prefer to fight."[64] Vang Pao asked the Americans for weapons, food, salt, and medical supplies. He then went off to consult Hmong clan leaders, who agreed to make a deal with the Americans after some of them had a chance to question Colonel Billy. One clan leader recalls that Colonel Billy promised them that should the Hmong succeed in pushing the North Vietnamese Communist forces back, the Americans would help the Hmong as much as possible, and if the Hmong should suffer defeat, then the Americans would "find a new place" where they could help the Hmong.[65] Other accounts suggest that the CIA promised the Hmong an autonomous kingdom.[66] The first American shipment of five hundred guns to the Hmong arrived soon thereafter. The CIA's chartered airline, Air America, now began airdropping arms, ammunition, food, and medical supplies to the Hmong as well as to General Phoumi's forces.

As the combined forces of Kong Le and the Pathet Lao captured more and more of the Plain of Jars, Vang Pao had to evacuate more than a hundred thousand Hmong from their villages. He moved them to refugee camps set up on seven mountaintops southwest of

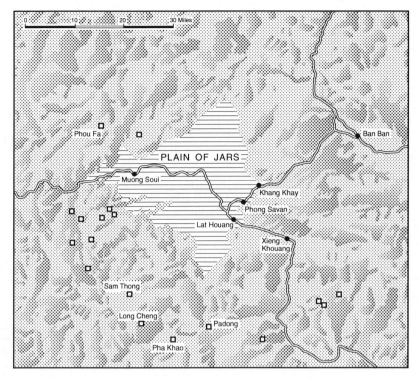

□ Air America landing strip
=== roads

The Plain of Jars in Xieng Khouang Province, Laos, showing the landing strips for Air America planes, 1960s. (Redrawn from map in Fred Branfman, *Voices from the Plain of Jars: Life Under an Air War,* p. xv.)

the Plain of Jars, establishing his headquarters first at Padong and, after Padong was overrun by Communist forces in June 1961, at Pha Khao, then finally at Long Cheng. From then on, instead of relying on their traditional slash-and-burn agriculture for subsistence, the Hmong depended largely on CIA supplies for survival.

After John F. Kennedy became president, he reviewed U.S. policy toward Laos thoroughly and came to the conclusion that the only way for the United States to avoid sending ground troops to Laos would be to accept a new coalition government. At the same time, however, he decided it would be expedient to strengthen the Hmong mercenary army, which might be used to fight on behalf of American interests. He renamed the Special Forces teams in Laos the White Star Mobile Training Teams and ordered them to train the Hmong secret army in earnest. By September 1961, there were three hundred Green Berets in Laos, while another one hundred and twelve men were being readied for deployment at Fort Bragg, North Carolina and in Okinawa. At the height of their strength in July 1962, four hundred and thirty-three Green Berets worked in Laos.[67] In that same year, there were an estimated fourteen thousand to eighteen thousand Hmong under arms, organized into shock companies and dispersed throughout the highlands to harass Pathet Lao and North Vietnamese forces. The Hmong also received training from Colonel Billy's Thai Police Aerial Reinforcement Units, which were secretly imported into Laos.[68] At its peak in 1969, the Hmong secret army numbered about forty thousand men. Until 1973, it was the main force holding back the Pathet Lao and North Vietnamese advance, providing exactly the kind of frontline defense that the United States desired in its efforts to "contain" the spread of Communism.

Laos during the Second Indochina War

The troops of Kong Le and the Pathet Lao not only fought against the Hmong under Vang Pao's leadership, but they also battered General Phoumi Nosavan's forces. Unable to withstand this onslaught, General Phoumi met with Souvanna in March 1961 to talk peace. In early May, General Phoumi and his ally, Prince Boun Oum, who now headed the government in Vientiane, Prince Souvanna Phouma, and Prince Souphanouvong agreed to a cease-fire. But the Hmong under Vang Pao persisted in fighting against the Pathet Lao and Kong Le's troops even after the cease-fire went into effect, while Air America planes continued to supply them. The Pathet Lao shot down an American helicopter and a transport plane, which gave them the proof they needed to accuse the Americans of violating the cease-fire. The Pathet Lao and their North Vietnamese ally seized the opportunity for retaliation. The Hmong base at Padong fell on June 7, 1961, though other Hmong outposts in Sam Neua and Xieng Khouang provinces were sustained by Air America's airdrops.[69] By this time, the Pathet Lao, aided by their North Vietnamese allies, had gained control over the entire eastern two-thirds of the country, north to south, while General Phoumi's side held only the major towns along the Mekong River in the western part of Laos.

In this tense atmosphere, the foreign ministers of those countries that had participated in the 1954 Geneva Conference plus their peers from several of Laos's neighboring countries met again at Geneva to discuss the situation in Laos. Meanwhile, President Kennedy sent Averell Harriman, his roving ambassador, to talk to the three warring factions. Kennedy himself and Soviet Premier Nikita Khrushchev agreed at their summit meeting in Vienna in June 1961 that Laos should have a neutral coalition government.[70] Apparently, at this time, neither the United States nor the Soviet Union wanted to become involved in a war with each other over Laos, a country in which neither superpower had any compelling interest.

From May 1961 through June and July 1962, two sets of negotiations went on simultaneously. The first was among the three Laotian factions—the rightists led by General Phoumi and Prince Boun Oum, the centrists led by Prince Souvanna Phouma, and the leftists led by Prince Souphanouvong, which occurred in Zurich and at various locations in Asia. Negotiations also took place among the participants of the Second Geneva Conference, who had to hammer out the terms of the cease-fire, the reconvening of the International Control Commission (ICC), and the creation of a neutral government. One of the chief hurdles blocking a settlement was the fact that no one could agree to a map showing where the troops of the three factions were stationed and what territory each group occupied at the time that a cease-fire was declared in May 1961. Furthermore, no side wanted the ICC to inspect the situation on the ground.

In early 1962, while the talks were still going on, General Phoumi Nosavan made a desperate attempt to test the CIA's commitment to him. He garrisoned his troops at Nam Tha, a city in northwestern Laos. But when Pathet Lao forces marched on Nam Tha, Phoumi's soldiers retreated pell-mell to Thailand. His ploy to lure American troops into Laos did not work: though the United States sent additional units to Thailand, none was sent into Laos to defend General Phoumi.[71]

After more than a year of painstaking and complicated discus-

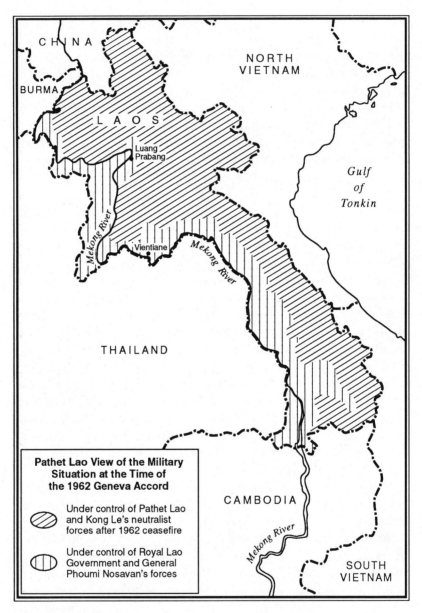

CHINA

BURMA

NORTH
VIETNAM

L A O S

Luang
Prabang

Mekong River

Vientiane

Mekong River

Gulf
of
Tonkin

THAILAND

**Pathet Lao View of the Military
Situation at the Time of
the 1962 Geneva Accord**

Under control of Pathet Lao
and Kong Le's neutralist
forces after 1962 ceasefire

Under control of Royal Lao
Government and General
Phoumi Nosavan's forces

CAMBODIA

Mekong River

SOUTH
VIETNAM

Pathet Lao and Royal Lao Government claims on Laotian territory, 1962.
(Redrawn from maps in Nina S. Adams and Alfred W. McCoy, eds., *Laos:
War and Revolution*, pp. 210–11.)

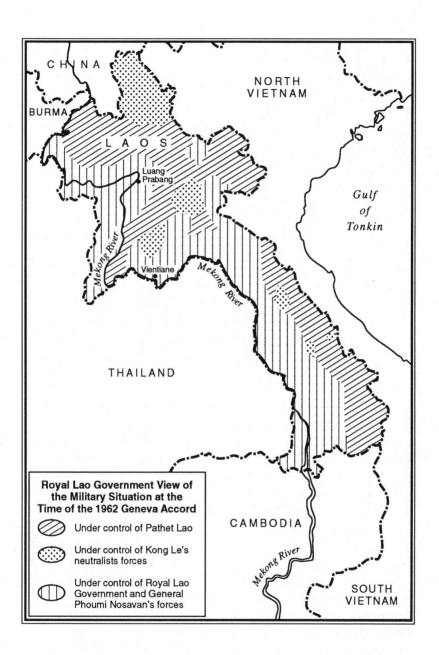

CHINA

BURMA

NORTH
VIETNAM

L A O S

Luang
Prabang

Mekong River

Vientiane

Mekong River

Gulf
of
Tonkin

THAILAND

CAMBODIA

Mekong River

SOUTH
VIETNAM

**Royal Lao Government View of
the Military Situation at the
Time of the 1962 Geneva Accord**

Under control of Pathet Lao

Under control of Kong Le's
neutralists forces

Under control of Royal Lao
Government and General
Phoumi Nosavan's forces

sions, the three Laotian factions agreed in June 1962 to set up the Provisional Government of National Union, to be made up of seven neutralists under Souvanna Phouma, four leftists from the Pathet Lao, four rightists from General Phoumi Nosavan's group, and four so-called rightwing neutralists—men who had remained in the Vientiane government but who had not shown any political commitment to General Phoumi. Souvanna was to become prime minister, while Souphanouvong and Boun Oum were both to become deputy prime ministers. On July 23, 1962, the international participants signed the Geneva Protocol, a comprehensive statement to guarantee the neutrality of Laos.[72]

In compliance with the Geneva Protocol, the United States pulled out all its military personnel—numbering more than a thousand—by October 1962, although U.S. military aid to Laos continued.[73] Vang Pao had by now been promoted to a general in charge of all of Military Region II in northeastern Laos. (Laos was divided into five military regions.) As a general in the RLA, he commanded some Lao troops as well as Hmong and other hill tribesmen organized into Special Guerrilla Units (SGU). He stockpiled arms and supplies at Long Cheng and was responsible for all civilians in the Plain of Jars and its surrounding mountains. U.S. advisors, dressed again as civilians, stayed behind to coordinate the distribution of the covert military aid given Vang Pao's forces. A new Requirements Office replaced MAAG; it was henceforth used as a convenient cover for the CIA's activities.[74] The number of CIA agents was not large, but they were placed in strategic locations to coordinate and direct the once-again-secret war. Each CIA agent was accompanied by a radio operator who could speak English, Lao, Hmong, and sometimes Vietnamese, in order to maintain contact with the CIA's Southeast Asian headquarters in Udon, Thailand, and with RLA troops and Hmong SGUs on the ground, and to pick up radio messages sent by the enemy.[75] By 1963, Air America's planes were dropping forty tons of supplies a day to the Hmong.[76] When the number of aircraft operated by Air America proved insufficient to handle the cargo load, another private airline, Continental Air Services, bid successfully for USAID and CIA contracts to supply the troops and civilians under Vang Pao's care.[77] The North Vietnamese were also supposed to withdraw their forces after the Geneva Protocol was signed, but no accurate count was ever done of how many of the latter actually left Laos. The Americans estimated that approximately six thousand North Vietnamese troops remained in Laos.[78]

Meanwhile, conflicts erupted among Kong Le's neutralist troops, on the one hand, and between them and the Pathet Lao, on the other hand. In February 1963 men under a colonel who had once been loyal to Kong Le but who had quarreled with him and joined the Pathet Lao killed one of Kong Le's officers. This dissident neutralist group, with the support of the Pathet Lao, fought against Kong Le's forces sporadically throughout the spring and summer of 1963. The dissident neutralists succeeded in ousting Kong Le's men from Khang Khay, Xieng Khouang town, and an airstrip on the Plain of Jars. As Kong Le retreated, he changed sides and joined forces with General Phoumi Nosavan's men, which enabled his troops to gain access to American weapons.[79]

In April 1963 after a leftist minister friendly to the Pathet Lao was assassinated in Vientiane, Souphanouvong and another Pathet Lao minister left the capital for Khang Khay, by then the Pathet Lao head-quarters. After two more neutralists were assassinated later that year, virtually all of Souphanouvong's followers left Vientiane, thereby bringing to an end the second coalition government.[80]

As the United States began supplying Kong Le's army, the North Vietnamese stepped up their support of the Pathet Lao. The USSR, however, withdrew from the scene and ceased its airlift to the Plain of Jars in October 1963, partly because it was embroiled in an ideo-logical war with China that was commonly called, at the time, the Sino–Soviet split. The Soviet Union did not resume an active role in Vietnam and Laos until American intervention in Vietnam intensified after August 1964.

At the beginning of 1964, Pathet Lao forces began pushing Kong Le's army off the Plain of Jars. They succeeded by mid-May. In the process, they also attacked Hmong strongholds, turning thousands more Hmong into refugees.[81] At the same time, they began a cam-paign to gain more territory in central and southern Laos. In despair, Souvanna Phouma announced he intended to resign. But before he could do so, the commander of the Vientiane Military Region, act-ing in conjunction with the head of General Phoumi's secret police, arrested him.[82] The United States and other Western nations successfully exerted pressure on the coup leaders to release Souvanna because by then the United States was committed to keeping him in power. Key American policymakers had come to believe that he was the only alternative to a Communist government.[83] General Phoumi's standing in the eyes of Americans, meanwhile, declined; he went into voluntary exile in Thailand in 1965. Kong Le, too, left Laos in 1966 and settled in France.[84]

Seen in a broader light, the second coalition government in Laos, like the first, was also a casualty of larger forces—this time, the Second Indochina War. This war can best be characterized as a civil war between Communist North Vietnam and anti-Communist South Vietnam, which soon became a testing ground for the larger Cold War between the Communist bloc of nations and the Western allies.

In 1959, as the American-supported government in South Vietnam increased its suppression of dissidents, the North Vietnamese decided to infiltrate cadres and transport war matériel to the south. The following year, a National Liberation Front (the NLF—commonly called the Viet Cong) was established in South Vietnam. Since the demilitarized zone (DMZ) along the 17th parallel, which divided North Vietnam from South Vietnam, was heavily guarded, the North Vietnamese had to find a way to get around the DMZ in order to get their supplies into the south. They laboriously hacked out a network of jungle treks that came to be called the Ho Chi Minh Trail, part of which ran through eastern Laos, adjacent to the Laotian–Vietnamese border around the 17th parallel. Down this trail, under cover of the thick jungle canopy, came trucks, bicycles, and people, all carrying supplies to aid the Viet Cong's war effort.

To prop up the successive governments that came to power in South Vietnam, the United States first sent military advisors, then air support, then bombing raids, and ultimately half a million ground troops to that country. To impede the southward flow of men and armaments, American planes bombed not only targets in North Vietnam but also the Ho Chi Minh Trail (and hence, Laotian territory in the vicinity of the trail). In this manner, Laos was drawn inexorably into the Vietnam War. In fact, whenever there was a pause in the American bombing of North Vietnam, the bombing of Laos intensified. By 1972, approximately 70 percent of all American air strikes in Indochina were aimed at targets in Laos and 80 percent of those were in the region of the Ho Chi Minh Trail. From a daily average of fifty-five sorties in 1965, the number grew to three hundred in late 1968.[85] The neutrality of Laos that was supposedly guaranteed by the 1962 Geneva Protocol, therefore, was violated with impunity by both the Communists and the Americans in the widening war.

The bombing of Laos was done in secret. It began in May 1964 when American reconnaissance planes started flying over southern Laos and the Plain of Jars. Souvanna Phouma gave verbal permission to the American ambassador for these flights. But as Communist antiaircraft units shot at and occasionally shot down the reconnaissance planes, fighter escorts began flying with them. At the same time, the United States began supplying bomb fuses to the Laotian Air Force to make operational the bombs that had been delivered to the Laotian government earlier. But since the number of qualified Laotian pilots was very small, Air America pilots as well as Thai pilots began manning some of the Laotian planes. The use of Thai pilots became public knowledge when, in June 1964, they bombed the Pathet Lao headquarters at Khang Khay and destroyed the Communist Chinese mission there. Souvanna Phouma, greatly embarrassed by this incident, tried to stop the air strikes, but the United States prevailed upon him to allow them to continue. The United States called all its air operations in Laos over the next six years "reconnaissance flights," even though over two million tons of bombs were dropped on Laos in the 1960s—more than the total tonnage dropped during World War II.[86] To conceal the true nature of its activities, the United States based all its bombers across the border in Thailand, keeping only reconnaissance, supply, and rescue aircraft on Laotian territory.[87]

Tactical air navigation systems were installed on Laotian soil to guide the American planes in their bombing missions against Communist targets in both Laos and North Vietnam. One such base was set up on a fifty-five-hundred-foot mountain, Phou Pha Thi, located in northern Laos, only fifteen miles from the Laotian–Vietnamese border. The sophisticated radar equipment was operated by more than a dozen American technicians—U.S. Air Force personnel dressed in civilian clothing—who were guarded by two hundred Hmong at the site, with another eight hundred Hmong stationed at lower elevations.[88] The radar system at Phou Pha Thi guided all the American bombers flying into North Vietnam until the base was captured by the Communists in March 1968.[89]

The secret war in Laos was fought on four fronts: (1) RLA and Communist troops battled each other around the major towns; (2) the Hmong guerrillas fought against Pathet Lao forces in northeastern Laos; (3) American B-52s rained destruction over northern Laos in coordination with the ground war fought by the Hmong; and (4) a second air war took place over the southern panhandle in the vicinity of the Ho Chi Minh Trail.[90] CIA personnel played the key role in directing both the ground and air wars.[91]

The fourth facet of this war took on added significance after March 1970, when Prince Norodom Sihanouk was deposed by one of his own generals, Lon Nol, in neighboring Cambodia. Up to this point, the Communists had managed to ship supplies into South Vietnam through Cambodia, but Sihanouk's successor was avidly pro-American, unlike Sihanouk, who tried to maintain Cambodian neutrality by playing various factions against each other. After Lon Nol came to power, he cut off all shipments through Cambodia of food and war matériel destined for the Viet Cong. Thus, the Ho Chi Minh Trail that ran through Laos became the only lifeline left for the Viet Cong. The North Vietnamese struggled to keep the trail open, while the Americans tried to bomb it out of existence.

Despite official denials, countless numbers of civilians were killed and entire villages wiped out during this unpublicized war. The Hmong, in particular, suffered so many casualties that Hmong and other hill tribesmen from Thailand, as well as regular Thai troops, had to be brought into Laos to help replenish Vang Pao's army. Bringing in Thai troops was part of a broader change in U.S. policy. When President Richard Nixon realized that the only way to extricate American ground forces from Vietnam was to "Vietnamize" the war by forcing the Vietnamese themselves to do more of the fighting, an effort was also made to "Thai-ize" the war in Laos.[92] Americans did not try to force more Laotians to fight because American military advisors in Laos were now fully aware that the RLA could not fight well. The Hmong were the only effective indigenous fighting force in Laos, but they paid an extraordinarily high price for their valor. According to one estimate, 25 percent of the Hmong who enlisted were killed.[93] According to another estimate, seventeen thousand Hmong troops and fifty thousand Hmong civilians perished during the war.[94]

The Hmong who survived also suffered greatly. Both the male and female narrators in this book talked about the extreme hardships they experienced. While men such as Xang Mao Xiong, Xia Shoua Fang, Chou Nou Tcha, and Boua Neng Moua, who have told their stories in this book, fought in the jungles and on the open plains, their wives and parents moved from place to place trying to farm while keeping one step ahead of the Communists. Often, they could not stay long enough in one place to harvest the crops they had grown, so to survive they had to eat leaves, wild fruit, tree bark, and whatever else they could find in the jungle.

As the 1960s unfolded, more and more North Vietnamese troops entered Laos: by 1970, their estimated number was sixty-seven thousand. As the People's Republic of China and the Soviet Union supplied the North Vietnamese with increasingly more sophisticated weapons, these were used against the Hmong, who could no longer hold their positions. By the late 1960s, Pathet Lao and North Vietnamese forces had captured the entire Plain of Jars.

General Vang Pao was determined, however, to retake the Plain of Jars. In August 1969, he launched an offensive and the following month he succeeded in reoccupying two key points—Xieng Khouang town and Muong Soui.[95] During 1969 and 1970, as American, Thai, and Hmong pilots retaliated against the Communists with the heaviest bombing to date, almost the entire population on the Plain of Jars had to be evacuated.[96] For the first time, President Nixon authorized the use of B-52s against targets in northern Laos. The number of refugees doubled, and airdropped relief supplies could barely keep them all alive.

In February 1970, the Communists began their counteroffensive to recapture those parts of the Plain of Jars that Vang Pao had taken in late 1969. Vang Pao's troops were forced to withdraw. The town of Sam Thong, where more than eight thousand Hmong refugees had gathered, was leveled in March 1970.[97] Civilians were also evacuated from Long Cheng, while Thai "volunteers" were flown in to help defend it. By this time, however, in the face of mounting antiwar protests in the United States and the continued loss of American lives in Vietnam, the United States was determined to find a way to end its involvement in Southeast Asia. Americans, therefore, did not provide Vang Pao with the air support he requested when he needed it most. By the time Long Cheng came under siege again in December 1971, little military air support was available, though airdrops by Air America and Continental Air Services continued to supply the people remaining at the base.[98] When the last RLG stronghold in northeastern Laos fell—the air base at Xieng Khouang town—the Pathet Lao and their North Vietnamese allies controlled most of the country.[99]

It is obvious that during this war neither the North Vietnamese nor the Americans cared much about the needs of Laos or of the Hmong. Both sides in the Second Indochina War and, by extension, the larger Cold War, made use of Laos for their own ends. It was possible for the U.S. government to hide this war from the American public—indeed, from Congress itself—because reporters were forbidden to interview pilots who left on bombing missions over Laos from American airbases in Thailand. (This policy was not applied in Vietnam, which allowed the American public to read daily newspaper accounts and see television footage of U.S. military actions in Vietnam.) Moreover, with the nation's attention riveted on the war in Vietnam, few people paid any attention to that lesser-known country, Laos. It was not until 1969 that the U.S. Senate Foreign Relations Subcommittee on U.S. Security Agreements and Commitments Abroad, chaired by Senator Stuart Symington, finally held hearings to find out what was going on in Laos. At the hearings, William Sullivan, the American ambassador to Laos at the time, maintained that the war in Laos had to be kept secret in order not to abrogate the verbal agreement that John F. Kennedy and Nikita Khrushchev had reached in Vienna in 1961! Only in March 1970 did President Richard Nixon make any public statement about American actions in Laos. But by then, the United States was determined to end its involvement in Southeast Asia and was looking for a way to extricate itself "with honor" from a conflict that had cost more than a million lives (all participants combined) and left a legacy of ecological destruction that still boggles the mind.

The Lao People's Democratic Republic and the Hmong

After three years of secret talks, on January 23, 1973, President Richard Nixon's national security advisor, Henry Kissinger, and

North Vietnamese negotiator, Le Duc Tho, finally reached an agreement on terminating the war in Vietnam. Four days later, a formal cease-fire agreement was signed in Paris, over the protest of South Vietnam's President, Nguyen Van Thieu. The United States pulled all its troops out of South Vietnam by the end of March.

Influenced by developments in Vietnam, the Pathet Lao decided the time had come to consider anew a political settlement in Laos and offered to negotiate with Souvanna Phouma's government without preconditions. Souvanna was happy to accept the offer and talks began in Vientiane in October 1972. Less than a month after the Paris Peace Agreements were signed by the United States and North Vietnam, the Laotian factions signed their own Agreement on the Restoration of Peace and Reconciliation in Laos on February 21, 1973. It specified that all foreign military forces were to be withdrawn within sixty days and provided for the formation of another Provisional Government of National Union, with an equal number of Communists and non-Communists, as well as a National Political Consultative Council (NPCC), a parliamentary body. When this third coalition government came into being in April 1974, Souvanna Phouma became its prime minister, while Souphanouvong became chairman of the NPCC. Three Hmong held high positions in this government: Touby Lyfong (representing the rightists) served as deputy minister for posts and telegraphs, Lo Fong (representing the leftists) as vice chair of the Culture and Education Committee of the NPCC, and Yang Dao (a neutralist and the first Hmong to receive a Ph.D. in France) as vice chair of the Economy and Finance Committee of the NPCC.[100]

For several months, the coalition government functioned smoothly and the cease-fire held. RLA and Pathet Lao forces jointly controlled Vientiane and Luang Prabang. Unfortunately, Souvanna Phouma suffered a heart attack in July 1974 and left for France to recuperate. During that interregnum, a series of strikes by students and workers disrupted the peace, and fighting broke out again between Pathet Lao and Vang Pao's troops in April 1975.[101]

Meanwhile, in neighboring Cambodia, the Khmer Rouge (Cambodian Communists) marched into Phnom Penh, the capital, and proclaimed a new regime on April 17. The South Vietnamese government in Saigon fell on April 30, 1975. In light of these Communist victories, the Pathet Lao decided they should speed up their own assumption of power. At the beginning of May, five rightist ministers (who held the defense, finance, foreign affairs, health, and public works portfolios) and seven rightist generals were forced to resign. People's Revolutionary Committees, with the support of Pathet Lao troops, took over many towns. Students then occupied the large USAID compound in Vientiane on May 21, whereupon the U.S. embassy closed down the agency on June 30. In early November, elections were held at the *ban, tasseng,* and *muong* levels for people's administrative committees. The elected officials replaced the former chiefs of these traditional administrative units. At the end of the month, the king was coerced into abdicating, thereby bringing to an end a monarchy that had ruled Laos for more than six hundred years. The coalition government and the NPCC were dissolved, and the Lao People's Democratic Republic was proclaimed on December 2, 1975.[102]

The Hmong did not fare well during this period of transition. After the Vientiane Agreement was signed in February 1973, some eighteen thousand Hmong troops were disbanded, while the rest were supposed to be merged into the regular army by the end of 1974.[103] All American military advisors in Laos left the country. Only a small number of USAID men and one CIA agent remained to help the Hmong. The USAID staff felt it was too dangerous to stay overnight at Long Cheng, so they flew into Long Cheng daily. The CIA agent, who was very devoted to the Hmong, remained at Long Cheng as long as he could, but eventually he was asked by his superiors at CIA headquarters in Udon, Thailand, to inform the Hmong that the Americans could no longer help them. He urged Vang Pao and some of the key Hmong leaders to leave the country, but Vang Pao refused.[104]

The Hmong who remained under Vang Pao's command clashed with Pathet Lao soldiers in March 1975. When Pathet Lao forces advanced toward Vientiane in April, Vang Pao tried to repel them with aerial bombardment. This action angered Souvanna Phouma, who very much wanted the third coalition government to succeed. He relieved Vang Pao of his command on May 10, 1975.[105] As this was happening, Hmong clan elders were meeting at Long Cheng to discuss and evaluate their situation. Though some wanted to remain to fight, most realized that they had no choice except to flee. But where could they go? Vang Pao flew to Udon to negotiate with the CIA: he felt the CIA was obligated to evacuate *all* the Hmong who had fought in the war, but the CIA replied that only the most important Hmong officers and their families could be taken care of. When Vang Pao asked for several C-130s to be dispatched to Long Cheng, he was informed that though a few such planes were still sitting on the runway in Udon waiting to be flown back to the American air base in the Philippines, only one C-130 pilot was available.

More than ten thousand Hmong swarmed into Long Cheng, hoping to be evacuated, but only one plane load of people was taken out by the C-130, which did not return to pick up any more passengers. Hmong and Lao pilots then flew in two old C-47 cargo planes they had commandeered and evacuated several hundred people over the next three days amid utter chaos. The last flight out of Long Cheng was made by a C-123, which was so overloaded that it could not take off until some twenty people were pushed out of the plane. On May 13, an emissary from the American embassy in Thailand came to Long Cheng and ordered Vang Pao to leave. He did so in a helicopter the following day.[106] In all, only about a thousand Hmong were evacuated. After arriving in Thailand, they were bused to a temporary refugee camp in Nam Phong. Stunned by the failure of the Americans to keep their "promise," allegedly made by the CIA in 1960 to help and protect the Hmong, those who were left behind either fled into the jungles or started a long trek on foot westward toward Thailand.

As Pathet Lao troops took over Long Cheng, those Hmong who were still in uniform were disarmed and sent to reeducation camps on the Plain of Jars and later at Nong Het, the traditional center of Hmong life. When the "confessions" they were forced to make were deemed unacceptable, their food rations were reduced. Many died from malnutrition and hard labor, while a few managed to escape. At the end of 1975, Touby Lyfong and one of his sons were sent to a reeducation camp at Sam Neua, where it is rumored he died of malaria in 1978. More than forty thousand Hmong, including some of the narrators in this book, managed to flee on foot to Thailand.[107] Thousands of others, who did not try to escape initially, retreated to the Phou Bia Massif, the highest mountain in Laos that rises to almost ten thousand feet, to resist the new government. Two groups of rebels hid in the thickets of Phou Bia: one band followed a messianic leader who preached that a Hmong king would return to lead his people; a second was made up mostly of ex-soldiers who tried to ambush government troops.[108]

On the other hand, a number of Hmong who had supported the Pathet Lao since the 1950s gained high office. Faydang Lobliayao became vice president of the Supreme People's Assembly. Nhiavu Lobliayao, his younger brother, became an alternate member of the Central Committee of the Lao People's Revolutionary Party as well as chairman of the Nationalities Committee within the new government.[109] Yang Dao and Lo Fong, who had served briefly in the third coalition government, however, were not appointed to any posts. Yang Dao escaped to France, while Lo Fong disappeared from sight.

The Lao People's Democratic Republic has pursued a rather contradictory policy toward the Hmong since 1975. From 1976 to 1979, the government sent Lao and Vietnamese troops, supported by artillery and Soviet-made MiG-21 airplanes, to attack the Hmong hideout at Phou Bia, dropping napalm, defoliants, and, according to Hmong refugees who managed to survive and escape, biological and chemical poisons on them, in order to crush the remaining pockets of resistance.[110]

Survivors report that the poisons came in several colors. The yellow poison fell like rain and made people dizzy and nauseous. The victims vomitted and had diarrhea until their bodies became so dehydrated that they died. The black poison came in larger drops and emanated a vapor that suffocated those who breathed it within three hours. Not only did the chemicals make those who came into direct contact with them sick, but they also poisoned the soil, plants, and streams, so that even those who were not covered with them became ill from the rice and vegetables they ate and the water they drank. Some airplanes spewed colored smoke that made people dizzy, gave them headaches, and caused them to vomit. Poisoned nails blasted out of airplanes also inflicted injury, misery, and death.[111] Those who believe the stories the refugees tell think the biological–chemical poisons had probably been provided by the former Soviet Union. Many observers, however, do not believe the refugees' tales and insist that no evidence of any poisons has been found.[112] Whatever the truth may be, the fact is, thousands of Hmong descended from Phou Bia and tried to find their way to Thailand.

In spite of this treatment, the Republic tried to dissuade the Hmong from leaving by telling them they could continue to grow the opium poppy (something that had been banned in 1971), and a radio broadcast beamed at the refugee camps on the Laotian-Thai border promised that the Hmong could return home without retribution.[113]

Hmong resistance against the Lao People's Democratic Republic has continued, however. Hmong refugees living in Thailand, allegedly with support from the Thai,[114] slip back across the border from time to time to harass Laotian government troops as well as the forty thousand Vietnamese forces still stationed in Laos. Several thousand Hmong have also made their way to China and have reportedly found some support there, both from their fellow Hmong and from the Chinese government, which fought a border war with Vietnam—Laos's number-one ally—at the beginning of 1979. The suspicion that the Hmong were receiving help from the Chinese government was based on the fact that a number of Hmong who were captured near the Chinese border in the early 1980s were wearing Chinese army uniforms and carrying Chinese-made arms, which they may have got from the Khmer Rouge, whom the Chinese supplied with arms. According to a former rightwing Laotian politician, the People's Republic of China was operating military training centers for the Hmong and several other minority groups along the Laotian–Chinese–Vietnamese borders.[115]

Resistance has also taken other forms. Hmong and other Laotian refugees who settled in France established a "Lao government-in-exile" in October 1978.[116] Former generals Vang Pao and Phoumi Nosavan announced in July, 1981 that they were forming a United Lao National Liberation Front.[117] The front has troubled the present regime in recent years. Insurgent guerrilla activities began to increase in northern Laos from December 1989 onward, after the United Lao National Liberation Front announced that it was creating a provisional government, with Vang Pao as the defense minister.[118] The Hmong resistance fighters were apparently inspired to step up their activities by uprisings in Burma in 1988, by the pro–democracy movement in China, and by the fall of Communist governments in Eastern Europe.[119]

The front gets most of its funds from Hmong refugees in the United States.[120] In 1989 and 1990, the *Washington Post* and the *New York Times* published articles about how the Hmong in the United

States were being required to—indeed, coerced into—making monthly payments to support the provisional government and its officers. In addition, for a certain sum, people can supposedly buy positions in a future government.[121]

Although perhaps as many as a hundred and fifty thousand Hmong have escaped from Laos since 1975, about that same number still live there. The latter are very unhappy about the government's attempts to force them to abandon their slash-and-burn agriculture (because it destroys valuable timber—one of Laos's few exportable items, aside from opium) and to move to lower altitudes to work on collective farms. In 1978, the felling of trees to clear land for farming was banned altogether.[122] It is also decreed that their rice harvest must be divided into three parts: a third to be given to the government as tax, a third for the village rice bank, with only a third reserved for the household's own consumption. The Hmong are, therefore, often short of food. In addition, they suffer from a shortage of other necessities, such as salt, cloth, and various items that used to be offered them by Chinese or Lao traders, but such a petit bourgeois trading system has been abolished. Finally, the Hmong are still sometimes subject to labor conscription, a practice that harks back to the *corvée* during French colonial rule.[123] The fiercely independent Hmong find these drastic changes from their traditional way of life most difficult to accept. Moreover, many of them do not want to live in the lowlands where, they claim, their health suffers. Such hardships make it unlikely that the exodus of Hmong refugees will stop in the foreseeable future. Given the family reunification provisions in current U.S. immigration laws, more Hmong—mostly family members of those already here—can be expected to continue coming to the United States, even though the total refugee outflow may eventually slow to a trickle.

Adapting to Life in the United States

A large proportion of the Hmong who found their way to refugee camps in Thailand endured harsh living conditions for months and, in many instances, years before being resettled in a third country. By far the largest number has come to the United States, with smaller numbers going to France, Australia, and Canada. Little has been written about life in the refugee camps. Four of the narrators in this book, who were children at the time, provide some of the more vivid glimpses of life in these camps. Maijue Xiong alludes to tensions within her family, as her parents toiled to earn a little money by working outside the camp, while leaving her and her sister (at the time aged three and five, respectively) to take care of themselves. Lee Fang and Thek Moua remember going to school—a new experience for them and for many Hmong children. Vu Pao Tcha recalls the gnawing hunger he experienced during his days in the refugee camp. The story of how he was branded a thief and was severely punished by his father for licking a little powdered milk from a carton that some other children had taken from another refugee family is especially poignant.

Thousands of Hmong spent years in Thai refugee camps. Unlike the one hundred and thirty thousand Vietnamese who were evacuated in late April 1975 by the Americans and allowed into the United States under the "parole" power of the U.S. Attorney General, the Hmong and other ethnic groups from Laos did not win that privilege until December 1975, when Congress admitted 3,466 Hmong under parole.[124] Since Laos did not capitulate to Communists overnight as South Vietnam did, the status of the Hmong who had fled Laos in the wake of General Vang Pao's departure remained ambiguous. General Vang Pao himself was held up for more than two months in Thailand before being flown to the United States because he had several wives. Polygamy is illegal in the United States, and he had to divorce all but one of his wives before he was allowed to land on American soil. (Several of his former wives have followed him to the United States and remain members of his household.)

In May 1976, another eleven thousand Laotians were granted entry under parole (there is no information on the ethnic mix of this group). Then in August 1977, Congress paroled eight thousand "land people," most of them from Laos, along with seven thousand Vietnamese "boat people."[125] By the early 1980s, some fifty thousand Hmong had been resettled in the United States. Their numbers were close to a hundred thousand when the 1990 U.S. census of population was taken.

Many studies have been made of the Hmong who have settled in the United States in the last two decades. These include several books, some twenty dissertations, dozens of journal articles and book chapters, and many newspaper stories. The most commonly studied topics are various aspects of Hmong acculturation,[126] literacy and the schooling of Hmong children as well as adults,[127] their health and mental health,[128] and their economic status.[129]

After reviewing the existing literature, I came to the conclusion that it is well-nigh impossible to generalize about how well the Hmong as a whole are adapting because their conditions in different localities vary a great deal. The locales of the existing studies stretch from Providence and Philadelphia on the East Coast to Seattle and San Diego on the West. Furthermore, there are not only variations across space but also changes over time. Given the fact that researchers who have studied the Hmong asked disparate questions, used different methodologies, interpreted their empirical findings according to theories in several disciplines, and obtained information from varying numbers of informants, it is difficult to synthesize the available information in any systematic way. For this reason, I shall discuss only the more interesting findings in the studies that have been done to date.

Anthropologist George M. Scott, Jr., has analyzed various facets of Hmong adaptation more carefully than anyone else. He noted how, despite the fact that social service providers report the almost universal failure of the adult Hmong to learn English and find employment, the Hmong, in fact, try actively to make cost–benefit calculations and to engage in "active, strategic, internal negotiation."[130] He examined four premigration variables and five postmigration or situational variables to assess the nature and degree of Hmong acculturation. The premigration variables are language, traditional occupations, war experience, and a kinship-based network of authority. The situational variables are postmigration settlement patterns; the ethnic composition of the neighborhoods where Hmong settled; the socioeconomic or class status of those neighborhoods; what resources were provided by the federal, state, and local governments, as well as by private agencies; and the values of the host society.[131]

Scott pointed out that long before the Hmong came to the United States, they had already encountered great disruptions in their lives. During the war, most of them had to abandon slash–and–burn agriculture in the mountains and either had to depend on American air-drops of food and other necessities while they lived in the refugee camps General Vang Pao had set up or move to lowland areas to learn wet-rice cultivation (as did Jou Yee Xiong, the first narrator in this book) or engage in white-collar wage labor (as did Ka Pao Xiong, the second narrator). In the lowland towns, Hmong became acquainted with such items of modern material culture as radios, clocks, bi-cycles, milled lumber, and tin roofs, and more generally learned to function in a monetary economy.[132]

The war also had a social impact. As men left home to become soldiers, the extended kinship network lost some of its importance as a system of social organization and control. Those who moved to the lowlands came increasingly under the jurisdiction of the RLG: they now had to obey government officials as well as their clan elders. Children in Hmong families that moved to the towns finally could attend school. One consequence was that young people were able to meet a broader range of potential marriage partners. When they mar-ried, more couples were able to live as nuclear families, away from the husbands' parents, brothers, and unmarried sisters. As Hmong fighters perished, widows married the brothers or cousins of their deceased husbands, as dictated by Hmong custom, thereby increas-ing the prevalence of polygamy.[133]

After their arrival in the United States, the Hmong have faced even greater changes in their material culture, means of livelihood, social organization, religious practices, and patterns of political leadership. In America, they cannot practice slash-and-burn agriculture nor de-pend on Air America to drop them food. Clans elders no longer control how land is used or when clan members should move to another locality. Instead, in San Diego in the early 1980s, when Scott did his field work, more than three-quarters of the Hmong depended on either federal refugee assistance or welfare. The only feature of the traditional Hmong economy that survived was the sharing of food and basic necessities among members of an extended family.[134]

In terms of social organization, most Hmong in the United States can no longer live as extended families. American landlords, govern-ment housing authorities, as well as fire and health department codes forbid too many individuals from living in an apartment or house. Thus, many Hmong extended families have had to split up physically, although family members still maintain strong emotional ties to each other. Social service agencies also affect the Hmong's sense of what constitutes a "family" because they use the nuclear family, and not the extended family, as the unit of distribution for various kinds of assistance. Instead of being a unit of production as it was in Laos, the extended family has become primarily a unit of consumption and distribution in America.[135]

The power formerly held by the larger clan has also declined. Clan elders used to perform traditional ceremonies but now seldom do so. Many of these rituals require chickens, pigs, and cows to be butchered, so that the animals' blood can be used as a sacrifice. It is not possible to buy live animals in urban supermarkets in the United States. Moreover, some of the ceremonies involve chanting and playing loud and, to American ears, strange music. The Hmong are painfully aware that such noise draws adverse attention. Besides, some Hmong are no longer certain about the efficacy of their beliefs and rituals. Those who live in rental housing wonder whether the spirits they used to worship are still accessible: after all, can such spirits reside in houses that are not owned by Hmong? As though to comfort themselves, some individuals draw a distinction between the pantheistic spirits dwelling in the jungles, mountains, streams, fields, and villages of Laos and the spirits of their own ancestors. They like to think that while the former may not reside in America, perhaps the latter continue to smile down at them from the heavens.

But ceremonies, particularly those associated with the Hmong New Year, remain important. In fact, the symbolic role of such celebrations has increased because they provide meaning, security, and, as Scott put it, "familiar relatedness."[136] However, what used to be *rituals* have become *performances* that are similar to the traditional version only in form because "they have taken their traditional ritual practices out of the context of everyday life and deposited them in the protective gallery of a public theatrical performance." These "serve as mnemonic repositories of religious beliefs whose daily utility has ended but whose importance in maintaining a sense of ongoing ethnic identity is still very much in evidence," and are being retained primarily as emblems of Hmong culture.[137] Nancy Donnelly, an anthropologist who studied Hmong women in Seattle, has made a similar observation. The Hmong New Year celebrations in Seattle, like those in San Diego, have likewise become "cultural displays," rather than "lived rituals." They are now "icons of identity rather than true natural expressions of an understood reality."[138]

In the political sphere of Hmong life, researchers have noted the emergence of a new leadership: educated, English-speaking young men who serve as officers in branches of the Lao Family Community, Inc.—a mutual aid association founded by General Vang Pao—that have been established in communities with enough Hmong to support them. These men function as cultural brokers vis-à-vis the larger society. As Scott cautioned, however, it would be a mistake to assume that members of this small but noticeable Westernized elite are supplanting the clan elders. The young men continue to show tremendous deference to their elders and are able to serve their communities only with the latter's blessing.[139]

One of the most subversive effects of the surrounding Euro-American culture on Hmong social organization is the greater equality accorded women in the United States. Despite the crucial contributions made by women in traditional Hmong society to economic subsistence and childbearing and rearing, they had a very low status. Women had to obey their menfolk in every aspect of life. Not only was bride kidnapping an acceptable practice, so were wife beating and polygamy. Donnelly has noted that tensions are growing in many Hmong households "because men [feel] they are losing their basis of command." Because they have few transferrable job skills, cannot find jobs that pay them enough to support their families, and consequently are forced to depend on welfare, many Hmong men suffer from depression. In those households where the wives have found employment, however marginal, the husbands often experience a loss of prestige, self-esteem, and authority.[140] Their fear of losing power in their families is very real for another reason: as Donnolly points out, "the state could circumscribe the authority of a man within his own household, for instance, by forbidding him to beat his wife."[141]

The ability of the police to intervene in family affairs is something that troubles many adult Hmong. Xang Mao Xiong, one of the narrators in this book, sighed about the difficulty of disciplining children in America because "we parents can be thrown in jail for trying to teach them what is right"—the method for such teaching being "a good beating."

Given the greater freedom as well as greater protection that women in the United States enjoy, it is not surprising that several available studies indicate Hmong women are adjusting more eagerly than Hmong men to life in America.[142] Donnelly discovered that "no Hmong woman has ever told me she wanted to live in Laos again."[143] Similarly, Goldstein found that "Hmong girls . . . did not want to return to the harder lives they lived in Laos."[144]

The women narrators in this book confirm this finding. While two of them complain about their lives—Vue Vang, who misses her siblings and longs to return to Laos someday, and Tchue Vue, who seems overburdened by the financial difficulties her family has experienced as farmers in the San Joaquin Valley of California—the rest sound quite happy. As Mai Moua said to her grandnephew, Lee Fang, "Ever since I have been in America, I have not done anything strenuous except to babysit my grandchildren. I am very happy to be alive today, seeing my family so well and happy." Ka Xiong put it this way: "I am so happy that we are now able to all live together in a country that is free . . . I am so happy to have all my children here with me and to see them doing so well." Pang Yang indicated that "the longer we have lived in the United States, the better our lives have become. . . . My sons often speak of this country as the land of opportunity. At first, I did not understand why they called it that, but now I do. Not only are there public schools, but there are lots of jobs, friendly neighbors, and a rich environment." Xer Lo, meanwhile, has been quite observant about the difference between the status of American women and that of Hmong women in Laos: "Women have more rights here in the United States, where wives and husbands have the same rights. Back in Laos, women have fewer rights than men. In fact, they have few rights at all. They must submit to their husbands. [Here in the United States] . . . their rights are protected, so they do not have to listen to their husbands. If husbands mistreat their wives, they can call the police. In Laos, wives have nobody to call when their husbands mistreat them."

Christianity, particularly its Protestant form, has also played a role in undermining traditional gender relations in some Hmong families. French Catholic and American Protestant missionaries have been active among the Hmong in Laos for many decades. At first, the Catholics were more successful in winning converts because Catholicism has shown itself quite capable of taking on elements from other religions in a syncretist way. Given Catholicism's own penchant for liturgy, Hmong who become Catholics feel little conflict when they retain some of their animistic rituals. In contrast, Hmong who become Protestants are compelled to renounce all of their old religious practices: instead of being an additive element like Catholicism, Protestantism completely replaces animism.

After the Hmong came to the United States, several of the major Protestant denominations—the Baptists, the Presbyterians, and the Church of Christ—as well as the Mormons, Jehovah's Witnesses, and the Christian and Missionary Alliance Church have all worked hard to gain Hmong adherents. Christianity has had a significant effect not only on the Hmong's religious practices but also on gender relations within some families. The various denominations involved with the Hmong do not approve of polygamy, which continues to exist *de facto,* if not *de jure,* among some Hmong in the United States. Christianity has affected other marriage practices as well. The payment by a groom's family of a bride price to the bride's parents, arranged marriage, bride kidnapping, and the tradition of girls marrying within a year or two of reaching puberty are all frowned upon—indeed, are deemed uncivilized—by the church, and those Hmong who have converted to Christianity have either modified such traditions or abandoned them altogether.

While Euro-American culture and Christianity have helped to change, however imperceptibly, the gender relations among some of the Hmong, certain American institutions, particularly the public schools, are eroding traditional Hmong intergenerational relations. Countless studies of immigrant adaptation have shown that children acculturate—that is, learn the values, the behavior that is considered appropriate, and the ideas that members of a culture hold about "reality"—much faster than adults. In the words of Henry Trueba and his associates, "Children are a focal point of the integration of cultures. They move in and out of home and school environments that are in sharp contrast to each other."[145] Immigrant schoolchildren quickly learn that what their parents expect is not necessarily the same as what their teachers and classmates approve of. The children also soon sense that the two cultures are not only different but are considered unequal: the Euro-American one is almost invariably treated as superior, the immigrant one as inferior. Until very recently, most teachers in American classrooms considered it their duty to help eradicate all traces of foreign cultures. Historically, one of the main justifications for using taxes to support a system of free, public schools in the United States has been the belief that education can play a central role in Americanizing newcomers from other lands. In short, schools in American society have functioned as major agents of assimilation and as builders of national unity.[146]

Unlike many Hmong adults, who received no education at all in Laos and are therefore illiterate and lack basic classroom skills,[147] Hmong children are able to benefit more from their schooling in America. In a study of Hmong first-, second-, and third-graders in Minneapolis, Renee Lemieux found that there is a positive correlation between a child's English proficiency and his or her perceived level of adjustment and his or her degree of self-esteem.[148] Thus, from a Euro-American middle-class perspective, the faster the children of refugees master English and internalize American values and norms, the better they will feel about themselves and the more easily they will fit into the larger society.

What is seldom recognized, however, is that Hmong families are paying a heavy price for their children's acculturation. Some children have become a source of distress to their parents and a cause of family disunity. The dilemma that Hmong parents face can be simply stated: while they very much want their children to become educated (good academic performance is viewed as an achievement in and of itself, and also as the only means that Hmong families have to ensure their future economic security), they are realizing that, paradoxically, school is the very place where their children are learning behavior that contradicts the parents' own teachings. While the adults appreciate the ability of the children to serve as cultural brokers— to read documents written in English, to communicate with various authorities, to interpret in all kinds of settings—they, in particular the fathers, cannot help but resent the "power accorded the children by their schooling, a power that underscores the men's inability to support their families and the reduced status that results."[149]

Older men—commonly understood to be those over forty, given the premature aging that Hmong experienced as a result of their hard lives in Laos—are having an especially difficult time adapting to life in the United States. The contrast between Hmong culture and

American culture is especially great in the honor accorded the aged. In Hmong society, as in most Old World cultures, old people are very much respected, so that individuals do not fear growing old. Even when old people are no longer economically productive or occupying positions of authority, they continue to enjoy respect within their families. There are multiple ways in which deference is shown to old people: reserving special seats for them, serving them choice foods, using honorifics to address them, assuming certain postures of deference, such as bowing in front of them, taking care of their bodily needs, and holding special celebrations in their honor.[150] Among the Hmong, age is defined not only by number of years but also by a person's status within his or her family, by his or her ability to perform hard, physical labor, and by the use of generational titles. That is to say, kinship terminology is used to reinforce respect for age.[151]

In American society, on the other hand, old people are often pushed aside to make room for those who are younger and more vigorous. The nonwhite elderly, in particular, faces what one scholar has called "double jeopardy"—suffering not only from old age but also their minority status.[152] Even more so than other minority elderly people, the Hmong elderly experience further privation due to their poverty and social marginality in the United States. The most painful moments they endure, however, occur when their own children and grandchildren no longer consult them, listen to their advice, or show them any respect. Unable to speak English, dependent on others to drive them places, fearful of taking public transportation in case they get lost, victimized by crime in the low-income neighborhoods where many of them live, many older Hmong men may sit at home with nothing to do except watch television. Having lost their traditional roles as elders—wise men who solve problems, adjudicate quarrels, and make important decisions—they feel useless and helpless. As one of them put it, "Where is my dignity if I cannot do anything for myself?"[153] Said another, "We have become children in this country."[154]

Some of the narrators in this book have had similar experiences. As Lee Fang wrote in his autobiography, his parents were quite disoriented during their early days in the United States. "Not only did they feel lonesome but they became children, wandering around the house without anything to do. Whenever someone knocked on the front door, they became hysterical. They hesitated to answer the door because they were scared to see people they did not know—mainly English-speaking people." Fortunately, not all older Hmong men have had such wrenching experiences. The two oldest male narrators in this book, Jou Yee Xiong and Boua Neng Moua, have both adjusted well. In general, older Hmong women also seem to be coping better. They remain active and useful by continuing to embroider, cook, do housework, and take care of children, as they have always done.[155]

Such changes in gender and intergenerational relations are very threatening to the Hmong because among all the ethnic markers they consider important—speaking Hmong, performing certain acts related to rites of passage and the New Year, engaging in slash-and-burn agriculture, growing the opium poppy, living in the mountains, wearing distinctive clothing and silver jewelry, expressing paramount loyalty to the clan and respect for elders, observing the sexual division of labor, and accepting the subordinate status of women—they regard the ability to speak the language and the retention of their gender and age hierarchies to be the most essential for maintaining their ethnicity.[156] As Kent Bishop put it, "They referred to the clans and the family as the 'Hmong way.' "[157]

But social service agencies, public schools, health clinics, and the judicial system all seem to conspire against them as they attempt to retain their ethnic identity.[158] And it is the "people in the extremes of traditional Hmong society"—the clan elders, the male heads of households, and the shamans, on the one hand, and women and children, on the other hand—who are undergoing the most profound changes in their lives, as status hierarchies are undermined, if not entirely turned on their heads.[159] Like many other immigrants, Hmong adults, as Goldstein has observed, tend to

> believe that economic integration is possible without socio-cultural integration. Their perception of how they formerly survived as an independent ethnic minority community is that they were able to maintain geographically separate residential enclaves while drawing on the national economy for their cash needs. Superficially, their re-settlement in the U.S. resembles this pattern, in that they are successfully re-establishing residential enclaves and reuniting kin. . . . [They] hope that they can again become an independent ethnic minority as

long as they successfully reproduce their kin networks. By this they mean not simply that relatives must live close together but that youth must be socialized into Hmong concepts of group identity and shared responsibilities.[160]

This intense desire to retain their culture may help explain one phenomenon that has frustrated resettlement workers and others who have tried to assist the Hmong since the 1970s. To avoid over-burdening any single locality and to encourage the refugees to learn English as quickly as possible, the federal government followed a policy of dispersing the refugees among communities across the face of the nation. However, as soon as the refugees learned enough to function on their own in American society, they began moving from the places of their initial settlement to other cities and towns. This arduous process of secondary or even tertiary migration confounded observers who tried to understand why it was taking place. Expla-nations included the desire for family reunification, the search for employment, the inability to continue living in places with high rents, hostile actions by the host communities, and difficulties in their relationships with their sponsors.[161]

Cheu Thao, a Hmong writer, has offered a more insightful expla-nation for the phenomenon. He sees a direct parallel between sec-ondary migration in America and the Hmong tradition of moving from one place to another either in response to adverse conditions or to find more fertile land. He believes that Hmong in the United States now move either to reunify their clans, whose members may have become separated during their tortuous journey from Laos to Thailand and finally to the United States, or to better their lives. But the motivation for the latter kind of move is not just economic—that is, to find locations with more employment possibilities, better voca-tional training, lower rents, or larger public assistance payments— but political as well. By that he means that the more members of a clan there are in a town or city, the more power its leaders can exert. Just as in Laos where "clan leaders could use moving as a means of consolidating clan and personal power," so clan leaders in the United States can attempt to gather together in one locality as many of their followers as possible in order to maintain their social stand-ing and influence vis-à-vis the new, young, educated, and English-speaking leaders who today control the Western-style mutual aid associations.[162]

Another possible motivation that Cheu Thao does not mention is that by increasing the size of the Hmong community in a particular locality, it becomes easier to maintain those social relations that form the basis of Hmong ethnic identity. Members of self-contained communities need not interact much, if at all, with the outside world as they find companionship among their own kind. Perhaps most important, in such a setting they can exert social control over the young and the female Hmong with, they hope, greater effectiveness.

Though there are many unique aspects to the Hmong migration experience, in a larger sense it is really not so different from that of other immigrant groups in America. Like other newcomers, the Hmong have tried simultaneously to hang on to some facets of their cultural heritage while adapting to American society with the hope of achieving economic success, social acceptance, and a measure of political power. It will be some time before the Hmong attain these goals. But if the reflective essays by the four student narrators in this book are at all representative, then the day when Hmong refugees and their Hmong American progeny will become an integral part of American society may be closer at hand than scholars seem to think.

The Xiong Family of Goleta

Jon Yee Xiong in California, 1985. *Courtesy of Jou Yee Xiong.*

Ka Pao Xiong in Laos, early 1970s. *Courtesy of Ka Pao Xiong.*

Jou Yee Xiong's Life Story

as told to Lee Fang, Thek Moua, and Vu Pao Tcha

My name is Jou Yee Xiong and I am sixty-six years old. More than a hundred years before I was born, the Hmong people had migrated from China into Laos and other places in Southeast Asia. The Hmong had been fighting with the Chinese; those who were not taken prisoner moved southward, while the captives remained in China. Many Hmong were captured and tortured during their migration.

After arriving in Laos, the Hmong lived in the jungles and sometimes fought against the French in Xieng Khouang Province, and especially on the Plain of Jars. We had a leader named Chao Ba Chay who led this resistance. The French asked the Hmong, "Why are you always fighting?" The Hmong responded it was because they were not allowed to rule themselves. So, the French gave them control of the region where many Hmong lived.

The Hmong lived only in the highlands, because every time we went to the lowlands we got sick. Our elders believed that the lowland Lao had put a curse on us, so that anyone going to the Lao towns would get very sick and die. Just as Hmong knew how to use black magic, so, too, did the Cambodians and Lao. The Hmong believed that the Lao, especially, could kill people by slitting their throats internally. We sometimes visited the towns, but only during our New Year's festival in January. Otherwise, we never went there.

Up in the mountains, we farmed with only a few simple tools. Each village had only two or three axes and hoes, which people used in turn. Only one in every three families had a large butchering knife for slaughtering pigs and cutting up the meat. We purchased iron from the townspeople to make these tools.

Everyone between the ages of eighteen and forty* had to pay taxes to the French as well as to the Lao chieftains who protected the villages. If a father served on the village council, however, only two of his sons, rather than all of them, had to pay taxes. Paying taxes was not easy. The Hmong were not educated enough to know how much gold and silver or diamonds were worth. We only knew how to grow rice, corn, and vegetables to feed ourselves and to raise animals which we sold for profit. There were a lot of wild animals, including wild boars, in the jungles that we hunted for meat. These wild animals often came to eat our crops at night. They especially liked young ears of corn. Without guns, we could not eliminate them. Since the crops we grew were not sufficient to feed us and the wild animals as well, we were poor and had a hard time paying our taxes.

My grandfather was a leader in our village. He had nine daughters and two sons. The younger son was my father. While my mother was still in labor with me, my father died. My grandfather cried for a year because he had fond hopes that my father would succeed him as the village leader. Then my grandfather, too, died. We suffered greatly. Our crops were not sufficient to feed us.

The most helpful individuals in my family were my two grandmothers. They cultivated *mang,* a kind of hemp whose fiber was used to make thread and cloth. Its skin had to be removed and its stem sliced with great caution. The skin was then pulled apart and the fibers rolled together to make thread. During our long treks to our fields, we rolled the *mang* between our palms as we walked. On the way home, we did the same thing. After dinner, we also worked on the *mang* till we fell asleep. Our grandmothers used a machine with a pedal to weave the threads into fabric, with which they made us clothes. Since it took so much energy to make cloth, each of us got only two new suits of clothing a year. We were so poor we had

*According to Alfred W. McCoy (1970), those between eighteen and sixty had to pay taxes. [*Ed.*]

no shoes. The Hmong did not know how to make shoes, so there were countless times when thorns pricked our soles and our feet were bruised all over. When I was young, we even went hunting in our bare feet.

Since there were a lot of lice and fleas where we lived, our grandmothers boiled water to bath us every two or three days, as well as to wash our clothes. We had to use hot water to kill the fleas. When our hair got long, our relatives shaved our heads, so that the lice had no place to hide. However, in those days, many Hmong liked to wear a bundle of hair on top of their heads, covering it with a cap.

At age fifteen, I began to learn the lowland Lao language. By the time I was twenty, I could read and write it. When I was sixteen, I started working as a messenger, going from town to town. Every year, one month before the French started collecting taxes, they sent a letter to each village. My job was to deliver these letters to the leaders of the villages. Those who could not pay the taxes had to work without wages for fifteen days, paving roads, building bridges, and constructing houses. Sometimes it took two or three days just to get to the work site. People had to bring their own food. Since the French did not work on Thursdays and Sundays for religious reasons, it took almost a month to finish the work. Sometimes people died while working and never went back to their villages.

Around this time, the imperial Japanese army came to Laos. Up till then, even under French colonial rule, the Hmong had been controlled by Lao chieftains, though each Hmong clan had its own leader. Nong Het [the center of a Hmong autonomous district east of the Plain of Jars] was governed by Hmong. Other parts of Laos were under the central government. When the Japanese seized power from the French, the leaders of the Lo clan joined the Japanese. They drove away the French and the latter's Hmong allies, the Ly and Moua clans. Captured French soldiers were taken to prison camps in Vietnam. They were later released and sent back to France. A number of the French soldiers who were not captured went to live with the Ly and Moua clans in the jungle. When the United States bombed Hiroshima and Nagasaki, Japan lost World War II and the Japanese soldiers in Laos returned to Japan.

During the war, after working for two years as a messenger, I became a servant to some government officials. I watched over their property. I got married when I was twenty and had two children by age twenty-five. Then I was given the title of "tax collector," even though no one under thirty-five was supposed to serve. I helped those who were too poor to pay; they promised to reimburse me later. Also, I gave them suggestions on how to come up with the money to pay their taxes.

In 1953, missionaries came to our village. I, along with my family, converted to Christianity. I stopped teaching my sons many of the Hmong ways because I felt my ancestors and I had suffered enough already. I thought that teaching my children the old ways would only place a burden on them. Instead, I began to teach them how to do things differently, so that they would not suffer as Hmong had in the past.

Our suffering was due to the fact that we had no country of our own. We did not live in any stable community. We were always moving. Hmong never had any land or any permanent place. We have always practiced slash-and-burn agriculture, moving from place to place. We lacked education, but we did learn bit by bit [to live in the modern world] from lowland Lao merchants who came to our villages to sell us sugarcane in exchange for our opium.

After the Japanese left, members of the Ly and Moua clans, carrying handmade weapons, went looking for the French soldiers who were still hiding in caves and took them to their villages. The French soldiers sent word back to France that they were still alive. Soon, French airplanes dropped them weapons [on the Plain of Jars]. Because we had helped the French to win, they gave us greater autonomy after the war. Touby Lyfong was put in charge of all the Hmong villages in the Plain of Jars. He asked for help to send some Hmong youth to school. Three of these students later helped General Vang Pao govern the Hmong between 1960 and 1975.

The parents of Touby Lyfong, and of Vang Pao, Lon Hong, and Nhia Vue all belonged to the Hmong aristocracy. That was why they were able to educate their children by hiring teachers to come to their homes, there being no schools available. Touby and several other Hmong later went to study in Vietnam, since there were no colleges in Laos. One of them then went to France, while Touby returned to Laos. After the Japanese were defeated, those Hmong studying in Vietnam returned home, and Touby and his sons were recognized as leaders.

After World War II ended, the Ly and Moua clans continued to help the French to fight, this time against the Communist Pathet Lao and their ally, the Lo clan. Initially, the French and their Hmong allies were victorious and drove the Red Laotians and the Hmong of the Lo clan into Vietnam. However, the latter soon returned and fought the Ly and Moua warriors all the way to Nong Het. But the Ly and Moua men regrouped and drove the invaders back to the Vietnamese border.

Later, when the Red Laotians came again, they came not as fighters but as thieves. They robbed the rich in Nong Het. Those who were not robbed migrated elsewhere. These thieves came to our village also and they tied up our leaders, including me. When we yelled for help, however, they ran away. This incident scared us, so we fled to the jungle, where we lived for several years without any decent houses. The thieves took over more and more territory and became powerful. The Laotian central government tried to capture their leader, Prince Souphanouvong. They succeeded and imprisoned him in Vientiane. Souphanouvong's brother tried to get him released but failed, so he persuaded an air force commander [named Kong Le] to turn sides. A civil war broke out in Vientiane, during which Souphanouvong escaped.

The Laotian central government, as well as the Hmong leaders, knew they could not win the war without modern weapons. So, they went to the Thai government and asked for help. The Thai gave them some cannon, with which they pushed Kong Le and his forces out of Vientiane and into Vang Vieng. But, unable to hold their ground, Kong Le and his troops moved to Mount Hang Hed. There, they battled Vang Pao and his followers. Vang Pao lost and sought refuge in the jungles.

Vang Pao came to our village and asked for help. With our aid, he made his way to Camp Padong, where airplanes dropped us food, weapons, medical supplies, and other miscellaneous items. Six months later, Kong Le shelled the camp repeatedly for three months. Everything was destroyed, so we could no longer live there. We fled to Phakhao to build a new base and an air strip. Laotian planes supplied us with military and construction materials. Vang Pao was made a general, with authority over the Phakhao base and the region surrounding it. He became responsible for all military, economic, and social affairs.

In 1966, I decided to leave the war zone, so I told our leader, Tou Pao, that I did not want to fight anymore. I did not want to be a soldier; instead, I wanted to farm. I asked for permission to go to Sayaboury [a province bordering Thailand]. Tou Pao allowed my family and several other families to take a plane to Vientiane. We stayed there for twenty days to get papers for going to Sayaboury. We left Vientiane on an American airplane. When we got to Sayaboury, we built a village at the edge of the jungle where some Hmong had already settled. We called our new village Nam Hia. As soon as we had enough people, our elders decided to build an irrigation system. The Americans supplied us with equipment, while the Hmong and Lao did the construction. It took three years to complete the irrigation works, after which we could finally farm.

Since the Hmong had always practiced slash-and-burn agriculture in the mountains, we initially did not know how to farm in the lowlands. Each family was given a certain amount of land—usually a plot measuring 300 by 100 meters. We had to learn how to talk to buffaloes. If you do not know how to talk to the buffaloes, they will not listen to you. To plow the land, we had to use buffaloes. It is not like here in America where you can use tractors. I did not know how to speak the buffaloes' language, so I had to learn it in order to get them to work. I had to learn to say, "Go. Go. Go to the right, go to the left."

We grew wet paddy rice [in contrast to the dry upland rice grown in the mountains] to feed ourselves, corn to feed our animals, bananas, sugarcane (whose stalks we chewed, as we did not know how to make sugar), pineapples, and all kinds of vegetables. The first seven years we lived in Nam Hia, our harvests were very good and we had an abundance of rice in storage. Laotians from Luang Prabang came to buy our rice, sugarcane, and pineapples. We prospered and our standard of living reached that of the lowland Lao.

We lived in Nam Hia for nine years. We were happy finally to have homes and land that belonged to us. We gained hope and worked harder. But our happy life did not last long. We had become friends with the missionaries there, so we knew that if the Communists from Vietnam ever came to our village, both the missionaries and those of us who were Christians would be persecuted.

When General Vang Pao left the country, we had to leave also, because there was no one left to protect us. I had three sons. Pao, who had graduated from a college in Vientiane, was working for the Americans; another son was in school in Sayaboury; a third was in Luang Prabang. My son Pao, who had a telephone in his home, called us when he heard the news that General Vang Pao was fleeing. He told me, "We Hmong can't stay in Laos. Vang Pao is going to Thailand. He is leaving today. Decide if you want to go or stay."

I cried because I did not want to go without my sons. But I thought it over and decided to leave. We left our home without taking anything. I did not want to sell our stored rice, but my wife wanted to do so. I told her, "If we cannot make it to Thailand, we will come back here and eat it." But my wife insisted, "No, we'll sell it." So we sold half of it for two hundred thousand Laotian *kips* [Laotian currency]. We could have sold the other half for five hundred thousand, but we had no more time, so we just left it in storage, along with five buffaloes and our house that had cost us fifteen thousand Laotian *kips* to build.

We only brought along three small children who were still feeding on condensed milk, a number of older ones—all members of our clan—and some silver money. Nam Hia was very close to Thailand. When we went there on foot to do business without carrying a lot of goods, it took only three days at most to get there. However, when we fled Laos, we had to carry a lot of food and had our children along, so it took us twenty-eight days to get to the Thai border.

When General Vang Pao left, he told everybody that if we did not cross the border within a month, we would no longer be allowed to do so. We were very scared. We did not know if we could make it. My son Pao eventually caught up with us. He hid his important documents in his hat. (We, on the other hand, had stored our money and other important items in a suitcase back at the village.) My son told me that the journey by land to Thailand would be difficult, so he suggested we turn back so that our family could fly to Thailand. He said he still had access to either a helicopter or an airplane. However, there would be room for only our family. I had a meeting with the other elders and they said, "If you leave us, we will face greater difficulty. So, if you choose to go back, all of us will return with you. But if you want to proceed to Thailand on foot, all of us will follow." We realized that should we retrace our steps, we might very likely encounter robbers, so we decided to continue on foot toward Thailand.

The first day we walked the whole day and camped by a stream for the night. At midnight, the male leaders had a meeting to discuss our situation. "What should we do with our guns and other weapons?" we asked ourselves. If we kept them and got caught, our captors would think we were soldiers and would kill us, but if we hid them or threw them away, then they would think we were only peasants trying to flee the war. Thus, we decided to go without our weapons.

On the second day, three families who had planted a lot of opium decided to return to their village to harvest the crop. The rest of us continued on our way. No food was available, so we could buy only corn, which was usually used to feed the pigs. We ground the corn to make bread. On the third day, it took us three-quarters of the day to reach a Lao village.

During our journey, we came upon a village settled by non-Christians who still performed evil rituals. The son in one of the families who were with us was attacked by demons and he got really sick. His family fell back while the others went on. Soon I decided some of us should go back to help the family. Many disagreed, so I went back alone to help them. The boy died and I asked his parents to let me bury him the Christian way. I said a prayer and we continued on our journey.

When we got to the border after twenty-eight days, the Thai officials would not let us cross. They did not want us to take refuge in their country. They said there was no war going on in Laos, so we were not being persecuted. We could not do anything to convince the Thai officials, so we stayed near the border for a week waiting for permission to enter. We consumed all our rice and had to buy food from the Lao families nearby. There were about two hundred families amassed near the border and we ate all the rice we could buy. I was in charge of sixty families, all of them Christians. Other families were led by their own leaders, some of whom had been teachers, community leaders, or army officers.

The weather was very bad. It rained heavily. People were in the worst condition. Many were sick. There was no shelter. I told the other leaders: "Let this young man, my son, go talk to the Thai. He knows how to speak Thai." That night, I called all my fellow Christians for a meeting. I took the Bible and read from it. Then we all prayed to Jesus Christ to help us convince the Thai officials to let us in. We prayed all night. Thank God, Jesus answered our prayers. While we were praying, the Thai came and told us we could go and that nobody would stop us. I was very happy. The news made everyone happy. It took us four more days to reach Thailand. Some elderly men and women could not walk and were carried by young adults. When we finally reached Thailand, we felt free.

We stayed in a refugee camp in Thailand for three months, then we were sent to Bangkok, where we stayed another three months. Our food ran out after the first two months and we went hungry. We had only ten thousand Laotian *kips* left. In Laos, such a sum could have bought food to feed us for a long time, but when it was changed into Thai currency, the money was not worth much and we could buy only a little food. Our papers still had not arrived, so we could not leave for the United States. We called long distance to our American Christian friends in Isla Vista, California, to ask them to send us some money. It cost sixty *baht* [Thai currency] to say just six words on the phone. Our friends sent us eight hundred U.S. dollars. We changed it to Thai money and rented a place and bought a lot of rice and kitchen utensils. During our stay in Thailand there was a flood. Our children caught the small fish in the water and we cooked them. We also ate other animals that lived in the water. We now laugh about those days, but they were very degrading.

Our papers finally came. We went to the airport at three o'clock in the morning. Since it was still dark, we never saw what Bangkok looked like. The place we had lived in, in Bangkok, was downtown near a square where four streets intersect. There were a lot of soldiers standing around, so we were afraid to go out to see the city. We lived like caged animals. Nobody knew the city and we did not know anyone who wanted to show us around. We went out only once during those months, when a Hmong who had studied at a university in Bangkok rented a small car and took us to see the stores.

On our way to the airport, twenty-seven of us were squeezed into a tiny bus. When we got to the airport, two Americans greeted us and took us to a big airplane. It was morning, around eight o'clock. The sun had risen by the time we got into the plane. So we left

Thailand. We flew in the air but we did not know where we were
going, only that it was some place in America. We stopped in Hong
Kong for an hour, during which the flight attendants were changed.
From there, we flew to Japan. It was already dark when we landed
in Japan. After the plane was refueled, we flew to Hawaii. The trip
from Japan to Hawaii did not seem very long. We stopped for an
hour and changed planes. The American airport inspectors, who had
never seen Hmong silver money, said nothing when they searched
our bags. But when I walked through the security gate, it made a
sound. So, they searched me and found my silver money, which I
was wearing around my waist. In Thailand, I had told the airport
officials that the silver was my property and my good luck charm.
They understood and let me keep it. But I did not know how to explain to the Americans what it was. They took all my money in front
of everybody. My children laughed at me and said, "See, you did not
want to use it to buy us food, now they are taking it all away from
you." After they inspected the money, however, the Americans gave
it back to me. We then flew to Los Angeles.

We were the first people of such short stature to come to the United
States, so people were very frightened of us. They had been told that
we had long tongues and ate humans. Two very courageous persons
came to pick us up at the airport. The Americans in Thailand had
telephoned them and told them our names and said that we would
have tags around our necks with our names written on them. When
we arrived in Los Angeles, we put our tags around our necks and got
out of the plane. Suddenly, there was a couple in front of us, saying,
"Pao?" My eldest son did not hear them, so my second son told him,
"Pao, those people are calling you." The Americans took us to the
bathrooms first and then we rested for three hours before catching
another plane to Santa Barbara.

We had left Thailand on December 29, 1975. When we arrived in
the United States, it was still December 29 [since we had crossed the
international dateline]. After spending one night here, it was December 30. The day after that was December 31. Then came January 1,
1976. So, it is easy to remember when we came: at the end of 1975
and the beginning of 1976.

Our American friends from Isla Vista took us to the house where
we were to live. Life was very difficult for my two oldest sons be-

cause they had to take care of everything but they could not speak English. Our friends brought us food—mostly bread, peanut butter, and jam, but we could not eat such unfamiliar things. We fed the sandwiches to the children, while the adults ate rice. My younger sons wanted to eat some meat but they did not know how to ask our friends for any. My sons spoke some French, but the Americans did not know French. So my sons took a piece of paper and drew a pig. The Americans finally understood. After that, they brought us some pork every week.

Our American friends took care of us for seven months. Then they found us jobs. They took my two sons, my son-in-law, and me to work for a company that built speed boats. We worked there for a month. The work was very difficult. We came home with bruises all over our arms. When our American friends saw our injuries, they took us to the hospital. Then they found us lighter work at a pharmaceutical company. When they discovered that Pao could speak some English, they sent him to another place to work, while the other three of us continued in the same company. There were forty Hmong working there and none of us knew a word of English. My boss used to joke with me. He asked, "Why do you never speak? If you just say 'coffee,' then I will get you some coffee." I did not want to talk, but he kept bothering me. I finally asked my boss for some coffee, but he told me, "All you have to do is pour it in a cup. You can do it yourself." And that is how I got coffee.

I did not try to learn English because I felt I was too old. Although I know some words, I will never be able to express myself correctly. In Laos I used to be a very good speaker and had no trouble expressing my thoughts. But with English, I know it will not be the same. I do not like people to make fun of me, so I never bother to say anything.

After three months, the four of us got our paychecks. We now could buy our own food, but our American friends still paid our rent. When we realized that we had enough money to both buy food and pay our rent, our American friends told us now that we were able to support ourselves, they were going to stop helping us. They told us not to be unhappy about the situation. Should we need help, they said, we could still call on them.

So, with the help of God, we have worked and found good jobs.

After we had been in the United States for a year, we were allowed to sponsor our relatives in Thailand to come here. After our relatives arrived, we sought financial assistance for them. We Hmong did not have any association to help us get public assistance, so we joined the Vietnamese one. A Vietnamese leader helped our relatives to get on welfare. But our American friends did not want to sign the papers to put us on welfare. They said they had not brought us to the United States so we could be on welfare. They wanted us to depend on ourselves. They said, "In life, if we do not learn, we will never be able to do a lot of things. If you wait and depend on others, you'll never learn." They signed the papers only for those who were in a really bad situation. The latter lived on welfare for two years until they, too, found jobs.

[After we saved some money,] the first thing we did was to buy a car and learn how to drive. It was a new experience. We were all afraid of cars but after a while some of us learned how to drive quite well. At that time, Isla Vista was not so crowded, so we could drive without any problem. There were rarely any cars in Isla Vista during weekends. My son drove people to the store, to work, or to other places. But after a while, he got tired of taking care of everyone. So, we decided to buy another car. Soon, the person driving that car also thought people were asking him to do too much, so we bought additional cars until almost everyone had a car.

After a few years, life became harder as our rent went up. There was also a law saying that too many of us could not live together in one place. So we had to find another place but the ones we liked were all too expensive. Places for which we could afford the rent we did not like. One of my sons-in-law decided to go to Stockton where, he was told, he could find cheap houses to rent. Four families went with him. After a year, however, two families came back, and the year after that another family returned because they could not find jobs in Stockton. But the one family that stayed helped other Hmong to settle there. That is how Hmong got to Stockton. There are a lot of Hmong there now.

My son-in-law, who remained in Stockton [for a while], could not find a job either. Fortunately, he met a Chinese who worked for American growers. The Chinese worker took my son-in-law to a place where his family did not have to pay rent. They just had to buy their own food. They worked for the American growers picking fruit and doing other farmwork. After three years, however, they had differences with the American growers, so they came back to Isla Vista. They had managed to save a little money, so they decided to buy a house, because no landlord would allow our entire family to live together. In two years' time, when our family grew too big, we bought another house—a large one—in Lompoc [where the real estate prices are lower].

My sons and I are not wealthy people. We are just workers who want to survive. We are not ambitious. We do not wish to go into business and get rich. We live like poor people but we are happy and do not envy others. We like living quietly and simply. I have three sons who have very good jobs and two other sons who are in college. I am waiting for the last two to complete their education. Since I have so many grandsons, relatives, and friends, it is hard for me to become wealthy. I cannot say whether I will continue to live like this for the rest of my life. If, one day, God wishes me to [become wealthy enough to] take care of my fellow Hmong, I will do it. But if that is not God's wish, then I will continue to live the same way as I am living now.

My family was one of the first Hmong families to come to the United States. My sons were among the first Hmong to study in the American educational system. One is studying in Los Angeles and the other is at the University of California, Santa Cruz. We arrived in two families with a total of twenty-seven persons. Since then, my sons-in-law and sister-in-law have sponsored their parents and other relatives who were living in refugee camps in Thailand to enter the United States. Through this process, we have brought our entire [extended] family here, but we have no difficulty buying food or paying our bills, even though at first it was hard financially. But we always help each other out and no one starves. Most members of my family now live in Lompoc.

Before we came, we were asked, "When you lived in Laos, did you know anything about the judicial system? Did you ever commit a crime, a misdemeanor or felony?" I answered, "No, I have not committed any of those things." They also asked me, "What was your occupation?" I answered, "In Laos, I farmed and grew my own food." One month after we arrived, our sponsors took us for a drive along the Santa Barbara coast to Solvang. Along the way, we saw some deer, which seemed very friendly, so we started hunting for squirrels, pigeons, and deer. We were sworn to abide by the hunting regulations, but we assumed that so long as we did not shoot other hunters, we could hunt. If Hmong have violated the regulations, it was because we did not understand them.

Before I left the refugee camp, I was also asked, "What is your religion?" "Christianity," I replied. Since coming to the United States, I have not feared anything. With Jesus as my guiding light, I am not afraid wherever I may be. That is why I was able to bring my family and close relatives to the United States, in spite of the fact that others in Thailand warned us it would be very difficult for us to survive. Many people tried to persuade me to remain in Thailand, but I ignored them and came. I told them, "If my family perishes in America, then none of you should follow in our footsteps. But if we succeed and have a good life, then you can decide whether or not you want to go."

Soon after we settled here, I recorded a cassette tape and sent it to my son-in-law in the Thai refugee camp. I told him, "If you want to come, I shall sponsor you. If I am able to survive, so can you." On the tape, I told about what life in the United States is like. I said there would be no way for Hmong to farm or build their own houses because Americans use machines to do those things. When Americans wish to remove half a hill to build the foundation for a house, they can do it. I also reported that Americans do not raise animals the same way Hmong do. Animals here are raised by the thousands. The eggs they collect from hens are also in the thousands, compared to the twenty or thirty we gathered in Laos. However, there was other work we could do. If I have not died, I said, others would not either. After listening to my tape, everyone wanted to come. We have, in time, sponsored all of them. That is why there are quite a few Hmong living in this area today.

Nkag Pov Xyooj's* (Ka Pao Xiong's) Life Story

as told to Thek Moua

In Laos, I worked for the American Agency for International Development (USAID). I lived in Ban Houei Sai near the Mekong River in the northwestern part of Laos. In April 1975, most of the Americans in Laos left the country. Many Laotian employees and I went to Vientiane [the administrative capital of Laos] for a meeting to discuss what to do. Since the newly formed government was a coalition government, every position was held by two people—one from the Communist side, and one from the pro-American side. The Americans who worked in Laos at that time had come under various auspices. Some were in the embassy, others worked for USAID, while yet others served as military advisors. The Laotian government asked all the American military personnel to leave the country. They wanted only the American ambassador and a few civilian officials to remain. The government also asked all the Communist troops from [North] Vietnam to withdraw. At the meeting in the USAID compound, I and other workers were assigned to certain positions. We were given three months' pay before we even started working. We were told that should the political situation prove stable after three months, we could return to receive additional salary.

At this meeting, the Americans told us that South Vietnam had

---

*Ka Pao Xiong requested that his name in Hmong script be indicated here. [Ed.]

77

been invaded by troops from the North, and that many South Vietnamese had already fled to the United States and the Philippines.
They said that those of us who feared for our lives had the right to go
to the United States as well, but that the U.S. Congress had not yet
passed any laws with regard to the admission of Laotian refugees, so
everything was in flux. But the Americans emphasized that those of
us who had worked for them could apply to enter the United States
as refugees, even though they were not making any promises about
whether or not we would be admitted.

After the meeting, I returned to Ban Houei Sai to continue working at the USAID mission. We had communication radios; thus I was
able to contact my parents in Sayaboury, where there was another
USAID headquarters. We talked about the political situation and especially about how General Vang Pao was evacuating Long Cheng. We
discussed what we should do. The word of Vang Pao's departure
spread like wildfire. My parents and I decided that all the members
of our family should meet at Udon [in Thailand] in sixty days. This
was the beginning of our journey to freedom.

I sent my wife and children to Sayaboury because it would be safer
for them there, as Sayaboury is on the other side of the Mekong
River. I stayed in Ban Houei Sai for another week. My brother-in-
law, Touby Lo, radioed me to tell me that my father wanted me to
find my brother, who was in school in Luang Prabang, before I left
for Udon. Since Air America was no longer flying its planes in Laos,
it was difficult to find air transportation. Only with the payment of
a huge fee could one hope to get a flight out. (There are no roads
from Ban Houei Sai to other parts of Laos.) I found only an Air Lao
cargo plane available. I used my USAID documents to obtain seven
plane tickets, so that my brother and I could fly back to Ban Houei
Sai where I had a Thai friend who worked with me. He was a good
friend of the Thai consul in Ban Houei Sai and he agreed to get a pass
for us to go to Udon legally.

I then flew to Luang Prabang to look for my brother at the
Christian-sponsored dormitory, but when I got there I was told that
all the Hmong students, including my brother, had already departed.
The overseer at the dorm said that my brother had gone to Sayaboury to join my parents. Later, I discovered that my brother had
missed my parents because they had left Sayaboury three days be-

fore he arrived. Failing to locate my brother, I did not know what to do. I went back to the airport to continue my flight to Sayaboury but there was no plane available. All the taxis had been rented out as well. After looking for a day, I finally managed to hire a taxi to take me to Sayaboury. When I got there, Vietnamese forces had already taken and occupied the town. They restricted the movement of the airplanes and taxis.

The only person left whom I knew was Moua Yia, a teacher in the high school. Since he had a well-paid job, he had decided to stay. He took me to his house and fed me. I then went to my parents' house in the same village and saw that other Hmong families had already moved into it. They were in the process of killing two cows and some pigs to feed the conquering Vietnamese general and his troops. I stayed and ate with them before leaving to look for my parents.

Near the town where my parents lived there was a small military base that General Vang Pao had built. After walking for a whole day and arriving in the middle of the night, I found my parents there. They had been told that airplanes would come and pick them up. Many of the refugees wanted to return to Sayaboury, but others, who had worked for Americans, were afraid that if they did so, their lives would be endangered. So the people told my father, who had been a community leader in Sayaboury, that should he decide to return, they would go back with him, but if he decided to press forward, they would follow. Peasants had their farms and houses to return to, but those who had held office jobs or who had worked for Americans had nothing left. So the latter did not want to return. They tried to convince the peasants that they might be killed along the way if they attempted to go back. My father gathered together all the elders and told them we should all go forward toward Thailand. He said that General Vang Pao and his forces would not be coming to rescue us. The airplanes and helicopters that were supposed to come for us never showed up. So we started walking.

Since my father has already talked about our journey, I shall not discuss it in detail. My family suffered greatly along the way. Since my wife is Lao, and not Hmong, she was not used to walking up and down the mountains and through rough terrain. Also, my three daughters were very young at the time—their ages were two and a half years, one and a half years, and six months. All of them still depended on condensed milk for their nutrition, so we had to carry many, many cans. Some people had infants strapped to the front of their bodies, while I had one in front and one on the back. So our pace was very slow. It also rained heavily, and the ground was very slippery. There were nearly two thousand people along on this journey. Those walking in front chopped down bushes and other obstacles in our path, but that meant those of us at the back had nothing to grab on to when we slipped. People also cut firewood for cooking and banana leaves for their makeshift shelters, but by the time we who were at the back got to the places where we camped for the night, there was nothing left. After suffering greatly for the first two nights, we decided that some of the strong, young men in our family should move ahead, so that they could chop the banana leaves and bamboo that we needed before they were all gone. In this way, we suffered less during the rest of the journey. God was with us all the way. Even though we were the last in line, He provided for our needs.

When we reached the Thai border, there was no refugee camp waiting for us. Refugee camps had not yet been built. There were also no taxis to take us to the temporary refugee camp. Those who walked to the camp were robbed by thieves. We kept walking and I soon encountered two empty taxis. I hired both for two hundred and fifty *baht* [Thai currency] and got driven to a newly built but plain-looking city hall, where the Thai authorities were keeping all the refugees. As soon as we got out of the taxis, we were surrounded by Thai policemen. We were afraid they might harm us, but instead, one of them asked who had hired the taxis and when I said I had, he asked me how much fare I had paid. When I told him two hundred and fifty *baht,* he said it was too much and made the Hmong taxi driver give me back a hundred *baht.*

The policeman directed us to a newly built house, which had no fence or garden around it. He said we could live there until we built our own house. The mayor of the town was very kind and understanding. Even though there were three thousand Hmong gathered there, he told us to buy wood or bamboo, if we had the money to do so. He said we could build temporary shelters on his extremely large fruit farm. His farm was filled with all kinds of fruit trees and he told us to be careful not to harm the trees. He started keeping a record of every family. He advised us to go look for work in order to earn some money. He even hired some Hmong to help him take a census and to plant grass in the city hall's yard. He paid each person who worked for him fifteen *baht* a day. But after all the work was done, we began to suffer because no other jobs could be found. Many of the Thai residents in the town protested the help their mayor was giving us. The quarrel between them was finally settled by the governor. The mayor told the governor that he had placed all of us on his own land because he did not want the Hmong to step on the rice fields of the Thai residents or steal their rice. He said he was only trying his best to help us. The governor, therefore, sided with the mayor. Since the work I had done for the Americans was very light, I found the job of helping the mayor build a store very hard. So, I became a fisherman instead, and fish became our main source of food for a while.

At this time, some Christian students from the University of California, Santa Barbara, came to visit our camp. They had established a church near their campus and recruited a number of Vietnamese students who [had been evacuated to the United States and] were in Camp Pendleton, as well as a number of Cambodian students, to join them in their work. They wanted to find some Hmong students to work with them also. One of these Americans came to see Pastor Torgerson, a missionary. Pastor Torgerson brought him to the section of town where we were living. They found Xay Her Xiong, my brother, and some other Hmong students and wanted to take them to the United States to train them for evangelical work. But when they went to the American embassy in Bangkok, they were told that Congress had not yet passed any bill to allow Hmong refugees to enter the United States. They were told that only individuals who had worked for the Americans during the war would qualify for entry. The young American came back to tell us what the situation was. I told him that I had worked for the Americans as an administrator. He offered to take me, my wife, and my children to the United States. My father spoke up, however, and said that since I was his eldest son, they could not take me without taking my parents and brothers and sisters also.

The Christian student from Santa Barbara took down my name and submitted it to the man who was supervising the refugee outflow from Thailand. By coincidence, this man had been my old boss in Ban Houei Sai. He was shocked to see my name and asked the student where I was. He sent the student back to get me right away. When the student arrived, I was fishing. My brother found me at the river to tell me the good news. The student and I started on our return journey the very same day. It took us a whole night of travel to get to Bangkok, where my old boss was. I was very happy to see him. He asked where my family was. I told him they were in Nan Province. He told me to go get my whole family as soon as possible, because the number of authorizations for aliens to go to the United States was running out. I rushed back to my family and returned with them, my parents and all my brothers and sisters.

My old boss presented my family of twenty-seven people to the immigration committee and told them that I had worked for him in Laos and asked if I and my family would be eligible to go to the United States. The committee members said that so long as my boss knew me, there was no need for us to go through the application process. The committee asked those who were members of my family to raise their hands. Everyone did so. Our papers were approved immediately but, as it turned out, we had to stay in Bangkok for three months, because the number of aliens authorized for resettlement in the United States had been filled and Bangkok was flooded for a long time. So, it was not until December 29, 1975, that we boarded a plane headed for the United States. We flew first to Hong Kong, then Japan, Hawaii, and finally Los Angeles. Something weird happened during our trip. It was December 29 when we began our journey and it was still December 29 when we got here, even though we had been traveling for a day and night. That was something I could not understand. Eventually, someone explained it to me [i.e., crossing the international dateline].

At Los Angeles International Airport, a couple from the church came to greet us. They helped us transfer to another plane and then they themselves drove back to Santa Barbara. When we landed at the airport in Goleta [the airport for Santa Barbara], many people from the church came to welcome us to the United States and especially to their community. When we got off the plane, we stood out from the crowd. People stared at us. The people welcoming us hugged all the members of my family. That made us afraid [because Hmong do not hug each other]. Each person hugged us and shook our hands and passed us on to another person in the large crowd. We were afraid these people were trying to scatter us so that they could steal one of us. But we also felt thankful because we realized we had arrived in a land of freedom and we could feel the love and care of the church right there at the airport. Many people were standing on the roof of the airport terminal shouting, "Praise God!" My spirit was touched.

The people took us to a house and gave us a lot of clothing. Each room in the house was labeled with our names. The Christian students from the University of California, Santa Barbara, were our sponsors. They were led by a pastor who used to be a Baptist but who later became a revivalist. Each month, the group met at a member's house for Bible study. Each member of the group also put their money into a common account. One of the students resided with us to help us buy food, show us how to do the laundry, take us to the hospital when we were sick, and help us with other chores. At first, we had no way of earning money, but before I left for the United States, the Americans had paid me for the work I had done for them in Laos. My total wages came to about two thousand dollars. I used this money to buy food and other necessities for my family when we first got here.

Our friend, the Christian student, taught us English. When we could comprehend the language a little, we were taught how to look for jobs and other means of survival. The basic principle that these Christian students followed was that when they understood the Gospels well enough to share their faith with others, they would move on to another town to spread the Good News.

My father, my brother, Xay Her Xiong, and I soon went to work for a medical supply company. We worked there for almost a year. We took the bus to work everyday. We were the reason that so many Hmong came here. Those who got here in the early days sponsored their relatives who were living in the refugee camps in Thailand. My wife is lowland Lao and she brought her side of the family here. Her relatives in turn helped other Lao to come to the United States. My father and I have only two immediate relatives left in Laos: my uncle and aunt. My uncle is a teacher at a school near Ban Houei Sai. But since he and my aunt have twelve children, I don't think we can sponsor them. However, if we have enough money, we would like to bring them here for a visit.

When our numbers grew to around eight hundred [in the Isla Vista and Goleta area], we went to the social service agencies to apply for federal aid. These agencies soon hired some of us as interpreters and social workers. Touby Lo and I were hired and I worked for them for four years. I also worked part time as an English-as-a-Second-Language teacher's aid for two years. As more Lao and Cambodians showed up in Isla Vista and Goleta, they needed public assistance. That was why I was offered the job as a social worker because I could speak not only Hmong but also Lao and some English.

During those years, we helped everybody. Lowland Lao, Hmong, Cambodians—we helped them all alike. Touby Lo and I took them to the hospital if they were sick; we took them to apply for federal aid for refugees or for Aid to Families with Dependent Children if they needed financial assistance; we took them to the store when they had to buy something; we helped them find a house if they needed a place to live. When our family first came here, we had a sponsor, but many of the refugees who came after us had no sponsors, so they relied on us for guidance and support.

As the rents went up in Isla Vista, my family decided to move to Goleta, where we bought the house we are still living in today. Many of our relatives, when they arrived in this country, were resettled [by the voluntary agencies working under federal contracts] in Los Angeles County for some unknown reason. We went down there to help them and to move them here to live with us. As refugee resettlement workers, we worked closely with the state Employment Development Department (EDD), especially the Work Incentive (WIN) program, to place anybody who needed work into a job befitting his or her ability. The WIN program supported our efforts to introduce our people to the job market. This meant that EDD/WIN paid an individual's wages until he or she had learned the necessary skills to do the job, or gave a tax incentive to the employers who hired such applicants. Through the good example set by those who were lucky enough to get hired and who proved their willingness to work hard, many employers contacted us for more workers. We are thankful to those employers who have offered us jobs.

We tried to live in harmony with our neighbors. [Soon after we came here,] the Hmong decided to help clean up the neighborhood. We picked up trash first in the streets of Isla Vista, then along the beach, and finally along the freeway. The city was very appreciative of our community service.

General Vang Pao came to visit us and told us about the Central Valley. He wanted all the Hmong to be together. He said that the Central Valley is ideal for farming, but we knew that so long as we had to farm with our bare hands, we could never compete with farmers who have tractors. So, we decided to stay in Goleta where we were already employed.

[I will tell you about how my family became Christians.] My father used to be a great shaman. He performed many rituals to see why so many people in the Xiong clan were dying. There was a rumor that a curse had been placed upon our clan. It was said that those families with sons and lots of money were sure to face death. Due to such suffering, my father wanted to find a way to break the curse. Fortunately, missionaries came to our village in Laos. My father spoke to them and asked them many questions. They told him the only way to break the curse upon our clan was to become Christians. Therefore, our entire family became Christians. After that, whenever people called on my father to perform rituals because he used to be a great shaman, he refused. So, many members of the Xiong clan began to hate us. They didn't want to be our relatives any more. We found other Christians families and they became our new relatives. We adopted Christian beliefs and still keep them today. We thank God for his faithfulness. Before we came, we were told we might be eaten alive by giants, but instead, we have become heirs of the Blessed One.

It has been very difficult for us to adapt because we had no professions or trades and we suffered from culture shock. Here in America, both the husband and wife must work simultaneously to earn enough money to live on. Many of our children are very ignorant of the Hmong way of life. Our children are assimilating into American society, so they no longer listen to us. They are growing up to be part of the American melting pot. Even the old people are forgetting about their life in Laos, as they enjoy the prosperity and good life in America. They are happy that their children are growing up in this society. This country has become ours and we will live the rest of our lives as good citizens.

The Xiong Family of Lompoc

Vue Vang with her eldest daughter, Mai Kou
Xiong, on her knee, 1971. The older girl is her
sister-in-law. *Courtesy of Vue Vang.*

The Xiong family in Lompoc, 1993. *Back row:* Vue Vang (*second from left*),
Xang Mao Xiong (*third from left*), and Maijue Xiong (*right*). *Courtesy of
Maijue Xiong.*

Xang Mao Xiong's Life Story

as told to his daughter, Maijue Xiong

My name is Xang Mao Xiong. My father's name was Xiong Cher Doua and my mother's, Ly Sao. I have four brothers, three of whom are dead. The other is now living in Fresno, California. I had one sister, but she died when I was very young.

My mother gave birth to me on May 14, 1941, in a small village called Pakdom in Xieng Khouang Province. After I was born, we moved to another village called Xanghoe, where we lived for about ten years. We moved again to Muong Cha when I was eleven years old. It took two days on foot and on horseback to journey to our new village.

In Laos, we lived in mountainous areas far away from any towns. Our houses, which we built ourselves, are different from the ones in the United States. The roofs are made of a special kind of long, sturdy grass stitched together into thatch. The walls are made of split bamboo slats tied together. From the inside, you can see the outside through the cracks. But at night, when the lamp is out, no one outside can see inside. Later, when my parents had accumulated some money by selling our animals and opium—our cash crop—to Chinese, Vietnamese, or Cambodian merchants, we were able to cut down trees, make boards, and build a nicer house of wood.

As a young child, my duties included clearing land for farming, cutting and chopping wood for fire, plowing the fields, harvesting the rice, tending the animals, and hauling water to the house from nearby streams and springs. In 1959, my parents decided that we should get an education. Since Muong Cha is many mountains away from any town, my brothers and I could not attend school, so my parents hired two Tai Dam [Black Tai, another ethnic group in Laos] teachers to start a school in our village. The cost per student was two silver bars per year. We studied French and Lao. The two Tai Dam teachers taught us for only a year.

My two older brothers and their wives helped my parents farm while my two younger brothers and I attended school. After school was out each day, I went to the fields to round up the cows, buffaloes, horses, and goats. At that time we owned twenty buffaloes, thirty cows, three horses, fifteen goats, and over fifty pigs and piglets. We also had several dozen chickens, six dogs, five cats, twenty pigeons, and two quail. I fed the animals before cutting wood to make a fire so my mother could cook dinner. We usually ate rice, with some chicken or pork or beef, and mustard greens. After dinner, my brothers and I did our homework. Due to the shortage of paper and pencils, homework consisted of memorizing short stories, poems, and songs.

After the Americans came, we attended a public school they established in another place that was quite far away from Muong Cha. General Vang Pao hired a few military men who had been former teachers to teach there. In 1963, he paid one of my relatives to teach the children in Muong Cha. A few years later, several more teachers were hired. In addition to learning to take dictation in French and Lao, we also studied arithmetic and the history and geography of France and Laos.

Every morning, all the students lined up around the Laotian flag in front of the school. Two students raised the flag as the rest of us sang the Laotian national anthem. Then we marched to our classrooms, where we had to remain standing by our desks as the teacher entered. Only after he was seated could we sit down. Each student was called to the front of the class to recite the homework assigned the day before. It was usually a poem or a passage from a reading. Those who could not recite the assignment were punished. They were made to kneel for twenty minutes, and then the teacher hit their hands before they were sent back to their seats. This punishment was to discipline the students so they would study harder in the future. I was never punished because I was determined to learn. My parents were poor, so when I was given an opportunity to acquire knowledge, I wanted to be the best student possible. In each class, the pupils were ranked and I was almost always number one or two.

At home, when my brothers and I did our homework, we did not have comfortable chairs to sit in or desks to sit at. We used a long board as a makeshift table in one corner of the house and sat on logs. There was no electricity, so we studied by the light of oil lamps. All evening long, my brothers and I memorized and recited the passage assigned. We did not go to bed until we had it completely memorized and we could recite it perfectly. The next morning, while walking to school, which was several miles from our house, we continued to recite it to ourselves.

There were a thousand to fifteen hundred students in our school, with thirty-five to forty students in each class. After my brothers and I had completed the highest grade, we took a test in French and we all passed it. My brother Pao Lo then went to school in Vientiane where he received a diploma. I could not do the same because I had decided to enroll in the army.

During the war in Vietnam in the early 1960s, the American CIA [Central Intelligence Agency] recruited many Hmong men to help them fight against the Communists. The CIA knew that the northeastern region of Laos [which the 1954 Geneva accords gave to the Communist Pathet Lao to control] was occupied mainly by Hmong, so the CIA recruited Hmong to fight there and farther south along the Ho Chi Minh Trail [that ran along the border between North Vietnam and Laos, and between South Vietnam and Cambodia] to prevent the North Vietnamese from transporting weapons, soldiers, and food to their men fighting in South Vietnam. Many American pilots were shot down in Laos, so our job was to rescue them also.

When the Hmong were asked to help, we did so because we knew the United States of America is a powerful country that will help us in return in the future. Though we were uneducated and without skills, we received no military training before we were sent into battle. We fought first, then trained afterwards. We helped fight the Communists from 1960 to 1975. After the Communists came to power, they started bombing our villages. Many Hmong military leaders left on May 14, 1975. For that reason, we also had to seek refuge elsewhere. That is why we are here in the United States.

Before the CIA started its "secret war" in Laos, we Hmong had lived in peace. We had no wars and no worries. We gathered vegetables from our gardens, harvested rice from our fields, and hunted in the jungles for meat. Our cattle, when sold, provided us with money. Life was simple. Anyone who was not lazy and was willing to farm could feed himself and his family. Because there were no roads to the cities, we lived on what we grew ourselves.

Life in the village revolved around the agricultural cycle and everyone looked forward to the New Year celebration—a time when everyone could rest from a long-year of hard work and come together for a joyous celebration. The New Year celebration gave young men and women a chance to meet. They got dressed up in their traditional clothing and looked for potential wives or husbands. During the celebration, they stood in two rows across from each other and tossed balls back and forth—an activity that gave them a chance to talk and to get acquainted. During the celebration, which normally ran about two weeks, there were many marriages.

We Hmong have never been a lazy people. We have always worked very hard. Because we had no modern machinery to help us farm, we did everything by the sweat of our brow. Living in the mountains, we had to plow uphill to prepare plots for growing our vegetables. During harvest, we carried the crops back to our houses on foot, for we did not have cars or trucks. Our fields were usually one whole morning's walk away from our houses.

In 1964, I decided to enlist in the army because my parents did not have enough money to allow me to finish school. From 1964 to 1967, I fought in northern Laos. I shall tell you about my experiences as a soldier with the CIA later. In 1967, I came home on leave and got married. My wife and I were married for only seven days before I had to return to the battlefield. I was gone for a whole year before I could come home on leave again. When I returned, my wife and I felt very shy toward each other because we never had a chance to get to know each other after our wedding.

We moved to Long Cheng where we built a new house. [The CIA had built an airstrip at Long Cheng, where the Hmong Armée Clandestine, or secret army, had its headquarters.] But soon I had to go back to the battlefield once again. That year, 1968, when I was away, my father became very ill and died in Muong Cha. I returned to give him a proper burial. In 1970, my wife and I had our first baby. We named her Mai Kou. Two years later, we moved back to Muong Cha where she gave birth to two more daughters, Mai Jue in 1972 and Mai Neng in 1974.

When the Communists took over Laos and General Vang Pao fled with his family, we, too, decided to leave. Not only my family, but thousands of Hmong tried to flee. I rented a car for thirty thousand Laotian dollars, and it took us to Nasu. There, we met with other relatives to discuss our plans for fleeing to Thailand. We felt compelled to leave because many of us had been connected with the CIA. From Nasu we walked to Hienhep. Thousands of Hmong were traveling on foot. Along the way, many of them were shot and killed by Communist soldiers. We witnessed a bloody massacre of civilians.

Those of us who survived decided to go back to Muong Cha, where we stayed for ten days to plan our escape by a different route. I asked my younger brother Pao Lo to go to Vientiane to apply for passes. I myself went back to Nasu where, after waiting for three days, I got our passes. I sent word to my wife and children to meet me in Nasu. When they arrived, we and two other families rented a taxi which cost us fifty thousand Laotian dollars per family. We shared the ride to Hienhep, but we were not allowed to proceed any farther, even though the leader in Hienhep had given us a pass.

In late June 1975, we made another attempt to escape. This time, we walked through dense jungles, over many mountains, through rice fields and flat land, and ended in a refugee camp at Pakxom on July 30. Shortly afterward, we were moved to another refugee camp at Nongkhai, where we lived for three years. My youngest daughter died there. We came to the United States on October 2, 1978. We landed in Los Angeles and stayed there with my brother for ten days. We then settled in Isla Vista [a small community contiguous to the campus of the University of California at Santa Barbara].

Since I spoke very little English, it was hard to find a job. We received public assistance for several months. On August 5, 1979, I was hired as an assembler at Joslyn Electronic Systems in Goleta, where I have worked ever since. Today I have nine daughters and one son.

Two of my daughters were born in Laos, one in Thailand, and the rest in the United States.

Now I shall tell you about the Hmong way of life in Laos. Our mothers, fathers, grandparents, and ancestors lived in the mountains. Their villages were in remote areas in the wilderness. There were no roads for automobiles. We traveled on foot from one village to the next. To survive, we farmed, hunted wild animals, collected edible plants, and raised our own cattle.

We grew rice with our bare hands. Each year, in January, we cleared the land for farming by chopping down trees with axes, saws, and knives. Blacksmiths made the axes and knives from abandoned vehicles, such as tanks and trucks left behind by the Americans. We used knives to clear off the smaller trees and a two-man saw to cut down the big ones. We allowed the stumps to dry in the sun. In late March or early April, we burned the clearing. Burning took place only on sunny days. With a lit torch, we set fire to the leaves, bushes, twigs, and logs, which had been cut earlier. Then we waited until May, when weeds began growing on the burned land. We used hoes to dig them up and to turn over the soil. The men usually did the clearing and burning, while the women (mothers, daughters, and daughters-in-law) turned the soil over with wooden sticks measuring an arm's length, the ends of which had been whittled into sharp points. We poked holes in the dirt and put six or seven rice grains into each hole. After the field had been planted, we told the seeds, "Grow quickly before the weeds cover your heads." Then we went home.

By the end of May, the rice seedlings were knee high. If there were weeds growing among them, we pulled them out with our hands and sometimes with hoes. In October, the rice fields began to turn yellow. By November, they would be entirely yellow, which indicated it was time to harvest the grain. We cut the stalks with sickles, tied them in small bundles, and laid them out in the field to dry in the sun for a month. In December, we took two or three bundles at a time and threshed them against a wooden table, letting the grain fall to the ground, which was usually covered with large banana leaves or sheets of cloth, if a family was rich enough to buy cloth. Sometimes we also beat the stalks with sticks. In January, after the New Year celebration was over, we beat the grain again to separate the kernels from the husks.

We then built a ladder, made of poles six inches in diameter and five yards long. Two holes were dug in the ground, each about one and a half feet deep and placed eighteen inches apart. The poles were inserted into the holes and dirt was packed firmly around them. We pounded the dirt tight with a log or with our feet to make sure the poles would be sturdy and not fall over. Slats of wood two inches in diameter were tied to the poles with vines collected in the jungles to make the steps of the ladder.

When the ladder had been constructed, we carried the grain in baskets up the ladder and slowly poured it out onto a mat made of either bamboo or banana leaves, allowing the wind to blow away the unwanted dirt, grass, leaves, husks, and bits of stalk, as the clean grain, which was heavier, fell to the mat. If there was no wind, we pleaded, "Wind, please blow," and presently there would be a wind.

If a family did not have a storage shed near their house, they now built one by using wood, bamboo, thatch, and banana leaves. The shed was built at least five or six feet above the ground and stood on bamboo stilts. That way, the grain stayed dry and animals could not get to it. The floor of the shed was covered with bamboo and banana leaves, the four sides with bamboo slats. The husked grain was taken home in bags slung across horses or oxen and stored in the shed.

I shall now speak in greater detail about my experiences as a soldier. I enlisted not because I was recruited but because I saw our country in a state of war. Since my family and extended family all had rice fields, homes, and children, I felt it was my duty to help my government and the Americans to defend Laos. We did not want to give up our land and our country. We did not want a foreign government or Communists to step all over Laos, so I decided to enlist and fight on the side of the American CIA.

A military officer in Unit 204 named Vang Chao, who knew me well, requested that I be his secretary. He sent word to me in Muong Cha, so I went. We were stationed in Xieng Xam Nhia and fought to defend it. A small airport was built at Nakhang, where food and ammunition were dropped to us. My duties included reporting the conditions of each battle we engaged in, how many men were killed, and what territory the enemy might have taken. I was also the one who made the requests for backup troops, for bombers to cover our men, and for food, clothing, ammunition, and money.

We fought in many areas along the Vietnamese–Laotian border. In 1969, we were pushed back close to Long Cheng in Xieng Khouang Province, only about sixty miles from our home. But we drove the enemy back to the border and freed many Hmong and Laotians who had been taken prisoner. Most of them moved back to their villages. Many families lost members as well as their homes and fields during the bombing, because our planes, when bombing the enemy troops, sometimes mistakenly bombed our own villages. So the people built shelters in the jungles, which were hidden from the bombers.

In 1969, Vang Chao retired and another commander was appointed in his place. I did not wish to work for him, so I asked to be assigned elsewhere. My new job was to respond to orders from the dispatchers in the battlefields. If they needed supplies, I would get them and make sure they got delivered to the troops by the American pilots. In January 1970, Colonel Lo Tong Va and platoon commander Vang Chong Neng requested that I become the new assistant platoon commander. I declined the offer because I did not want to go into the battlefield. I wanted to stay at the base, instead. But the higher officers told me I had no choice and that I had to accept the position and go. They said that General Vang Pao, Colonel Lo Tong Va, and platoon commander Vang Chong Neng all had ordered that I take the position. Since there was nothing else I could do, I obeyed. I thought to myself, "If the higher officers believe I can handle the situation, I will give it a try."

The day after I accepted the position, we received orders to go into battle. Many of our soldiers were killed or injured. Our unit's doctor was shot and died instantly. Today, I still have a dent on my chin and a lump on my forehead because I, too, was hit. A bullet went through my helmet, but I was fortunate I was not severely wounded.

We were in the mountains for fifteen days. The enemy was coming toward us from a nearby town. I ordered a few soldiers to go down the mountain to find out how far away and how numerous the enemy troops were. It appeared there were many of them. Two nights later, they attacked us. We retreated to another mountain. I sprained my neck badly while we were retreating. I radioed to headquarters and was soon picked up by a chopper. I was taken to Long Cheng for medical treatment. After my neck healed, I did not want to return to the battlefield. I remained in Long Cheng for a month, but orders came for me to return to the battlefield because our soldiers were being pushed back rapidly. The colonel and other officers told me if I did not go back and we were beaten, they would hold me responsible. So I boarded an aircraft and went back to the front.

The night after I arrived, the platoon commander told me that since I was now there, he wanted to take a leave to visit his family in Long Cheng. He radioed for an aircraft to pick him up. Before he left, the troops requested that I ask him for whatever money was left so that I could buy food for the unit. He said he was going to take the money but that once he got to Long Cheng, he would purchase food and send it to us. The following day, four section leaders wrote a letter to headquarters saying they did not want the platoon commander to return, as he was uneducated and could not even read a compass or a map. He had no sense of direction, therefore he could never give accurate locations to the aircraft covering his troops. He also did not know how to estimate the time it would take to get from one location to another. Due to his poor judgment, he had repeatedly led his troops into danger zones or enemy territory. Many soldiers had died as a result.

I was contacted by an officer and told about the accusations against the platoon commander. I did not know that the section leaders had made such complaints and I was unaware of the problems. If the accusations were true, I did not want to stay with the unit. I did not want the platoon leader to think it was my idea to kick him out of his position. The soldiers wanted me to be their new platoon commander. I refused, but Colonel Lo Tong Va ordered that I take the position because, he said, the soldiers will follow a leader they can respect. So, in January 1970, I became a platoon commander.

Long Cheng was invaded a second time. The Communist army shot at us from every direction. We could not even lift our heads up. We did not have the proper weapons to fire at them. Many soldiers were killed. One of our commanders was also shot. I radioed to direct my platoon forward to help carry the commander to safety, but we ran into enemy troops. My soldiers ran in every direction and were separated. Only eleven soldiers remained with me—ten in front and one at the back of me. We were being fired at from behind. I was hit above my left ear, and the bullet came out of my forehead. I fell to the ground and bled profusely. I could not radio for help because the radio was covered with the blood dripping from my forehead. My vision became blurred and I could not speak at all. The soldiers bandaged me up. Since I could not speak, I motioned with my hands for five soldiers to move forward to the mountain ahead of us. When they reached their destination, they signaled for us to follow.

It was safe on that mountain. We took the radio apart and cleaned it so we could contact the unit with the injured commander we had left behind. We asked them to meet us on another mountain. When my remaining soldiers and I arrived there, one of our aircraft located us. I asked to be picked up because I was still bleeding, but the pilot told me he would send another aircraft for me. He lied to me. We waited for two days but no aircraft came. I could not open my mouth to eat. My soldiers fed me like a baby. After two days, however, a colonel who was looking for his unit found us. He went to Long Cheng and sent three T-28 planes and four helicopters to rescue us. By then, the other unit had joined us. Seven of us were injured. We got into the aircraft and were taken to Long Cheng. I was able to walk, but the other commander, who had been shot in the leg, could not. I had to carry him on my back to the hospital.

At the hospital, the doctors examined us. They cut the injured flesh and skin around my wound and cleaned it, but they did this without giving me any pain killer. They thought I was just another soldier. They did not know I had a handgun tucked away in my socks. As the doctors started cutting away at my flesh, I was in severe pain. Four nurses held me down by my arms and legs. I started to black out, but I was so angry that I reached down and pulled out my handgun and pointed it at the doctor operating on me. I shouted, "You! Doctor! Your job is to treat me so I can get well. How can you be so cruel? I'm going to kill you! I've been injured, and it hurts enough as it is, but here you are, operating on me and increasing the pain. Give me some pain killer or I'll shoot you!" When he realized I was a platoon commander, he apologized and gave me the pain killer.

I was in the hospital for a week. The enemy was bombing Long Cheng heavily. Though I was still bleeding, I knew it would not be safe for me to remain in Long Cheng. So I went to the hospital in Nasu, but it was filled with wounded soldiers and had no room for me. I was then taken by aircraft to a small hospital in Muong Cha. When I reached Muong Cha, my wife, parents, brothers, and other relatives were preparing to run off into the jungle. I asked them to remain in the village until we could figure out which direction the enemy was coming from, so that we would know where to go. If we ran away now, before they came, I explained, we might just run into them along the way. The same night that I arrived at Muong Cha, our headquarters at Long Cheng was destroyed. What happened was that when the Communist forces invaded Long Cheng, the American headquarters, located at the foot of the mountains, sent bombers into action. The enemy was firing from the opposite side of Long Cheng at the American headquarters. The American commanders sent signals up into the air to indicate where the enemy was. Unfortunately, there was a miscommunication between those in the headquarters and the pilots, who thought they were to drop CBUS [Cluster Bomb Units that opened in mid-air to scatter bomblets that splintered on impact] at the place where the signals were coming from—that is, the buildings of the headquarters.

I remained in Muong Cha until my wounds healed. Then I went to Long Cheng, which by then was no longer occupied by the enemy. I was ordered back into battle, but I refused to go: I had been on the battlefield for too long—from 1965 to 1972. I wanted to stay on base. By this time, I was supposed to have been promoted to captain, but I was cheated of my rank. The honor was given, instead, to a man who was related to the commander in charge of promotions. I was upset, but I could not say anything because doing so might have resulted in a bloody confrontation. Feeling furious, I walked away from the army. I also called upon members of my extended family who were still fighting and asked them to go home while they still had their arms and legs. So they, too, dropped their weapons. We all quit and went back to our village to start farming again. The war was still on, but our army days were behind us.

After I returned to my village, my wife and I had a chance to get to know each other better. When I married her, I did not know her well and she did not know me, either. It was simply our fate to become husband and wife. I was a soldier at the time. I lived in Muong Cha while she lived with her brother in Long Cheng. When I took leave to go home to get married, I had no idea whom I was going to marry. I did not even tell the girl I had chosen that I wanted to marry her. In the old country, if a man liked a certain girl and wanted to marry her, he simply gave her a gift of money or some small item, such as a scarf, as a token of his interest. During New Year, when we were tossing balls, I gave her some money. She kept it, so I figured she must be interested in me and might be willing to marry me. I did not even know whether she would have said "yes" had I gone to her house to ask for her hand. Because I was uncertain how she felt about me, I did not want her to reject me. So, my friends and I decided to kidnap her, as our custom allowed. One early morning, my friends and I waited outside her house. When she came out, we grabbed her by the arms and legs. We called out to her sister-in-law, who came out to see what the commotion was about. She asked if Vue (my wife-to-be) had accepted anything from me. I told her "yes." So all she said was, "Go ahead and take her with you if she has accepted a gift from you."

After three days, according to tradition, I bought her some new clothes and took her to visit her family. At her brother's house, we set up a date for the wedding. That night, Vue and I returned to my house. I had to find two elders and a best man. The two elders would negotiate on behalf of my family, while her family would find their own representatives. On the day we went to her home to make arrangements, custom dictated that we enter through the back door. It would have been disrespectful to enter through the front door. When we reached the back door, the two elders representing my family sang a traditional song inviting us to come in, as the woman's family waiting inside listened. Only after the singing was finished were we permitted to step inside. The two elders representing her family then sat down with those representing mine to talk. They asked if there had been any conflicts in the past between the two families. They also asked if she had accepted any gifts from other young men. If she had, she had to return everything to them.

We held the wedding in Long Cheng. I paid four silver bars for her plus another two for the feast. So, your mother cost me six silver bars. After the feast, we returned to Muong Cha. As I told you earlier, I could stay only a few days before returning to the battlefield. I left her with my parents.

The laws in Laos are very different from those in the United States. That is why people of my generation often feel frustrated living in America. One of the reasons that many Hmong are unhappy in the

United States is that back in Laos, a man must pay a price for his wife, but she does not have to pay anything for him. Paying a bride price is a ritual we have practiced for hundreds of years—ever since our ancestors lived in China. Because a man must pay so much money for his wife, if she has an affair with another man, the husband may sue the lover for damaging the marriage. The settlement is not reached in a court of law but between the families involved. In fact, when a wife commits adultery, if the husband is angry enough, he can kill her lover, and it would not be considered a crime.

Besides adultery, stealing is also not tolerated in our homeland. If a person is caught stealing, no matter what his age, he is thrown into prison and tortured. He is released only after he has been tortured so much that he pleads for his life and promises never to steal again. As everyone fears torture, there are very few thieves among the Hmong.

A problem that we Hmong parents face today in America is disciplining our children. It is so difficult! Not only are our children not listening to us, but we parents can be thrown in jail for trying to teach them what is right. In Laos, we disciplined our children by a good beating. If a child fights with other children or with his or her brothers and sisters, or talks back to his or her parents, or steals, then he or she receives a beating. After a few such beatings, children learn their lesson and become better persons. But today, here in America, if we hit our children, if they are smart they will tell their teacher or call the police. The children of today have no respect for their elders and do not fear their parents. Americans do not understand our culture, and we do not understand theirs. Therefore, we run into problems when raising our children in the United States.

Another major problem I have experienced since arriving in the United States is speaking and understanding English. I did not even know the difference between "yes" and "no" when I first came, yet I was required to find a job to support my family. I did not have the least idea where to start looking. I had no special skills and could not read or write English. How could I fill out employment application forms? I did not know how. Luckily, there were two Hmong named Touby Lo and Ka Pao Xiong who worked in Isla Vista for a social service agency called Indochina. This agency helped find employment for the new arrivals—for Cambodians, Vietnamese, lowland Lao, and Hmong.

My very first job in America, at which I am still employed, had very, very low pay. I started at $3.15 an hour. Though the pay was low, I was tired of being on welfare. I was tired of filling out forms and making monthly reports, tired of having to get papers signed for not working. If I did not fill out those papers and get them signed each month, my family and I would be removed from the welfare rolls. I decided, therefore, to take the job. No more papers! I could buy what I wanted without having to report to the welfare department. I was not used to depending on the government for financial support. In Laos, we had grown our own crops and earned our living by the sweat of our brow.

The American language is very difficult because a lot of different words can have the same meaning. One problem I have had in learning English is that after I learned what one word means, I got all confused when I found that another word had the same meaning. For example, good, nice, beautiful, perfect have similar meanings. In Hmong, different words have different meanings. American English is very hard for us adults to learn. It is easy for our children, but not for us.

When I first arrived in the United States, the first thing I noticed were all the cars on the streets and freeways. I feared crossing the street, even at a traffic light. I was also afraid to go to the grocery store on my own for I worried about getting lost. It really frustrated me that I was not able to be independent. It took me years to get adjusted and to learn my way around town.

Besides being afraid of getting lost in a strange place, I was homesick. I missed my country. The mountains, trees, flowers, and animals here are all so different. There is nothing here to remind me of my country, and that makes me sad. The sky, the earth, and the mountains in Santa Barbara County are not the same as those in Laos. The people and the social environment are also different. I am sad not knowing whether I will ever see the flowers and bamboo groves in Laos again.

Vue Vang's Life Story

as told to her daughter, Maijue Xiong

My father, whom I never knew, was named Yang Chong Moua. My mother's name was Joua Vue. My name was originally Yang Mai Sue, but it was later changed to Vang Vue. I was born on February 12, 1946 in a small village called Pusay.

I do not have many memories of my father because he had what we Hmong call "many hearts." My parents had three boys and two girls, but they did not love each other. My father had an affair with a widow. Soon he married her as his second wife, and she brought the son she had conceived with her previous husband with her to live with us. Two months after the wedding, she died. After her death, although my father still had my mother, he became very lonely. He then had an affair with another widow. This woman was not able to bear children, but my father married her, supposedly to care for the child that his second wife had left behind. However, because the baby belonged not to the Yang but the Her clan, his Her relatives did not want my father to raise him as a Yang, so they came and took him back to his clan after his mother died.

Before my father married his third wife, she insisted that he divorce my mother. To avoid complications, my father did so. My mother gave custody of my three brothers and a sister to my father. She kept me and the child she was still carrying inside her. My mother and I went back to Namphanoi, where my maternal grand-parents lived. Not long after we started a new life in Namphanoi, my mother gave birth to a boy. After he was born, my father came to visit us twice. Upon seeing what a fine son he had, he wanted to take my mother, me, and my brother back with him. But my mother was a stubborn woman. She refused to remarry my father. My father thus regretted his decision to divorce her, for he now wanted the son that my mother had just given birth to.

My father returned home to Pusay and visited us again a few months later. By this time, my mother had a new boyfriend. He was around when my father visited. My father was deeply hurt; he went home and never came back again. A very cruel man, he paid a Lao witch doctor to put a spell on my baby brother. During my father's visit, the baby had been well and healthy, but immediately after his departure, my baby brother became ill and died suddenly. It took two days to walk from Namphanoi to Pusay, but we sent a messenger to tell my father of his son's death. My mother requested that he come to the funeral, but my father never showed up.

After my brother's death, my mother started seeing many men. She left me at home with my grandmother. I was much loved by my grandparents, aunts, and uncles. Whenever they killed a chicken for dinner, they saved me the drumstick. In our culture, the most loved child always gets the drumstick. Despite their love, I missed my mother very much, but she was always away with her boy-friends. At night, when I wanted mother's milk, I would touch my grandmother's breast, thinking she was my mother.

My mother eventually married a man named Vang Cher Tou. He took my mother as his third wife. I went to live with my mother and adopted the last name, Vang. My stepfather lived in a small village called Bliahia. He had a big family. There were babies, teenagers, sons and daughters-in-law, all living together. He was very old, but that did not stop him from marrying my mother. In time, my mother gave birth to my stepsister, Yer, who is still living in Laos today. Soon after she was born, my stepfather became very ill. He passed away in 1960. After his death, my mother gave birth to another son. Unfortunately, there were complications and no doctors to attend to her. The baby died at birth. After my stepfather's death, his property was divided among the three wives, and my mother, my sister, and I built our own house with the help of my uncles.

Our village was located on a tall mountain. Our farm was really far from where we lived. We had to walk all the way down the mountain to get to our field. One day, when I was five or six years old, we went to the farm and camped there. A woman with a child who lived in the village next to ours came walking by. My mother asked her if she would mind keeping an eye on me as I walked back to our village to fetch some cooking oil. My mother gave me a basket to carry on my back and a hollow trunk of bamboo to put the cooking oil in. When I left our field, the sky was getting very dark and thunder was roaring in the distance. It started to pour and the wind blew from every direction.

Not caring how severe the storm might become, my mother insisted that I walk back to the village with the woman. As we climbed up the mountain, the rain pounded the earth. The woman cut two large leaves for me and her daughter with which to cover our heads. When we came to a small stream, the woman went ahead and told me, "I will go first. You two hold on to my hands and I will lead us across." The stream was rising quickly. The woman took her daughter's hand and pulled her across. She then tried to reach for my hand, but she could not reach me. I fell into the stream and was washed downstream about a quarter-mile. I did not know how to swim, but I knew God would help me. I felt it was not yet my time to die; surely I had a future waiting for me. Suddenly, I started grabbing on to whatever I could. Luckily, I was able to grab some tall grass near the edge of the stream. I held on tightly and pulled myself out of the water. It was really strange, but once I pulled myself out of the water, the storm subsided.

I found I was on the same side of the stream where I had been before I fell in, which meant I still had to cross the stream to get to our village. I had swallowed so much water that my stomach was really bloated. The basket on my back had long ago been washed away. I sat on a rock, feeling very uncomfortable because of the water in my stomach. The woman I was traveling with did not even bother to stop at my village to inform anyone of my accident. Only when she got to the far side of our village did she tell someone to look for me and to see if I was dead or alive.

The people she talked to quickly spread the news in the village. When my uncles heard about the accident, they knew the child she referred to had to be me, because this was not the first time that my mother had sent me home with strangers. Many times I had even been sent home alone. My uncles gathered some men, and they came looking for me. I was still sitting on the rock when I heard voices from the opposite bank. My uncles waded across the stream and took me home.

The next morning, they sent word to my mother about my accident. She returned home immediately. I felt very sick and sad because I had no father, and while I had a mother, she did not love me. She expected a lot from me, even though I was still very young. She summoned a shaman who performed a ritual on me, calling my soul out of the water. After this incident, my mother no longer made me walk home alone or with strangers.

We depended on agriculture for our subsistence and cash income. I recall clearly how every morning, my mother, my sister, and I woke up before the crack of dawn to go to our opium farm. The path to our fields was very steep and rugged. We had to climb over many big rocks to get there. The men from our village had cleared a path through the jungle for our horses. We had many fields of opium, which sold for good money. The opium collected was carried by the horses to locations where Lao, French, and Chinese dealers bought it. When I was growing up, there were no Americans around.

The walk to our opium fields took an hour and a half each way. Since we had no flashlights, torches lighted our path. We had to leave in the middle of the night because we had to reach the opium fields before dawn. Once the sun comes up, the latex that drips from the incisions we cut in the poppy buds dries up too quickly, making it impossible to remove the opium resin from the plants. The tool used to cut the poppy buds is made of a long piece of bamboo with three brass blades attached. Each poppy bud receives nine cuts, but only on one side. It is very hard work because every bud has to be slit. The resin is scraped off with a special spoon shaped like the letter P. The edge opposite the half circle, which is very sharp, is used to scrape the resin off.

Since I was too young to help my mother, she left me and my sister in a small hut that she had built with bamboo and thatch. Inside the hut, there was a bamboo mat for us to lie on. There was also a fire pit where we built a fire to keep warm at night. One morning when my sister and I were in the hut, which was at the bottom of the hill, there was a terrible thunderstorm. Strong wind was blowing from every direction and lightning lit the sky. I was carrying my sister in a baby pack made of an embroidered piece of cloth. We were both terrified. My mother ran down the hill as the strong wind and rain knocked the hut over, burying my sister and me under the bamboo and thatch. My sister, who was still strapped to my back, was crying very loudly. The fallen bamboo made a deep gash in my leg. (Today I still have a scar on my leg.) My mother dug us out, removed my sister from my back, and put her on her own back. She took my hand and we ran to a nearby hut belonging to one of our neighbors. My mother did not notice my gash until we reached our neighbor's hut. It was our neighbor who pointed out to her that I was bleeding heavily. My mother wrapped my leg with a piece of cloth. We remained in the hut with my neighbor till the storm ceased. Today I have aches in my body because as a small child I had to work so hard and was hurt repeatedly.

In time—I no longer remember which year—my mother married again. My new stepfather's name was Vang Nau Qhua. He was a married man with two sons. He, too, was very old, but that did not stop him, either, from marrying my mother, who became his second wife. We moved from Bliahia to Muong Cha. A few years later, my mother gave birth to a son, whom we named Chou. We then moved to Long Cheng.

Unfortunately, nine months after Chou was born, my mother became very ill. She had a severe case of diarrhea and a very high fever. My stepfather put her and my baby brother on an airplane to fly them to a hospital in Sam Thong. He told my sister and me to walk to the hospital the next morning. It took us a whole day to get there. I was about twelve at the time, and my sister was about six. We arrived at Sam Thong by nightfall and found my mother at the hospital. She was lying in one bed and my brother Chou in another.

After two weeks, Chou got better but not my mother. We all thought the time had come for her to leave this earth. She was unconscious and her breathing became very shallow. My stepfather asked me to go find the doctor. I told the doctor my mother was dead. He followed me to my mother's bed and examined her. He told my stepfather and me that she was not dead. If she could survive the night, he said, her chances of recovering would be better. Later that night, my mother became conscious. I told her she was going to be all right and urged her to eat in order to regain her strength. After a few days, it looked like she would recover. We all felt very happy and grateful. The doctor wanted my mother to remain in the hospital for a few more days before releasing her. Quite unexpectedly, she became very ill and weak again. My stepfather wanted to take her home to see a shaman, who might be able to do something for her. We got on a small plane that landed outside the hospital and flew back to Long Cheng. But that same evening, my mother passed away.

I was told to take my brother to the house of one of my aunts, which was close by. My brother slept with me in my arms that night. He woke up crying whenever he was hungry. He searched and felt my chest for milk, but there was none to be found. Each time he cried, I got up and put him on my back and rocked him back to sleep again. I was so tired that my eyes were closed while I stood and rocked him. After my mother's funeral, we returned to my stepfather's house. At the age of twelve, I became my brother's mother. Raising him was the hardest task. I had a far worse time raising my brother than my own ten children.

Luckily we did not have to farm when we lived in Long Cheng. One of my uncles was in the army, and we received food from the government. I had to do a lot of cooking for the family, clean the house, and take care of my brother as though he were my own child. My mother had died in June. In November, I went with my uncle Chia Vue to Muong Cha. When I was sixteen, I got married. I am still married to the same man today.

I was really poor and had to work very hard as a young child, but after I got married, I had to work even harder. My husband was away at war, and I was left with his parents. Every morning, my mother-in-law woke me up to cook breakfast before we headed out to work in the fields. With my husband away, I had to sleep in the same bed as my mother-in-law. I did not want to sleep with her because she was an opium smoker. She always reeked of opium, but I was not allowed to have my own bed. Many times, I purposely went to sleep early in one corner of the room, with the hope that she would not make me sleep with her. However, when she came to bed, she always woke me up, saying, "Daughter-in-law, wake up! Come and sleep beside me." I could not say no to her, so I had to get up and sleep beside her.

Living with my husband's family was desperately hard. We grew opium poppies, corn, string beans, peas, mustard greens, cucumbers, squash, pumpkins, and rice. We had to work very hard every day. Not a single day was wasted with rest. The first year after my marriage was the hardest of all. I had to cut down trees with an axe so that we could cultivate the land. I had to chop the branches and trunks and carry them home for firewood. If you look at my hands, you will see they have been working hands. My palms used to be covered with big blisters.

A typical day for me was to rise at the first crow of the rooster. I cooked breakfast and prepared lunch to take with us to the field. I also helped my mother-in-law to husk the rice and my husband's oldest brother's wife to feed the chickens, horses, pigs, and goats. These chores had to be completed before we left for the fields. We spent the whole day there pulling weeds out with our bare hands and picking whatever needed to be picked. Before the sun set on the horizon, we had to gather food for the animals at home. As the moon came up, we headed for home, carrying freshly picked plants and leaves to feed our animals. It was a long walk back to the house. It was usually completely dark by the time we arrived home, but the day did not end then. I had to cook dinner, feed the animals, and complete other chores before retiring. The next day would be the same as the one that had just ended.

My husband was away at war for many months at a time. He came home on leave for only a few days and then had to return to the battlefield. My first child, a baby boy, did not breathe when he came out, even though his little heart was beating. There were no doctors to help me, so we held him for two hours, not knowing what we could do to save him. He never cried. His heart beat slowed down and eventually stopped. We carried him outside and buried him.

I remained in bed for a month, feeling empty with no child to hold. In our culture, a woman who has given birth to a child re-mains indoors for a month afterward. She is put on a diet of rice and chicken cooked with different herbs, intended to restore her strength and provide sufficient milk for the newborn baby. She is not allowed to drink cold water, which is thought to damage her reproductive system. I followed this tradition for a month, but without a child in my arms. During this period, I was in mourning. My husband had come home when I was in labor, but he had to return to Long Cheng immediately after I gave birth. I felt very sad.

After that month of rest, I refused to continue to live with my husband's family. They made me work too hard, constantly lifting heavy loads on to the horses and carrying equally heavy loads myself, with no one to help me. Many a time, I had to lead three or four horses, each with a heavy load on its back, up and down the mountain. I am not a very big woman, so, many times I got trampled by the horses. If I was behind them, I had to run after them, grabbing their tails in order to keep up with their pace. I felt such hard work had caused the complications that led to my son's death.

In 1970, I gave birth to my daughter, Mai Kou, in Long Cheng. Ten days later, Long Cheng was invaded. The villagers ran in every direction. My husband and I carried our newborn child and walked to Muong Cha, where my mother- and father-in-law lived. A month later, my husband returned to Long Cheng, only to discover that everything in our house had been stolen by thieves. When we fled our home, we had left our clothes, blankets, and pots and pans behind and closed the door. Now the house was empty. We had nothing left. My husband wrote me a letter telling me of the misfortune. Since he had to return to the battlefield, he asked me to remain with my daughter at my in-laws' house until he could return.

When my daughter could sit up at four months, I took her with me to the airport in Muong Cha and caught a plane to Long Cheng. By this time, the Communist troops were no longer occupying Long Cheng and people were returning to their homes. I cleaned up our house and bought new blankets, pots, pans, and dishes. When my husband came back from the battlefield, however, we moved back to Muong Cha. He felt it would be best for me to live there so that he would not have to worry about us constantly while he was away at war. He hired some Lao men to saw down some trees so we could build and live in our own house. But as soon as the house was completed, my mother-in-law and my husband's two younger brothers moved in with us. In 1972, I gave birth to my second daughter, Mai Jue. Shortly afterward, my husband left the army. My third daughter, Mai Neng, was born in 1974.

In 1975, when the Communists took over Laos, my husband, my children, and I moved to Nasu. People from many villages came to Nasu to make plans to leave Laos for Thailand. We left my mother-in-law and my husband's eldest brother and his family behind in Muong Cha. (My brother-in-law was sick in bed.) When news got out that General Vang Pao had left Laos, all his followers also made plans to leave. Those with money had escaped already. By this time, the Communist government had taken over many towns and villages. Posters were put up everywhere, announcing that the war was over and the Communists were in control. They wanted everyone to obey their laws. They said the country was now once again at peace.

I asked my husband, "Are we going to just stay here? The General and many others have already left. They have left their homes and farms behind. Are we going to leave or stay?" My husband responded that we must all leave. His eldest brother had always been a farmer and had nothing to fear. He did not want to leave, but he told my husband that we had to flee because my husband had been in the army and it would be unsafe for us to remain in Laos. So, my husband and I, our three daughters, and my husband's younger brother, Pao Lo, decided to go.

We traveled to Nasu. There were Communist soldiers guarding all the roads and preventing civilians from leaving. People were fleeing by the thousands; we were among them. We walked for two days toward the gate that leads to Vientiane, but when we got there, the gate was locked and no one was allowed to pass through it. Those walking in front of us were shot by the soldiers. Many innocent victims were killed or wounded. People ran back in fear of their lives. There was chaos everywhere.

We Hmong are used to living in the mountains. The hot, humid weather in the lowlands made many of us feel sick. Because it was so hot, my husband drank a lot of water and became very ill, so we had to take a taxi back to Muong Cha. A week later, my husband went to Nasu again to get official papers that would allow us to leave. Three days later, I received a letter from him requesting that his brother, Pao Lo, and I take our children by taxi to Nasu. I gathered what I could of our valuables and left everything else behind. My mother-in-law walked with us for about a mile. We could not find a taxi inside our village, because if a taxi driver picked anyone up and was caught, he would face severe punishment. To find a taxi, we kept walking until we reached the countryside where there were no soldiers.

The first time we escaped from Muong Cha, we had locked our black bull inside his pen. My mother-in-law, who was very worried about us, did not look after it. The bull got out and ran away. My mother-in-law looked all over for it, but it was nowhere to be found. When we returned to Muong Cha after the massacre at the gate in Nasu, the bull also came home. His eyes were watery and tears were streaming down his face. I had never seen such a sight. His nose had been ripped when he struggled to free himself, and it was still bleeding. I loved that bull very much and felt very sad when we butchered him a few days later. We hung his meat out to dry, and when we started again on our long journey toward Thailand, we packed some of this meat and took it with us.

I carried my youngest daughter, Mai Neng, on my back and held Mai Jue's and Mai Kou's hands. My mother-in-law carried a basket on her back containing a bag of rice and some of the dried meat. We waited for a taxi. When it arrived, my mother-in-law touched each of my daughters on the head and turned to go back to the village. This was the last time we saw her alive.

We arrived at Nasu by sunset. The next morning, we were going to begin our journey again. There were six or seven families traveling with us. When we came to the same gate where the massacre had occurred, soldiers guarding it refused to let anyone through, even though we had papers giving us permission to leave. We all went to a nearby village, where we met a Lao man. He was from the town of Banduan and agreed to help us escape. He went to the government officials and filed some papers saying that he was helping us to move to Banduan. If we managed to get these papers, he told us, it would be easier to get to Thailand.

Permission was granted, and the Lao came with his pickup truck to get us all. When we got to the gate, he showed the soldiers our papers and we were allowed to pass through. After driving a few hours, we had an accident. Because there were so many of us in the truck, it started rolling downhill when we were trying to drive uphill. When I recall this experience, I still feel frightened. The road was very, very steep. If the truck had rolled over, it would have been the end of all of us. As the truck slid downhill, its brakes gave out. Luckily, one of the wheels got caught in some bushes, and the truck came to a stop. We were all terrified and jumped out as fast as we could.

A taxi that came along helped pull the truck back onto the road. The taxi driver went and fetched another taxi. We piled into the two cars and were taken to Banduan. We arrived there at night. Reflecting on this incident, I feel very thankful. Without the help of God, we would not be alive today.

The next morning, two Lao men led us up a hill, where they gave us directions to our next destination. I carried my baby, while my husband carried our food and Mai Jue. I felt very weak and ill. I burned with a fever all the way. I was wondering whether I would make it safely to Thailand. We passed many deserted Hmong villages along the way. Chickens and pigs were running around freely, but there were no humans in sight. We rested in abandoned houses and ate the rice that people had left behind. In a little over a month, we reached and crossed the Mekong River and ended up in a refugee camp. We set foot on Thai soil on July 30, 1975. When we reached shore, several Thai officials picked us up and took us to a small village called Pakxom. There were about ten other families with us. We were taken to a bus station, where we spent the night. Movies were shown to keep us entertained. Each family took up a small amount of space and rolled out its bedding for the night. We gathered firewood from the surrounding area and cooked our meals outside the bus station. The officials stayed with us until morning.

A week later, the mayor of Pakxom sent some soldiers in a truck to where we were. Along with the soldiers, our husbands went into the forest to cut bamboo, which was used to section off the space within the bus station so that each family had a little privacy. We also built bamboo walls around the bus station, which had only a roof over it. The soldiers were kind enough to help us put up the walls. But the Thai government did not provide us with any food. We bought food with whatever money we had. When our money ran out, we exchanged our jewelry for food. Many of us earned a little money by clearing land, pulling weeds, and picking corn and beans for the Thai farmers in the area. Each day, we earned fifteen *baht,* which was enough to buy us only one meal. Only three months later did the Thai government begin to supply us with food. Because Mai Kou, Mai Jue, and Mai Neng were still very young, I did not work. My husband and his brother, Pao Lo, went out each day to work and brought home a total of thirty *baht,* with which we bought rice.

A month after we began receiving food from the government, we were transferred to another refugee camp at Nongkhai, which is about three hundred miles from Pakxom. There were already many Hmong families at Nongkhai. We did not have a place to live, so we squeezed in with one of my uncles' families. There were ten of them and five of us. A month after we arrived at Nongkhai, Mai Neng, my youngest daughter, became very ill. She and Mai Jue both had the measles and we took them to the hospital. Mai Jue recovered but Mai Neng did not. We brought her home and she died a few days later. We did not have money or any elders around to give her a proper funeral. She did not even have a nice coffin. Our uncle found a few pieces of wood and made a coffin for her.

Shortly after Mai Neng died, a family living a few doors away received permission to go to the United States. The wife came and told us that we could move into their house after they left. We remained in this house for about six months. By this time, the Thai government had built a new camp with apartment complexes. We were all relocated there. The housing was nothing fancy, but at least we had a roof over our heads. There were people with many different last names; all the people with the same last name were assigned to five apartment complexes, each of which had thirty rooms. Each family, regardless of how large or small it was, was put into one room. Every two weeks, trucks brought vegetables, fish, eggs, and rice to the camp. The food was given to two representatives from each apartment complex, who then divided it among the families. Each person was allocated a certain amount of rice, vegetables, and meat. Although we were grateful for this free food, we never had enough to eat. So our husbands went out of the refugee camp in search of work. They hoped to earn a little money to buy more food. The women remained in the camp, sewing *paj ntaub* [Hmong embroidered fabric pronounced in English as *pangdao*], which we sold to foreign tourists, students, and Thai who visited the camp.

Life in the camp was very hard. Each day was like the day before—lots of hard work, just trying to survive, with no future ahead of us. We heard many good as well as bad things about the United States. Those Hmong who had gone there wrote back to their relatives in the Thai refugee camps to tell us about life in America. Some wrote that life was very relaxing because they did not have to farm from dawn to dusk. Others wrote that life had become very complicated. They reported that many Hmong women had abandoned their husbands to be with American men. Wives in the United States, according to them, never obeyed their husbands. As funny as it may sound now, we also heard rumors that there were giants in the United States who ate people. We got the impression that America is the land where good and evil, life and death, all come together. Individuals who had died in Laos were said to have been seen in America.

Given all these rumors, many Hmong in the camps became frightened. My family, however, did not believe a word of it. We felt it was best to see things for ourselves [before forming any opinions]. Life was so hard in the camp that when we found out we could go to the United States, we did not hesitate to grasp the chance. We knew that were we to remain in the camp, there would be no hope for a better future. We would not be able to offer our children anything better than a life of perpetual poverty and anguish. Having fled Laos, we were determined to go all the way to America.

On October 2, 1978, my family and I arrived in Los Angeles where my husband's brother, Pao Lo, had already gone to live. We remained in Los Angeles for two weeks and then moved to Isla Vista. A month after we landed in the United States, I gave birth to my first son at the Goleta Valley Community Hospital. I spoke no English, so when our American friends came to visit me, I could express neither my sadness nor joy to them.

Some other Hmong women and I were eager to learn English so that we could understand and communicate with our American friends. We wanted to be able to go to the grocery store, read prices, and understand the cashier. When I first got here, I always brought extra money with me to make sure I would have enough to pay for the groceries I bought. I bought only those products I recognized—that is, meat and vegetables. At the cash register, because I could not talk to the cashier, I simply handed him or her all my money, with the hope that he or she was honest and would take the correct amount. The other Hmong women and I told our American friends we wanted to learn English, so a few elderly American women started coming to our homes to teach us. They brought apples, oranges, peaches, and many different fruits and vegetables with them, so that we could learn the name for each. We also learned to write our names in English.

A few months later, we had progressed so much that we could

communicate with our teachers in English, unlike earlier when all we could do was nod our heads, regardless of whether or not we understood what they were saying. When we started, there were just a few of us, but in time, so many people came that we had to find a building where we could hold our class. Fortunately, we were able to bring our children with us, because we could not afford babysitters. The children picked up a few words here and there, so they also were soon speaking English. We attended classes both in the daytime and at night at Isla Vista Elementary School. This education helped a great deal and made our lives a little easier. I now could go to the grocery store and read what the price for each item was and compute the total cost of my purchase. I could now give the cashier the correct amount of cash.

A few years later, I decided to learn to drive so that I could get around on my own and take my children to school. I had to try twice before I passed the test for a driver's license. The first time I took the written test, I was given one printed in Spanish. I did not realize it was in Spanish until I showed the slip of paper to my husband. A few days later, I went back and was given a test written in English. I passed this time. I passed the driving part of the test after two tries also.

In 1983, I got my first job in the United States. I worked at the same company where my husband had found a job. But I worked for only seven months before I was laid off. I have not been able to return to work since then because I have had one child after another. I now have ten children. The oldest, Mai Kou, is twenty-two, while my youngest is a little over two years old.

I have been in the United States for almost fourteen years now. In the beginning, life seemed very hard because I was not able to understand anything that was going on around me. Today, I lose sleep worrying about my children, about having enough money to pay all our bills, and about the family members we left behind in Laos. I feel there are good and bad things about America. The good part is we don't have to sweat over a piece of land to produce food for every meal. The bad part is, even though I am told that the United States is a land of freedom, I feel no freedom at all. Freedom, to me, is being able to farm our own land, raise our cattle, and own our own homes without obligation to anyone. I am happy to be here, but at the same time, I am very sad because many of my family members are not here. I would be so much happier if my brothers and sisters could be here with me. Even if we do not have much here, I would be completely content if I could have all my family here with me. [Because they are not here,] I would like to return to Laos some day. Day after day, I long to return to my country. My heart is not here in America. I fear that when it comes time for me to leave this world, my children will not give me a proper funeral. My children will be able to take care of themselves as they grow older because they have been educated here and life will be easier for them. But as for my husband and myself, we feel as though we are here only to earn money and to cook for them. We cannot help them much in other ways because we had little education and do not know a great deal about life in America. That is why [when my children are grown,] I hope to return home someday.

An Unforgettable Journey

by Maijue Xiong

I was born in a small village called Muong Cha in Laos on April 30, 1972. At the time I was born, my father was a soldier actively fighting alongside the American Central Intelligence Agency against the Communists. Although a war was in progress, life seemed peaceful. We did not think of ever leaving Laos, but one day our lives were changed forever. We found ourselves without a home or a country and with a need to seek refuge in another country. This period of relocation involved a lot of changes, adjustments, and adaptations. We experienced changes in our language, customs, traditional values, and social status. Some made the transition quickly; others have never fully adjusted. The changes my family and I experienced are the foundation of my identity today.

After Laos became a Communist country in 1975, my family, along with many others, fled in fear of persecution. Because my father had served as a commanding officer for eleven years with the American Central Intelligence Agency in what is known to the American public as the "Secret War," my family had no choice but to leave immediately. My father's life was in danger, along with those of thousands of others. We were forced to leave loved ones behind, including my grandmother who was ill in bed the day we fled our village. For a month, my family walked through the dense tropical jungles and rice fields, along rugged trails through many mountains, and battled the powerful Mekong River. We traveled in silence at night and slept in the daytime. Children were very hard to keep quiet. Many parents feared the Communist soldiers would hear the cries of their young children; therefore, they drugged the children with opium to keep them quiet. Some parents even left those children who would not stop crying behind. Fortunately, whenever my parents told my sisters and me to keep quiet, we listened and obeyed.

I do not remember much about our flight, but I do have certain memories that have been imprinted in my mind. It is all so unclear—the experience was like a bad dream: when you wake up, you don't remember what it was you had dreamed about but recall only those bits and pieces of the dream that stand out the most. I remember sleeping under tall trees. I was like a little ant placed in a field of tall grass, surrounded by a dense jungle with trees and bushes all around me—right, left, in the back, and in front of me. I also remember that it rained a lot and that it was cold. We took only what we could carry and it was not much. My father carried a sack of rice, which had to last us the whole way. My mother carried one extra change of clothing for each of us, a few personal belongings, and my baby sister on her back. My older sister and I helped carry pots and pans. My stepuncle carried water, dried meat, and his personal belongings.

From the jungles to the open fields, we walked along a path. We came across a trail of red ants and, being a stubborn child, I refused to walk over them. I wanted someone to pick me up because I was scared, but my parents kept walking ahead. They kept telling me to hurry up and to step over the ants, but I just stood there and cried. Finally, my father came back and put me on his shoulders, along with the heavy sack of rice he was carrying. My dad said he carried me on his back practically all the way to Thailand.

I also recall a car accident we had. My father had paid a truck-driver to take my family and relatives to a nearby town. There were about fifteen of us in the truck. My father, along with the driver and my pregnant aunt, sat in front. The rest of us were in the bed of the truck. While going up a steep mountain, the truck got out of control and, instead of going uphill, started sliding downhill and off the road. Everyone was terrified, but with the help of God, the truck was stopped by a tree stump. Everyone panicked and scrambled out, except for my pregnant aunt who was trapped on the passenger's side because the door was jammed. The impact affected her so much that she could not crawl from her seat to the driver's side in order to get out. My father risked his life to save hers. The rest of us stood back and waited breathlessly as he tried to open the jammed door. He managed to free her just as the truck slid down the hill.

Our adventure did not end then—many nights filled with terror were yet to come. After experiencing many cold days and rainy nights, we finally saw Thailand on the other side of the Mekong River. My parents bribed several fishermen to row us across. The fishermen knew we were desperate, yet, instead of helping us, they took advantage of us. We had to give them all our valuables: silver bars, silver coins, paper money, and my mother's silver wedding necklace, which had cost a lot of money. When it got dark, the fishermen came back with a small fishing boat and took us across the river. The currents were high and powerful. I remember being very scared. I kept yelling, "We're going to fall out! We're going to fall into the river!" My mom tried to reassure me but I kept screaming in fear. Finally, we got across safely. My family, along with many other families, were picked up by the Thai police and taken to an empty bus station for the night.

After a whole month at this temporary refugee camp set up in the bus station, during which we ate rice, dried fish, roots we dug up, and bamboo shoots we cut down, and drank water from streams, we were in very poor shape due to the lack of nutrition. Our feet were also swollen from walking. We were then taken to a refugee camp in Nongkhai, where disease was rampant and many people got sick. My family suffered a loss: my baby sister, who was only a few months old, died. She had become very skinny from the lack of milk, and there was no medical care available. The memory of her death still burns in my mind like a flame. On the evening she died, my older sister and I were playing with our cousins outside the building where we stayed. My father came out to tell us the sad news and told us to go find my stepuncle. After we found him, we went inside and saw our mother mourning the baby's death. Fortunately, our family had relatives around to support and comfort us.

Life in the refugee camp was very difficult. Rice, fish, vegetables, and water were delivered to the camp, but the ration for each family was never enough. Many times, the food my family received did not last until the next delivery. My parents went out to work in the fields to earn a little extra money to buy food. As a child, I did not understand why we had to work so hard and live so poorly.

When I left Laos, I was only three years old. I do not remember much of our life there, but my parents have told me that our family had been quite well off. We had our own house, cattle, rice fields, and a garden where all our vegetables were grown. The money my father received for serving in the army was saved, for there was little need for money. We had enough to eat because we grew our own food. The poor life in the camp is the only life I can remember. I saw my parents' suffering, but I was too young to understand why life was so difficult. Only later did I realize that I and thousands of other young children were victims of a cruel war. Our family remained in Nongkhai for three agonizing years, with our fate uncertain and our future obscure.

Our family life in the camp was very unstable, characterized by deprivation and neglect. My older sister and I were left alone for days while my parents were outside the camp trying to earn money to buy extra food. My parents fought a lot during this period, because we were all under such stress. They knew that if we remained in Thailand, there would be no telling what would become of us. We *had* to find a better life. Some people in the camp were being sponsored to go to the United States. The news spread that anyone who had served in the military with the CIA could apply to go to America. Since my stepuncle had already gone there two years earlier, he sponsored my family. Because my father had been in the military and we had a sponsor, it took only six months to process our papers when usually it took a year or more.

I can still recall the process of leaving the camp. Our relatives, whom we were leaving behind, walked my family from our house to the bus that was to take us to Bangkok. We boarded the bus with our few belongings. People hung out of the windows to touch loved ones for the last time. They cried, knowing they might never meet again. As the buses slowly made their way through the crowd, people ran after them calling out the names of their relatives. "Have a safe trip to your new home!" they shouted. "Don't forget us who are left behind! Please write and tell us about your new life!" Quickly the camp vanished out of sight . . . forever. The moments filled with laughter and tears shared with close friends and relatives were now just faint memories.

It took a full day to travel to Bangkok, where we stayed for four nights. The building we stayed in was one huge room. It was depressing and nerve-wracking. I especially remember how, when we got off the bus to go into the building, a small child about my age came up to my family to beg for food. I recall the exact words she said to my father, "Uncle, can you give me some food? I am hungry. My parents are dead and I am here alone." My dad gave her a piece of bread that we had packed for our lunch. After she walked away, my family found an empty corner and rolled out our bedding for the night. That night, the same child came around again, but people chased her away, which made me sad.

In the morning, I ran to get in line for breakfast. Each person received a bowl of rice porridge with a few strips of chicken in it. For four days, we remained in that building, not knowing when we could leave for the United States. Many families had been there for weeks, months, perhaps even years. On the fourth day, my family was notified to be ready early the next morning to be taken to the airport. The plane ride took a long time and I got motion sickness. I threw up a lot. Only when I saw my stepuncle's face after we landed did I know we had come to the end of our journey. We had come in search of a better life in the "land of giants."

On October 2, 1978, my family arrived at Los Angeles International Airport, where my uncle was waiting anxiously. We stayed with my uncle in Los Angeles for two weeks and then settled in Isla Vista because there were already a few Hmong families there. We knew only one family in Isla Vista, but later we met other families whom my parents had known in their village and from villages nearby. It was in Isla Vista that my life really began. My home life was now more stable. My mother gave birth to a boy a month after we arrived in the United States. It was a joyous event because the first three children she had were all girls. [Boys are desired and valued far more than girls in Hmong culture]. My family also accepted Christ into our lives. My parents still fought once in a while, but these fights were never like those they had in Thailand. The birth of my brother marked the beginning of a new life for us all.

I entered kindergarten at Isla Vista Elementary School. The first day was scary because I could not speak any English. Fortunately, my cousin, who had been in the United States for three years and spoke English, was in the same class with me. She led me to the playground where the children were playing. I was shocked to see so many faces of different colors. The Caucasian students shocked me the most. I had never seen people with blond hair before. The sight sent me to a bench, where I sat and watched everyone in amazement. In class, I was introduced to coloring. I did not know how to hold a crayon or what it was for. My teacher had to show me how to color. I also soon learned the alphabet. This was the beginning of my lifelong goal to get an education.

I loved it in Isla Vista. When my family first settled there, we shared a three-bedroom apartment with another family. Altogether, there were fifteen of us. My family of five shared one room. A few years later, our family shared another three-bedroom apartment with two other families. There were twenty of us in this household. By then, I had four sisters and a brother; we all lived in the same room. I never knew what it was like to have my own room or bed. From this experience of living with so many people, I learned many valuable lessons that helped me to grow. I learned how to share but at the same time to respect the privacy of others. I also realized the uniqueness of my people. No matter how tough a situation is, we all stick together and help each other get through it. So long as there are other Hmong around, no individual Hmong will starve in the streets.

The rising rents in Isla Vista soon made it impossible for my family to continue living there. We moved to Lompoc, which is where my family now lives. There is a sizable Hmong community in Lompoc today. I now have eight sisters and one brother. I am the second oldest. People are usually shocked to hear there are so many of us. I believe that being part of such a large family has helped shape the person that I am today. My willingness to share was reinforced because there were so many of us to care for. I also learned to value many aspects of life that many people take for granted. My family is not rich. We live on the meager salary that my father brings home each week, which is never enough. For as long as I can remember, we got new clothes on only two special occasions: on our traditional Hmong New Year and at the beginning of each school year. There was always food on the table, but just enough that we did not go hungry. We could never afford snacks like cookies, chips, sodas, or fruits. Toys were unknown to me as a child. I never had a Barbie doll or a playhouse—things one might assume every child [in America] has.

My family is very patriarchal. Very early in my life, I was taught the manners that any proper Hmong female should have. I was taught the duties of a daughter. In the Hmong community, there is a clear and stereotypical understanding of how a daughter should act and what duties she must perform. In other words, all Hmong daughters are expected to be alike. A Hmong daughter should know how to cook and clean. She must get up earlier than her parents in the morning. If she doesn't, she is considered lazy. No girl wants that reputation because every girl is taught that if she is known to be lazy, no man would want her. A daughter is expected to stay home to help with the chores. During her free time, she has to occupy herself with needlework, which is called *pangdao*. Sons, on the other hand, are free to do whatever they choose. They are never expected to cook or help around the house.

When I became a teenager, I was never allowed to go out with a boy alone. When I got older and proved to my parents that I was responsible enough to have a boyfriend, they did not object, but still, we could not go out on dates by ourselves. Some of my sisters or my brother always had to go along, or I had to be with a large group. But having adopted the American belief that an individual should be free to choose his or her friends, many times I have gone out behind my parents' back. I believe it is wrong of me to do so, but because I am not allowed to go out even with people I trust, I feel I have no choice. If my parents were not so strict about dating, I would not go against their wishes. In a sense, their attitude drove me to rebel. Although I disagree with the restrictions they impose on me, I understand their reasoning. My parents feel a need to restrict my sisters and me because they fear they would lose control over us otherwise. They want to protect us from embarrassment and shame.

Although my parents have always been very strict, I was really surprised that they did not object at all when I wanted to go to college. In my culture, girls get married at a very young age. So, even though my parents encouraged me to get a higher education, they do not feel certain that I shall complete my studies. Since they came to

America, they have seen many Hmong girls start college, but then get married and leave school before completing their degrees. They cannot grasp the idea that one can still get a college education after one gets married. My parents believe that a college education, which they understand serves as a ticket to a secure and comfortable future, is possible only when one is still single. They think once a young woman starts a family, she would not have time for school and a career.

As the first child in my family to go to college, and as a daughter, I face a lot of pressure. I feel it is my duty to prove, not only to my parents but also to other Hmong parents, that a daughter can do anything that a son can do—perhaps even more. My parents are very old-fashioned and set in their ways. In many respects, they raised us as they themselves were raised, but at the same time, they have pushed us toward a life they have never known. They do not understand that there is a gap between their generation and ours. Growing up in American society, I am caught between two very different cultures.

The kind of physical affection and words of praise that many American parents express are unknown in my family. My parents seldom converse with my sisters, brother, and me. They are very indirect in their communication and actions. They never tell us they love us, nor do they congratulate us when we accomplish something. They believe strongly that people should not show their feelings and emotions. I don't remember ever touching my parents' hands or embracing them. It is sad, but it would be awkward to hug them or hold their hands. Americans touch and hug each other all the time. In my culture, if a married man or woman hugs someone of the opposite sex, it is assumed the two individuals are in love, and rumors would fly, and jealousy would grow. Even married couples do not walk side by side. One, usually the husband, must walk in front of the other. It is considered disrespectful to elders if we touch them or walk in front of them.

My father never says much when he is home, but when he does talk to us, we know it must be serious. Because my father has to drive an hour each way to Goleta to get to work, our family sees him only for a few hours a night. On the weekends, he is too tired to spend time with his children. He hardly ever smiles. Many times, I think to myself, "He must be a sad and lonely man because he is one of only two survivors in his family as the result of a cold and deadly war." I feel sorry for him.

In one year, he lost two older brothers, whom we had left behind in Laos. One of them died after months of suffering. He had been in a car accident, but there was no medical care available to help him recover. My other uncle, after five years in a refugee camp in Thailand, decided he wanted to come to the United States. After studying for six months to prepare himself for the dramatic changes he and his family would encounter, he died suddenly in his sleep. This Sudden Unexplained Nocturnal Death Syndrome has affected many Hmong. We do not know the cause of his death, only that he died in peace. He went to bed and never woke up again. When my father received the news, he cried so much. It made me really sad to see him cry, because even though he has always looked sad to me, he has never said anything about how he feels or shown the pain he carries in his overburdened heart. Having learned the American way of expressing myself, I wanted to say something to him or just to hold him to let him know that I love him, but I could not bring myself to do so.

I felt awkward expressing my love to him either verbally or physically because my parents have never told us in words that they love us, nor have they shown any appreciation for the good deeds or services we have performed or for our achievements at school. They express their love only by the food they provide us with at each meal and the roof over our heads. It was not until this past summer (1992) that I learned that my parents in fact long to hear us children tell them, "*Niam thiab txiv, kuv hlub neb*" (Mom and Dad, we love you). This past summer, when I was at Maranatha Bible Camp in Nebraska for an annual conference held by the Hmong Youth Rally Zone, one of the pastors' sermons made me realize that should anything happen to my parents, I would not be able to live with the guilt of never having told them that I love them. That night, I called home and talked to my parents. And yes, I told them that for the past twenty years of my life, I have loved them with all my heart. In reply, my mother said that they loved me also and that they thought they would never hear any of us children tell them that.

My mother is very different from my father. She talks a lot and she is always complaining about how hard life is in America. She cannot go anywhere by herself because she cannot speak English well enough. My older sister and I have always been her interpreters and translators. For as long as I can remember, we have taken turns taking my mother to the grocery store, to parent–teacher conferences, to the doctor, and to other events that require communication. Every month when the utility bills come or when rent is due, she fusses about how we have so many bills to pay in the United States. She is right, of course. My mother is always making a comparison between our old life back in Laos and our new life here in California. "We didn't have to pay rent because we had built our own house. Electricity and gas were not available, yet we managed to survive. We had to haul water from nearby springs, but there was plenty of it. There were always fresh vegetables from our garden and our cattle provided milk and meat. We had no worries about what we would eat the next day or whether we had enough money to pay the bills."

Although her complaints get to me sometimes, I see in her a very courageous and caring woman. She has, in a single lifetime, gone through the worst I can imagine. When she shares with me her life story, I wish I had been there to help her in times of hardship. My grandparents divorced when my mother was only a few months old. She never knew her father. Her mother remarried shortly afterward. My grandmother died when my mother was only eleven or twelve years old, leaving her with her stepsister, who was five or six, and her stepbrother, who was a few months old. My stepgrandfather had two other wives, so these women were asked to care for my mother and her siblings, but they made my mother into their slave. My mother practically raised her brother and sister until she married my father at the age of sixteen. Even after her marriage, she worked hard. Throughout her life, she has never had a break. And now, she has ten children. Imagine how hectic that must be, especially in the United States, when the average number of children in a family is only two or three.

My mother is my mentor, my guide, and my shelter. Although I know I can never make up for the hard life she has led, I thank her for bringing me into this world. She has taught me to see through all the hatred and suffering in this world and to look at the good side that I know how to appreciate: my family.

When I was younger, lectures from my parents were dreadful to listen to. As I recall, the themes running through all their lectures were: "Don't forget where you came from and who you are! Nothing comes easy without sweat from your brow! Study hard and pursue your education to the best of your ability!" When I was young, I thought I knew everything about life. Those words of wisdom meant nothing to me. I was too busy trying to become a typical American girl, going out on dates, wearing nice clothes and makeup, and voicing my opinion when I felt my parents were wrong to tell me what to do and what not to do. I was ashamed of my heritage, of where I had come from, of who I was, and even of my parents who could not speak good English. I found it embarrassing and even shameful to speak my native language. I wanted so much to be like my "Americanized" Hmong–American friends. I felt I had to change my identity or risk rejection from my peers.

Now that I am older, I treasure the long but valuable lessons my parents tried to teach us—lessons that gave me a sense of identity as a Hmong. "Nothing comes easy. . . . ," my parents always said. As I attempt to get a college education, I remember how my parents have been really supportive of me financially throughout my schooling, but because they never had a chance to get an education themselves, they were not able to help me whenever I could not solve a math problem or write an English paper. Although they cannot help me in my schoolwork, I know in my heart that they care about me and want me to be successful so that I can help them when they can no longer help themselves. Therefore, I am determined to do well at the university. I want to become a role model for my younger brother and sisters, for I am the very first member of my family to attend college. I feel a real sense of accomplishment to have set such an example.

The Fang Family of San Diego

Mai Moua (*right*) and an unidentified companion in Laos.
Courtesy of Mai Moua.

The Fang family in Laos, mid–1960s. Xia Shoua Fang is on the left, Ka Xiong is on the right. The children are their three oldest. *Courtesy of Xia Shoua Fang, Ka Xiong, and Lee Fang.*

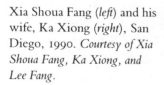

Xia Shoua Fang (*left*) and his wife, Ka Xiong (*right*), San Diego, 1990. *Courtesy of Xia Shoua Fang, Ka Xiong, and Lee Fang.*

Mai Moua's Life Story

as told to her grandnephew, Lee Fang

I do not know how old my brothers and I were when my parents died, but we were very young. My mother had her children one after another in a short period of time, so that when my father died, I already had three brothers. We killed five animals [to feed the people who came] for my father's funeral. One of my brothers, Yee, died a year after my parents did. An uncle of mine named Ying also died while we were living in Punong.

After my father, brother, and uncle died, we sent a message to my cousins in Mouaping, and they came and picked us up. Since I was still very little, they took turns carrying me on their back all the way to their village. I do not know what year that was. We lived in Mouaping until each of us was old enough to get married and have families of our own.

In Mouaping, my other two brothers, Vang and Wang Sue, also died, so I have no brothers left. My son, Xia Neng, died just as he became old enough to get married. Ten or eleven years later, another son, Cha Ying, and all six members of his family were killed. That same year, my husband died in June or July while yet another son of mine, Xao Cher, died in September. I felt miserable after their deaths. I had no one to turn to. Nu Yia, one of my two remaining sons, asked me what was wrong with me. He asked whether I had anything to do with all those deaths.

Chapter Three

When I was young, Hmong girls spent their time doing needlework and working in the fields. We did those two things all the time.
As an orphan, when my neighbors got up in the morning to go to
the fields, I had to go with them. We exchanged labor with other
people who were cultivating their fields, spending a few days here, a
few days there.

When I married your grandfather, Fang Soua,* I did everything
that his family told me to do. For a while, we had some luck. A lot
of people complimented me on the sons I bore. They told me my
sons would have great futures. When my daughter died, however,
my luck left me.

My relatives had not wanted me to marry your grandfather at all.
They scolded me so much that I did not know what to do. Some
of my relatives beat me, while others yelled at me. Then the elder
of the Moua clan, to which I belonged, came to ask me what had
happened. He wanted to know whether your grandfather was trying
to force me to marry him or whether I loved him. I said, "The truth
is, he is not forcing me. I want to marry him because I love him. In
this world, no one can force me to marry anyone unless I like him.
I want to go and live with him." After that, members of the Moua
clan did not pressure me any more. However, they demanded more
money from the groom and insisted that his family serve everyone
corn whiskey at the wedding ceremony. When we got home after the
wedding, the elder of my husband's clan was really angry. He never
forgot what the Moua clan had done to us. But all the money they
made my husband's family pay for me did not hurt as much as the
bad words they said about us.

After I married, my life was both happy and miserable—happy
because I had married someone to whom I was attracted, miserable
because your grandfather did not help me and the children with work
in the fields at all. He was always at home attending to his guests,
who came from other villages. He devoted most of his time to receiving guests every single day because he was the community leader.
I went to work in the fields while he entertained them. His guests

*Mai Moua is the wife of Lee Fang's grandfather's brother. But since Lee Fang's
real grandparents are no longer living, he calls Mai Moua "grandmother," while
she refers to her deceased husband as Lee Fang's "grandfather." [Ed.]

usually ate most of the food in the house as though it were theirs. When I came home from the fields, I had to get the grain, pound it [to remove the husks], and cook some more food—breakfast, lunch, and dinner for the next day. [By the time I finished,] all the people in the village were already asleep.

This was how I had to live through most of my life with your grandfather. Our family was big, but there were few persons who helped me. Other [women] could rely on their whole family. Their husbands did not go away as my husband did; they helped their wives in whatever way was needed. So the women were able to finish the planting without doing much work [themselves]. But for me, it was different. Since my husband had his personal business, my children and I had to do all the clearing and planting of the fields. Later, when I had daughters-in-law, I did not have to work as much. They helped me. Your grandfather came to the fields only once in a while and then just to tell us what to do.

We worked very hard in the fields. We started by cutting down trees. A few weeks later, we burned them. Two or three days after the burning, we planted rice and corn. We did not stay home at all. We did not even come home to sleep sometimes; we slept in little shacks in the fields. We had a few *rai* of rice, a few *rai* of corn, and a few *rai* of opium. We went back and forth among the different fields that grew these crops. We always had to make sure each was growing properly. We had good harvests in some years but in other years we did not. In bad years, we did not have enough rice to eat.

Each season, as soon as we finished cutting and stacking the stalks of rice, we would work in the opium fields. When the opium poppies bloomed, we felt very happy. We made incisions in the top part of the plants early in the morning. I could take care of a few *rai* and collect several bowls of opium latex by myself. Right now, my life does not have any meaning and I have no accomplishments to boast about, but back in the days when I worked in the opium fields, I was proud of what I could do. Since the poppy plants did not all ripen at the same time, the fast-growing ones had already been incised a few times by the time the slower-growing poppies started to bloom. When the good soil was used up or when there were weeds in the fields, it was difficult for the opium poppies to grow well.

Your grandfather was not a nice person. He did not give me any of his money. When our sons got married, they had to work hard because their father did not give them much. But once they started working for themselves, they were able to make some money, with which they could buy clothes and other things as they pleased. Everybody became happier.

Then war broke out and our husbands went away to fight the enemy. Those of us left behind ate anything we could find. We suffered a lot. After the Communist invasion, we had to move from place to place. Our lives changed a lot. We could not take good care of our crops because we had to run away from the Communist soldiers. We had to leave behind our stored rice and corn. The Communists must have been happy when they found so much food waiting for them.

Your grandfather died about a year after the Communists came. We were in hiding for several years after his death. We had to live like savages deep in the jungles on the mountains. We stayed at each place for only a few days and then moved on because we did not want the enemy to find us. Since we were constantly moving, we had no time to plant any crops. We ate anything that was edible to stop our stomachs from growling.

As we moved from place to place, we carried our belongings on our backs. The loads were so heavy that we cried when we could not walk any further. At first, we were able to walk long distances, but as time passed, we lost our strength. The strange thing is, though we were running for our lives, we took our chickens, pigeons, cows, horses, and pigs with us. Now that I think about it, that was very stupid of us.

We were constantly bitten by mosquitoes and other insects that sucked blood from our bodies. I was very scared of the blood-sucking insects that crawled all over me. There were so many of them that I did not know what to do except cry. But the more I cried, the more they bit me. We lived in the jungles for three or four years. Our lives were miserable like that until we left Laos.

When many people started leaving for Thailand, we decided we should also. We lived through many days and nights of hardship as we made our way to Thailand. I was carrying so much that I sprained my ankles, which gave me great agony throughout the trip. My two sons had to carry me for part of the way. We had been dressed in good clothes when we began our journey, but our clothes were in shreds by the time we arrived in Thailand.

We lived in Thailand for a year before we came to the United States. In the Ban Vinai refugee camp, I did what everyone else did: I sat all day and waited for the Thai officials to give us food. They gave us just enough to keep us alive. I tried to make some money by picking flowers, but we got chased away from the fields belonging to the Thai because it was illegal to pick their flowers. With whatever money we made, we bought the kind of food we wanted to eat.

I arrived in America in 1980—I think it was in the month of May. We lived in North Carolina for three months. My son had to find a job even though he did not know a word of English. All I could do was to grow some vegetables in our backyard. Our sponsors gave us clothes. One day my son had a really bad stomachache. We were very worried because we spoke no English. None of us could understand what the doctor told us about his condition. I promised the evil spirits that if my son got well, I would sacrifice a pig or some chickens for them.

Fortunately, my grandson, who had studied a little English in the Thai refugee camp, knew how to look up the phone number of some people who had just moved from California to North Carolina. We called them and they told us where our cousins were in San Diego. After my son had the operation on his stomach, we moved to San Diego. Ever since I have been in America, I have not done anything strenuous except to babysit my grandchildren. I am very happy to be alive today, seeing my family so well and happy.

Xia Shoua Fang's Life Story

as told to his son, Lee Fang

I am Xia Shoua Fang. I am fifty-eight years old. I was born in 1933 in a village called Nasigao in Mouaping. My grandfather had three sons and three daughters. I am the son of the eldest son, named Jou Kou. In Mouaping, my father was considered the most intelligent man. If there was a misunderstanding or a crime that no one could solve, my father was the person who dealt with and settled the matter. The people under my father were almost as numerous as those under the governor.

In 1945, my father hired four Vietnamese men to saw down some trees and build us a house. There was war that year, first with the French and then with the Lao Issara [the Free Lao, a group fighting for Laotian independence]. Some Chinese soldiers came to Mouaping and asked the Vietnamese carpenters to bring my father and Shoua Sher as well as another Hmong named Ying to them. The soldiers then went to the governor's home to try to capture him, but he had already escaped to the woods before the soldiers arrived. However, when the governor saw that my father and the other two Hmong were with the soldiers, he came out of hiding, whereupon they arrested him.

My father told his Hmong comrades, "Now that we have been captured, each of us must try to escape." Though they were being securely guarded by the soldiers, somehow my father managed to get away. The governor and the two other Hmong, however, did not. The next day, the soldiers took them to Nakong, with Shoua Sher and Ying tied with same rope. As they crossed a stream, Shoua Sher and Ying ran away together. The soldiers fired some shots, but these never touched them and they got away. The only prisoner left was the governor.

The commander of the army blamed my father and a man named Lao Sa for the capture of the governor. His soldiers took them prisoner and beat them up. My father asked his captors to send someone to his family to get money to pay for his release. Before our relatives could come, the soldiers beat up my father and broke all his opium-smoking equipment. His head was badly cut and blood dripped everywhere. His clothes were covered with blood. They tied him up like a pig. Uncle Youa asked a different governor named Blia Tia, to whom we paid a large sum of money, to help us. He agreed to do so. He promised not to allow my father to be tortured any more. My father and Lao Sa were released after our family paid another large sum of money to the captors. We had to sell our silver jewelry to get the money.

After this incident, we had nothing left in our family except one cow, one male water buffalo, and one female water buffalo. Eventually, the female water buffalo gave birth to a calf, which was given to me. When her second calf was born, my older brother, Wang, got it. The third calf was given to Uncle Chou. The fourth one went to my mother. The fifth was given to my other mother—my father's first wife. That one female water buffalo thus was the origin of all the water buffaloes we eventually raised. The cow, however, did not flourish as the water buffalo had. She had no calves. So we sold her. The money from this sale was divided between me and my brother Wang. We used it to buy some other cows. We could now also buy some clothes and salt for our food. Raising those animals and working in our fields, we no longer had to depend on others. We lived our life this way until 1960 or 1961, when General Vang Pao went to war.

I do not have a lot of intelligent things to say because I never had any real education, as my mother would not let me go away to school. In those days, the only way to go to school was to go to a town. The only thing I know about is farming. Instead of going to school, I joined the army. In 1962, some of the soldiers who could read and write were asked to teach those of us who were illiterate. That was how I learned to read and write.

After I joined the army, I moved around for several years until I got stationed at Long Cheng in 1964, where I remained for two months. Then I was sent to several other places before returning to Long Cheng. My job was to give the orders to deliver food to the troops in various stations and to the civilians as well. I did this work for two years.

In 1966 or 1967, I was sent to Thakhek, where I stayed for two years also. Around October 1969, my brother Wang passed away. I asked permission to attend his funeral, which gave me a pretext to leave the army. I returned to farm with my family. I was elected the village leader. In this capacity, I looked after the people and solved problems. I held this position until 1974. I paid some Lao men from the city to come and build a new house for my family in Namai, which is close to Thakhek. It was one of the best houses I ever saw in Laos.

After General Vang Pao fled, we were left behind with the Communists. Those Hmong who were able to follow General Vang Pao got out alive, but their numbers are small compared to those who did not make it. A lot of people were shot and killed by the Communists. Many drowned in the Mekong River as they tried to cross over to Thailand.

Two Communist officials came to our village and told us they had taken over the country. They told us not to be scared. They asked us to elect a mayor, but no one wanted to become mayor. They then asked us to join their army. We told them that if all of us Hmong could join at the same time, we would do so. But they did not believe us. They also promised to kill fifteen cows and fifteen buffaloes for a feast so that we and they could get to know each other. They said different groups of people had to sit at different tables—the older men, the younger men, the women, the children, the veterans, and the soldiers would each have their own table. The Hmong leaders discussed the situation among themselves. They came to the conclusion that the feast was a ruse to get everyone killed. So we decided not to go. The Communists were upset. They threatened to arrest us. This confirmed that the feast was a plot to kill us.

A little guerrilla war then broke out. It lasted for three days and nights. Some of our men were injured, but the Communists also suffered greatly. About a hundred and fifty of their men were killed. They turned back. But later they returned with big machine guns and other weapons. Fortunately, a Hmong who was an associate of the Communists asked them not to shoot us. He told them we were running out of ammunition and that they should send for more men. The Communists did what this Hmong told them. This gave us time to move deeper into the jungle, where we lived savage lives. Wherever we went, the Communists invaded the territory, killed our people, and burned our crops. We lived for four miserable years in the jungles.

In 1979, the Communists came in the thousands like swarms of bees. They crossed rivers, mountains, jungles, and open fields. They used big guns to shoot at places where they suspected Hmong were hiding. There was no way we could defend ourselves any longer. We did not have the weapons or enough people to continue to fight, so we began to flee.

As we fled, the Communists cut me off from the people who had gone ahead of me. I was with one of my cousins and his family. Of the twenty-seven people in our group, he and I were the only adult men. We went deep into the jungle. We walked in the streams so that we would leave no trails. We sneaked around the places where we suspected there were soldiers as we tried to find the groups ahead.

Finally, we came to a small village where we met some people we knew. We were very relieved. We thought everyone had gone on their way to Thailand. Our friends told us it was true everyone had left, but that they had come back to get their money. My cousin felt we should also return to Naga that overlooked Black Mountain to get the money we had hidden there. I argued we should not go back, since we had all our wives and children with us and we did not know what we might run into next. It was too dangerous to go back when there were Communists everywhere. In the end, we decided to send two of the older boys with [my cousin] to get our money, while I pushed ahead with the women and children.

Next we came to a village where my son-in-law and his cousins from the Moua clan lived. The people there told us the last of my uncles and cousins had left for Thailand the day before. The other members of my family had departed the day before that. A lot of people were gathering their belongings for the journey. We were told we would not be able to find rice in any of the villages ahead. I asked one of the villagers where I could buy [unhusked] rice and he told me where to go. But by the time I returned with some rice, people had already taken all the rice pestles with them. So we went on to the next village, but all the people there had also left. We did find a rice pestle, though, and finished pounding and husking our rice around midnight.

We slept for a few hours but were up at the first crow of the rooster. After eating a little, we left the village at dawn. It was lucky we left so early: just as we got to the edge of the village, a bomb hit it. We ran down the hill. We could see gunshots in the distance. We ran as fast as we could. We finally got to Nainoi. Everyone there had departed also; they had not even shut their doors. I went looking for my uncle, who had suffered burns when we were burning our fields, and my cousin, who had been shot in the leg by the Communists and had to have it amputated before we fled. But I could not find them. I rejoined my family and we moved on. We finally caught up with my uncle and cousin the next day.

We were able to spend only a little time with each other because the following day we ran into the Communists. A battle broke out. All I could see was gunfire everywhere, with bullets whizzing past our heads. This was all we could see because it was dark in the jungle. I split up my family that night. I took two of my older sons with me and left the rest of my family with my cousin Fang Nou Chia, who had never been a soldier but only a student. I figured that he would not be executed if he were caught. But the Communists definitely would kill me, should they catch me, because I had been a soldier.

We got to another village and waited there for news. I decided to let my two sons go ahead with my cousin, Fang Cher Chang, to Thailand. I stayed behind with two friends to try to free those Hmong who had been captured, but five days later, the Communists found us. They opened fire and we ran into the wilderness. The Communists burned all the houses in that village—about twenty-five in all.

We fled to Punyer, where we went to see a very important Hmong military commander. He had been raised with the Communists but he still had some connections to the Hmong. We asked him to help get our family and the other imprisoned Hmong released. He told us not to worry. He said he could get even those who were under the strictest supervision freed. He advised us to go to Mount Chai, as it would be easier to reach Thailand from there. Besides, he said, if we went there, we would not create any problems for him, as he would not be blamed for letting us escape to Thailand when his job was to stop us from leaving. He further advised us to act as though we were planning to live on Mount Chai. So we built two houses there and planted four to six *rai* of highland rice. Eight of us stayed there for two months, until the rest of our family joined us. We remained another two months in order to harvest our rice crop before leaving for Thailand.

When we reached the Mekong River, several Thai men came to meet us. They told us they could smuggle us across the river at night, but we had to pay a large sum of money for each person. The first night, the smugglers did not succeed in transporting us across because the currents were running too strong and fast in that section of the river. The next night we moved upriver to a safer place. The Thai said they would paddle all of us across only if we gave them all our money.

After three boatloads of us had been ferried to an island in the middle of the river, Uncle Vang Ser's wife, who was on the fourth boatload, fired her pistol at the Thai when they tried to take her money from her. The smugglers stopped midstream. Half of our party were still waiting on the other shore, while the rest of us were on the island. The Thai strip-searched the people on the island in retaliation for Aunt Vang firing her pistol at them.

We were stranded on the island for five days. When the Thai came back for us, we refused to leave. But they showed us a letter from someone belonging to the Vu clan then living in the Ban Vinai refugee camp, saying it was all right for us to follow the Thai. It took eleven boatloads and two hours to get us all across. We resided in Pasoo for two weeks before we went to Ban Vinai. We arrived in November and stayed there till March 24, 1980, when we left Thailand for the United States.

[The narrative ends here because Mr. Fang did not wish to discuss his life in the United States.]

Ka Xiong's Life Story

as told to her son, Lee Fang

My name is Ka Xiong. I was born in January 1935, but I do not know on what day of the month. My life has been very hard from the start. Both my grandparents as well as my mother died when I was still very young. I never met my grandparents. All I know about them is what my relatives have told me. My cousins told me that my great-grandfather was named Xiong Wang Lue and my grandfather Xiong Shoua Leng. Xiong Wang Lue had six sons; Shoua Leng was the fourth. My father, Xiong Xa Chue, was the son of Shoua Leng.

My mother's name was Moua Zoua. She had five children, two of whom died in their infancy. Three of us are left—my sister Xia Neng, brother Pang Ying, and me. My mother passed away when I was five or six years old, Xia Neng was seven or eight, and Pang Ying was a baby. We had to take care of the baby. He cried a lot. I noticed it especially at night. We did not have milk for him, so we boiled rice until it was very soft and fed him with it. We sometimes asked our cousins as well as neighbors to breast-feed him. I am still grateful to Yia Shoua's wife and Chai Ying's wife who breast-fed him. Those two women now live in Milwaukee, Wisconsin. Though both my sister and I had to take care of our baby brother, I spent more time doing it because I was too small to work in the fields.

Since I was still a child myself, I cried every time he cried, especially at night.

Though my father never showed it in public, I knew he missed my mother a lot, because I heard sobbing sounds at night from his bed. He also visited my mother's parents to help ease the pain. He kept in close touch with them until the day he died. In Hmong society, men whose wives have died seldom keep in touch with their dead wives' parents, but my father was different.

In time he must have got over my mother's death because he remarried. His new wife's name was Thao Chou, and she bore several children, none of whom lived to adulthood. My father died in 1961 and my stepmother a few years after that. My brother now lives in Milwaukee, Wisconsin, and has six sons and five daughters. My sister, who is living in Merced, California, has three sons and six daughters. I have six sons and four daughters.

When my mother was alive, she was very busy. She worked almost every day in the fields. I remember that because she usually took me with her. Since I was too young to do anything, I just sat and played alongside her while she worked. When she died, she left some clothes that we girls wore when we got bigger. That was how we managed to clothe ourselves since we were not old enough to sew our own. She also left some money behind. But after she died, whenever I saw a child holding his or her mother's hand, or when I saw someone else's mother coming home from the fields and smiling at her children who came up to greet her, I thought of my mother and cried. I kept thinking how, if my mother were still alive, she would be bringing food home and cooking it for us. I continued to cry for many years until I became old enough to accept her death.

My grandparents were rich. They had many bars of silver hidden away. My father inherited some of this wealth, so he did not have to worry about food or money. Part of this wealth eventually passed on to my brother, Pang Ying. [Despite our wealth,] my life was hard after my parents died. It seemed I did not have any luck at all. Why did my mother have to die so young? I have always had to act like a grown-up; I never had a chance to enjoy my childhood. I worked a lot and had little time for recreation. I never played with the other young girls in our village. Neither did I have time to go to school or learn to play the bamboo flute.

I worked throughout my childhood and teenage years until I married your father, but after my marriage my life did not change much. Your father's father had died as well, so only his mother was alive when we got married. Your father came from a big family. Your Uncle Wang had a big family of his own, and now your father started his. I gave birth to your eldest brother, Chou, then to your sister, Mee, and then your brother, Lao Mo, who died when he was a child. We all lived in the same household as your Uncle Wang's family. Your father and your uncle worked alongside each other in the rice and corn fields, but they cared for their opium fields separately. At first, I did not understand why, but later, I realized it had to do with money [as opium was our cash crop].

About five years after I married your father, he wanted to go to the city to study. He left me with your grandmother. When he left us, Chou had just been born; when he returned about a year and a half later, Chou could already walk. Your father did not succeed in enrolling in school, so he joined the army instead. While he was away, I worked with his relatives to grow rice and opium.

I worked almost as hard as I had done when I was a young girl. The only difference was that I was not as lonely because I lived with your grandmother and her family and I had your brother to care for. I worked so hard that I used up two bamboo buckets every year. That can be compared to your wearing out two backpacks carrying heavy books every year. My body ached constantly and my palms and fingers were covered with calluses. My clothes would be soaked with sweat by noon. The sweat sometimes got into my eyes and blinded me. Whenever I carried a bucket, it was fully loaded and was placed high on my back.

I was the only Xiong to be married into the Fang clan, which made life very difficult for me. Hard as I worked, some people still spread rumors that I was not hardworking. Such a rumor is what a Hmong wife fears the most. Usually, when villagers do not like a woman, they spread this rumor about her. Apparently, the villagers did not like me as much as they liked the other wives in the village. Only your uncle, Fang Yee, made nice comments about me. He said no wonder we were rich and had everything we wanted, seeing how hard I worked. Whenever your father was away trading, I had to become the man of the house. I did almost anything that a man did. I tilled the rice fields [by myself]; irrigating them was especially hard work. Such was my life until we left Laos.

When we were in Nali, our rice, corn, and opium fields were all close to our house, so we did not have to walk far to get to them. For that reason, we did not suffer as much. However, our neighbors often picked the vegetables and sugarcane in our yard without asking our permission, as though those things were theirs. By the time we found out, they had already eaten them. This upset me because I had worked so hard to plant them. But there was nothing I could do about it. I suppose they must have been very desperate to have taken our vegetables without asking.

I did not want to work so hard side by side with your grandma and uncle, but your father insisted that I continue to do so. We harvested the same amount of crops as they did and we had as many domestic animals, such as horses, cows, water buffaloes, pigs, goats, chickens, and ducks, as they did. We did not spend much of the money we made until our journey to Thailand because we ourselves produced everything we needed at that time.

After your Uncle Wang died, I went to Long Cheng to live with your father, where we made money without having to work as hard. Your father was doing business with people in the city. He made a lot of profit selling cattle and other animals. He hired people to care for them. So the time I spent in Long Cheng was very relaxing.

When we moved back to Namai, your father decided to build a big house against my wishes. I did not want to spend so much money on such a big house because somehow I had the feeling we would not be able to live in it for long. But you know your father; he never listens to me. He went ahead and had it built, anyway. He never bought me earrings, necklaces, or anything of that sort. Instead, he wanted to have something that would catch other people's eyes. In other words, he wanted to show off his wealth. It was one of the best houses in our village at that time. The carpenters, whom your father hired from the city, used wood for the walls and tin sheets for the roof. Hmong could never have built such a house. I don't remember exactly how much it cost, but it was a lot. We paid for it with a stack of money about five or six inches high. Your father had made that money selling cattle. The sad thing is, we lost that house when we fled from Laos. All our money also became worthless. Had he bought me some gold or silver jewelry, I might still have some things that we used to own.

Although we had a big and beautiful house, I never could spend much time enjoying it because I was always out working in the fields. I managed to spend only a few days sitting in front of the house sewing. I was at the house only when I had to clean it or rake the leaves in the yard. I got up early every morning to feed the pigs, chickens, horses, cows, dogs, etc. Just as the sun was rising above the horizon, I set out for the fields. I would already be on my way when the roosters started to crow.

I went to work in the fields every day. When the corn season was over, the rice season began. We used corn to feed our livestock. I hated having to go out into the woods to cut plants for our animals' feed. The worst part was carrying the plants back to the house. My back ached so much that I often had to crawl on my knees while going up a hill. I would be all muddy when I got home. The aching stopped only when I fell asleep. Since we raised livestock for sale, I had to take good care of them. I saved some of the money we got for each cow, horse, or water buffalo we sold. I used the money to buy you children clothes. At that time, all of you were so small you could not help me even if you wanted to. I had to do everything myself. Your father helped me sometimes, but at other times he would not. So I ended up doing all the work in the fields and around the house.

All that hard work made me feel like an important person, however. Now that I no longer have to work all day, I do not feel important anymore. When I worked to make money, I used my intelligence as best I could. But now I am useless. I have to wait for you children to help me with everything. I have to depend on you to take me to the store, to drive me to visit my relatives, or even to walk around the neighborhood. But you cannot imagine how happy I am that we succeeded in bringing all of you to the United States so you would not have to experience the hardships we had experienced in Laos.

Our family was just beginning to flourish when we left Laos. We would have become a very wealthy family had we been able to remain there. We had already built everything we needed and our rice, corn, and opium fields were large enough to make us wealthy. Life would have become easier as you children grew up to help us. But [, in retrospect,] I think your father would have put all of you in school [instead of keeping you at home to help me]. I know he would have done this because he himself never got a chance to go to school. We always wished for sons and daughters who could read and write. We would have done anything to let you children get an education. Paying the school fees would have been a problem, but not as big a problem as getting you accepted into school because the Lao educational system favored [lowland] Lao over Hmong students. This was especially true at the college level.

Now, my life is very different. I cannot do the things I used to do or want to do. Everything related to school is left up to you children. I cannot help you and I cannot even give you enough money for school. I feel so helpless. I was never helpless back in Laos.

Let me tell you some more about my life in Laos. When we moved to Kolue, your father took us there but he could not remain with us. He had to help the other men fight the Communists. We lived in Kolue for about a year, and then we moved back to the place where your father had built the big house. But when we got back, the house was gone. Someone had burned it down. The rumor was that it was the Communists who had done so, but the truth was, the Hmong people must have destroyed it because they were jealous of our big and beautiful house. I know that what we were told was an excuse because our house was the only one in the village that was burned. None of the other houses were burned. But, since we had not been there when it happened, we could not prove who had done it.

When you children were still very young, I often wished that you could be like needles and thread so that I could have simply sewn you children right on my blouse. It would have made moving around so much easier. After I slipped on a rock and broke my right wrist, my life and the lives of you children became miserable. It took more than a year for my wrist to heal. During that time, I could not do any heavy work since I could not use my right hand at all. I put a sling around my neck and rested my arm in it. People had to help me whenever I had to put my bucket on my back. I could not even wash myself. Your sister, Kazoua, had to wash my back for me. You children helped me, but I could not take care of you as well as I wanted to. Your older sister and brother had to help me cook.

In thinking back, I often ask, why did we have to rear you children during the worst period in our lives—in a time of war and misery?

Whatever hardships I had to live through, you children had to also. My sympathies really went out to you children. I am very happy that we came to the United States. I'm so happy because I still have all my children with me. If some of you had been separated from us and were still back in Laos, that would have broken my heart. It really would have.

Your other grandmother [one of the two wives that your grandfather had] died a day before the Communists reached our village. That was the last time we saw her. We never managed to give her a proper burial. We would all have been killed had we not left the village. Your father was the only person who saw her being buried because it was he who dug her grave and buried her. We left the ceremonial tablet for the dead in our house. Now that I think about it, I hate myself for having left her there. But at the time, it was the only thing we could do. Everything was happening so fast. Gunshots were coming from everywhere. It was that close. We were really scared. We panicked. We did not know what we were doing.

Later, when we came back to the village, everything had been destroyed. So, we had to start all over again. We used the same fields to plant rice, corn, and vegetables, but it was already late in the season, so the harvest was not a good one. The rains had come, and the heavy downpour destroyed the crops. I still remember one night when I was carrying your sister, Tang, and some chickens from our old village to our new village. I could not find my way because it was so dark and it was raining so hard. Your sister and I spent all night sitting under a tree. All we had was a small blanket, which I used to cover your sister. It was so cold. Fortunately, I found my way back to the new village just as your father came looking for us.

Your father had a reputation for being wealthy. He was very well known in our village and among our relatives. To this day, people still respect him for that reputation. But the odd thing was, we did not live as though we were a rich family. There was little difference between the way we lived and the way my poorer uncles and cousins lived. We mostly ate rice with peppers dipped in salt. We did not eat much meat even though we had the money to buy it. Our life stayed simple like that until we reached America.

We did not stay in the new village long either. After being there for about a year, we made our way to Thailand. The journey was a hard one, especially for you children. You were all still so small then. You were like little mice and piglets running alongside their mom. I loved you children so much then, and I love all of you so much now. You children meant and still mean everything to me. Sometimes, these days, when I see poor little children of other countries on television, it reminds me of how my own children were dressed in rags and were so very skinny due to the shortage of food and the difficulties we encountered along our way. We had just enough food to keep us alive. We had only rice with water and pepper; we had no meat or vegetables and only occasionally did we use salt. Your father said he had to be frugal with our money so that he could use it to get us all to America.

Though the journey was hardest on you children, it was a stressful one for me as well because I was pregnant with your youngest brother, Ger. I felt sick constantly, which added to our problems. Ger was born in 1979 during our journey. I felt very weak after he was born, and it took me a long time to regain my strength because I did not have enough rice or any chicken to eat and I could not rest. Ger cried a lot since I could not give him sufficient nutrition. But after that long, hard journey, I learned to love and admire myself.

When we were stopped in our tracks by Communist soldiers, we had to pay them a lot of money to let us go. That was one of the few times we had to spend a large sum of money. When we reached the Mekong River, we spent some more money to get ourselves ferried across. We had not brought all our money with us—we left some back at the village. We took only about thirty silver bars with us on our journey, but that was considered a lot of money. By the time we got across the Mekong, however, almost all that money was gone, because your father used his money to help many other families get across the Mekong River and to pay off the soldiers who held us up. He helped these people because they had no money of their own. I did not mind his using our money this way—at the time it was the right thing to do. Even today, I do not resent giving all our money to those boatmen who took us across the big river, though I may sound as if I am complaining. So our money was used to benefit not only ourselves but others as well. I hope all these good deeds your father did will be rewarded. I have suffered enough in my life; perhaps God will reward us for our good deeds now that we are in America.

I am so happy that we are now able to all live together in a country that is free, even though the environment here is not as peaceful and harmonious as it was in Laos before the war. I am so happy to have all my children here with me and to see them doing so well. In life, we must work hard to get what we want. In Laos, all we could do was work in the fields. In America, life is different. We must use our heads—our intelligence and our knowledge—to the fullest to bring about the results we desire. I regret that I never got a chance to go to school, as you children have the opportunity to do now. Without any education, I cannot go to work and bring home money. If you children love me and want to show your gratitude to your father and me for bringing you here, then please try to complete the highest level of education you can. Do it for your father and me. All we have now are you children. If you children don't do well in school, then all the hardships we have suffered will have been in vain.

When other people brag about their children to me, I want to be able to brag about you children to them. I want to be able to say that my sons and daughters have received at least as high or even higher degrees than their children. We Hmong believe that if one child in a family is well educated and successful, then the rest of the family will be considered successful also. I don't have the money to help you, so all I can do is to tell you to please strive hard and do the best you can. Here in America, your father and I have become like children: we can no longer do many of the things we used to do. So you have to help yourselves. Back in Laos, food and money were separate. Even if we had no money, we could still produce our own food. But here, without money, there is no food. Everything in America comes down to money. I want you children to study hard so that all of us can live well and be happy.

The Homeless Asian American

by Lee Fang

From the thick mountainous jungles of Laos to the open plains of Thailand, to the shores of endless-city southern California, I came as a desperate, homeless immigrant. I have become a part of the vast diversity of people who have come to America, like swarms of hungry mosquitoes, searching for security and a better life. I was an Indochinese refugee and have gradually become an Asian American, although I am still a Hmong. Life was, and still is, very hard. I have gone through many miserable experiences, trying to live a normal life and trying to fit into a new environment. At the same time, I have had to discard some of the morals I learned from my culture in order to adjust to my new surroundings because I was, and still am, a Hmong. Before all this took place, I struggled to stay alive from day to day, on a journey in search of a peaceful place and a better life.

At dawn on May 6, 1971, at a small village called Pouabang, near Vientiane, Laos, I was born. There, in the beautiful and vast countryside of Laos, was where I lived some of my most memorable early childhood years, babysitting my younger brothers and sisters while my parents were out working in the fields. Playing with my brothers, sisters, and cousins in the mud during the rains, going to and coming from the fields, and hunting and camping with my father and brothers during the off seasons are all I seem to remember doing. It is this memory of the many things I did and the free feeling of living in the countryside during my childhood that makes my homeland so unforgettable to this day.

I lived in an agrarian society where my family worked many acres of land, farming for ourselves and no one else. My family was considered well-to-do in the village because we had almost everything that a family could have in those days. Whenever my relatives or people in the village needed something from us, we gave it to them. Our meals consisted of rice (sometimes sweet rice), vegetables with meat, and some kind of soup. My family owned livestock, including herds of water buffaloes and cows. We also had seven horses to help us transport goods from place to place. We did not have to worry about our meals because it was easy to find land and grow food. Unlike rice, corn is easy to grow because it will grow almost anywhere on any kind of land. So, life was very happy for us as far back as I can remember until the Communists came.

By the time I was six or seven, though I could barely distinguish between right and wrong, I already had a vision of how I could end up as an old man: a farmer, with a big, happy family, successfully managing fields of rice and corn growing in the rich, sparsely populated countryside. That was a recurring picture I held in my mind for some years. I would brag about my vision to my family—usually my mother because she always listened to me. She laughed at first, but after I kept telling her about my vision, she told me to keep my dream alive and to work toward it. I was very happy every time my mother said that. She usually supported me. She was more lenient than my father, so we children usually talked to her. It is now difficult for me to believe how once I could have envisioned myself as an old man.

My father influenced what I envisioned I would become. He was a successful farmer in his forties, about five-foot-four, with dark brown skin from the long days working in the sun, and a strong, well-built body. He had quite an unusual character: he always examined and judged thoroughly whatever tasks he was to perform. He usually got things done right. He enjoyed hunting and camping; sometimes we spent weeks in the wilderness during the summer. He used to take me hunting and hiking and taught me how to fish and hunt. We went to places where my grandfather had taken him when he was a kid. He told me scary stories and sometimes I got really scared. Most important of all, he told me I should feel good and be proud of myself. He advised me to live my life as fully as I could. During those years, I got really close to him. However, our closeness did not last long because the Communists invaded our village, so we had no more time to spend together.

On a gloomy day in late summer of 1979, the clouds became darker and darker, closing the door on the fading sunlight. Then, it suddenly began raining, lightly at first, barely touching the leaves on the trees. Suddenly, the ruthless Communists came out of the pouring rain like thunder with lightning flashing here and there, from behind the trees in the darkness of the night, shooting across the countryside, destroying all the little innocent things that stood in their way. The wicked Communist invasion left an indelible mark on my family and me. It broke our hearts and ruined any smiles I had, as well as all the harmony I had felt with nature in my early life.

Besides bringing tears to my eyes and planting sorrow and distress in my mind, the evil thunderstorm-Communist invaders forced my family and me to take a long, desperate journey to unsettled places in the green, mountainous jungles of Laos. Nowhere to run any more! Trying hard to recover the love and comfort lost, trying hard to find security each day, I left my homeland, which I loved so dearly, with my family and a group from our village. It was an unforgettable nightmare as we suffered great pain, searching for a brighter day.

Through many days and nights, I walked countless miles alongside my family and fellow villagers through the jungles. I was burdened with a large sack of rice and other food, which pulled heavily on my shoulders, causing unbearable pain in my back. I walked in the quiet of the night, with the hungry mosquitoes feeding on me. My eyes were blind in the darkness, as I trudged through the thick jungles and hills and mountains. I could hardly see, nor could I keep up with the group. Whenever we stopped to rest, I felt exhausted, with every muscle in my body feeling dead from head to toe. I could not even sleep because my body was aching as if I had just been beaten up.

After days and nights of walking across the mountains, jungles, and rivers of western Laos, we came to the open plains of a new country, Thailand. By this time, the large package on my back had shrunk to an empty bag. The food I had carried had all been eaten and turned to waste. After this long, horrible journey, all I had left were my savagely torn clothes trailing down like the dried leaves of a palm tree in the desert, covering my badly scratched and filthy body. Even though I was now free from the evil thunderstorm-Communists, all I could feel was emptiness and frustration inside me.

But at the same time, I could already feel changes within me. I was growing taller, bigger, and stronger. I felt the impact of the destruction and catastrophe I had experienced changing me. I felt myself being conquered by a strange person who resembled me but who changed me into a different person I did not yet know. Moreover, the new person dominating the old one seemed to know what had happened and why we had left our homeland. He had a deeper understanding about life than the old one. I soon learned to like and admire this new person. After this transformation, I no longer felt like doing the things I used to do and I did not even think about the things I used to think about any more. I had become a new person. For a while, I did not know what to do. Silently, I flashed back to the moment when I had felt such tremendous emptiness and frustration, with my heart pounding as if I had just run a mile. Then I began to understand: I was developing a new personality.

[By the time I reached this insight,] six long, terrifying months had passed since my family and fellow villagers had set out on our journey. My family and I lived in a small but densely populated refugee camp called Ban Vinai for three long, hungry months before we received our papers to resettle in the United States. Our papers were processed by Americans, with blond hair and light skin. They also spoke a language I did not understand or had ever heard. I used to go to their offices to stare at them for hours. I do not know why I did that. Perhaps it was my curiosity: I had never seen anyone like them before. I did not know why the Americans were so different from me.

Life in the refugee camp was very harsh. Many people got sick and died due to the shortage of food and the terrible conditions. Disease was a major problem. A majority of those who died were old men and women and newborn children who did not have the strength or the immune system to resist diseases such as malaria, chicken pox, smallpox, or yellow fever. Luckily, no one in my family caught any of these deadly diseases, except for my little sister, who got chicken pox. Her sickness caused a lot of problems for my family, especially my mother. Fortunately, she healed not long before we flew to America.

During those three months at the camp, my father took me to attend a Thai school. I did not want to go because I had never been to school before and I did not know the Thai language. However, my father insisted. At first I cried, but after a while I went on my own. My first day at school seemed like the longest day in my life. Seconds seemed like minutes and minutes seemed like hours. After the first week or so, however, I began to like going to school. I had a lot of fun and the class was very interesting. I kept going to school until we left for America. Although I did not attend that school long enough to learn how to write, I did learn a few things about education and what it takes to become an educated person. I learned that education takes a lot of discipline and dedication. I owe many of the ideas I acquired to a teacher, whose name I no longer remember. In his thirties, he was a very strict teacher and I did not like him one bit at first. Gradually, however, I realized he was not trying to be cruel but was, instead, trying to teach us. He was a prime example to me because he taught me so many things I had never known before. I went and thanked him before we left Thailand.

These unforgettable experiences at school and in the camp changed me more or less for the better. My perspective on life was broadened ever further when the huge Delta Air Line plane in which we flew to America landed at San Francisco International Airport in April 1980. The moment the wheels of the plane touched the rough, hard surface of the runway, I was filled with a wonderful feeling of being alive and free. I saw so many different kinds of people whom I had never seen before leaving the plane: Koreans, Japanese, Chinese, Euro-Americans, and Afro-Americans. I was most amazed at the color of the Afro-Americans. I was very impressed with the many tall buildings and the beautiful scenery in San Francisco. Somehow, these new sights gradually helped me to overcome the nightmare of the Communists and slowly healed the great pain in my broken heart, granting me a sense of security and happiness. At the same time, I tried hard to hold back the tears gathering in my eyes and dripping down my chin. I was so glad to be in America.

Chapter Three

A few hours later, we flew to Lindbergh Field in lovely San Diego. During the flight, my consciousness was filled with great uncertainty. I kept thinking about my new life, my new beginning in America. I kept asking myself questions for which I could find no answers. The one question that kept running through my head until the time we landed was: what will become of me in this strange land they call America? I felt this way because all I could see was its beauty, but I did not have the vaguest idea about my new home or the people I was going to live with.

When the big airplane came to a stop in San Diego, I walked out slowly with my family, feeling a little dizzy. I stumbled along the walk tunnel like someone who has been drinking. The members of my family stayed close together because we were afraid of losing each other. We were all frightened by the many people walking alongside us. Of course, it would have been very difficult if one of us had got lost because none of us spoke a word of English. I noticed that people stared at us as they walked by. The expressions on their faces seemed to indicate that they had never seen people like us before. We were dressed in rags, so I felt embarrassed.

When we arrived in the lobby, my eldest brother, Chou, who had come with my uncle and his family to the United States two years earlier, was waiting for us. Behind him stood my uncle and his family. They were all very excited to see us, as it had been some time since we had last seen each other. They knew we were coming—my uncle was our sponsor. I noticed that my father and mother began to cry when they saw our relatives. The moment we met, my brother began embracing each member of the family one after another. It seemed very strange to me because in my culture people do not give other people hugs. After embracing the rest of my family, my brother tried to give me a hug. Even though I felt quite uneasy about it, I did not refuse his gesture. When he hugged me, I could smell the aftershave that he had put on. This made me feel even more embarrassed because I smelled from not having taken a shower for days and my clothes were filthy. At the same time, I felt very happy because my brother, who was a stranger to me, had hugged me. I did not remember or recognize my brother or any of my other relatives when I first set eyes upon them because I had been so little when I last saw them.

My brother took us to my uncle's house, where he was living. It was a beautiful place. We had never seen anything like it. Deep inside my heart, I felt ashamed of my house and the many things we had left behind in Laos. Everything here seemed to look so nice and advanced, while everything back there was so primitive. I felt happy because I realized that my new home would look like my uncle's.

A few weeks later, my family rented a three-bedroom apartment a few blocks from my uncle's house. My brother Chou could not come to live with us because the nine of us already filled the whole house. We did not want to live too far from my uncle and brother because we needed their help for shopping, interpreting, and especially for communicating with others in case of emergency. We could not do even simple things like go to the store to buy food or clothing—the things we most needed at first. Since they were the only people we knew, we would have felt completely isolated had we lived far away from them. For the Hmong, family relations are very strong and we feel more secure living close to each other.

In the fall of 1980, I was enrolled in an elementary school. Being a newcomer in a strange environment and seeing very unusual-looking people was exciting. Some of the other students were really nice to me, but others were not so friendly. I remember one day, when I was walking home from school with my two brothers, my sister, and my cousin, we encountered a group of Euro-Americans who were playing baseball in the middle of the street. They yelled and made faces at us as though we had done something wrong. It was the first time something like that had happened to me. I had neither the capacity nor the knowledge to fight against such cruelty. I did not know what they were saying but sensed by the way they acted that they felt great hostility and hatred toward us. I experienced for the first time what it was like to be discriminated against and hated simply because we looked different. This made me realize what kind of people I would have to face every day here in America. It made me realize I would be surrounded by hatred and hostility. It was the first time since we arrived that I longed for Laos and its beautiful countryside where prejudice did not exist.

I was not the only one longing for Laos. My whole family did. My father and mother suffered the most, though. They missed their old ways of life—their men's talk and their women's gossip with relatives and friends. The only people my parents could talk to were us children and my uncle's family. Since there was no one their own age for them to socialize with, my parents usually stayed inside the house for weeks, not coming out because they thought doing so would not make them feel any better. My parents were deprived of all the activities that had kept them busy in Laos. For example, my father, who always liked fishing, hunting, and camping, could no longer enjoy those activities. He had to turn to other things, but these were very limited because of his language problem. In their homeland, my parents never had to worry about whom they could talk to or where they could go. It was terrible seeing how lost they felt. Not only did they feel lonesome, but they became like children, wandering around the house without anything to do. Whenever someone knocked on the front door, they became hysterical. They hesitated to answer the door because they were scared to see people they did not know—mainly English-speaking people. For some reason that I do not understand, such strangers frightened my parents. They found it very difficult to confront people to whom they could not speak. This went on for about a year until my parents realized that their behavior would neither bring their friends and relatives to America, nor would it make them feel as though they were still in Laos. Once they realized this, they began to do more things for themselves.

I have been living with my family in America as an Indochinese refugee for more than ten years now. Life has not been as hard for my family as it has been for some other Asian immigrants because we were eligible for financial assistance from the government. At the beginning of our fourth year here, however, my father had to work to support us because our financial assistance was cut. He worked at a Chinese restaurant washing dishes. This created a lot of problems for my father and the family because he spoke little English [and no Chinese] and could not understand what his boss's directions were, which made him feel like a child. Even though he worked there until 1985, he did not like his job. He felt he was being discriminated against due to his inability to speak English. He was not treated kindly. In Laos, my father never had to do the dishes. In Hmong society, men were not supposed to do the dishes or the laundry. People would look down on them if they did. But regardless of what values he held, [he knew that refusing to work as a dishwasher] would not give him his traditions back.

Our struggles as an Asian American family slowly grew less difficult as most members of our family learned to speak English. Animosity towards us also became less visible, though I was still called a "Chink" and a "Jap." But I did not feel too offended because I knew I was neither Chinese nor Japanese. As I saw other Asian Americans victimized by the same name-calling, however, I began to develop a certain hatred for those stupid kids who had no idea what suffering we had gone through. It took a long time before the anger I felt inside me began to dissipate.

The animosity we encountered during our high school years was not so intense. There were so many minorities in my high school that it became an advantage for many of us. I met a lot of really nice people and made friends with individuals from many different backgrounds. Two of my best friends in high school were Euro-Americans, one a Chinese American, and two Vietnamese Americans. Each of them has influenced me as I was transformed from an Indochinese refugee to an Asian American and an American. Their friendship helped me realize how lucky I am to be a Hmong, even as I slowly became an American.

I have also encountered a lot of people who encouraged me. In high school, I had a really great teacher who encouraged me to pursue my education as far as I could. He told me that being myself is unique because there is no one exactly like me on earth. He meant that I should be proud to be a Hmong. From that day on, I have tried always to remember what he told me. The unfortunate experiences I have had in Laos and Thailand and the prejudices and animosity I have had to deal with in American society all set me apart from other people.

My life has changed in many ways in college. Being separated from my family when I left for the university was the biggest adjustment I had to make. I was living without my family for the very first time. Everything was new to me. My experience was probably very much like what my parents had felt when they first came to this country. Life was particularly difficult for me during my first year in college, but it has become easier as time passed. I have been struggling, trying to stay in school, but I am becoming more familiar with my new life and am learning day by day to put things in better perspective.

My relationship to people of other racial or ethnic backgrounds has not changed that much, however. My friends are still from a variety of races—Asian Americans, Euro-Americans, African Americans, Hispanic Americans, and others. The only difference is that I have tried to see each of them as a person, rather than as an Asian American, an Euro-American, a Chicano, and so forth. I have tried to look into the hidden parts of each person, rather than just what seems obvious. I constantly ask myself, what has led them to do the things they do? Why do they do these things? Although the kind of animosity and hatred I experienced when I first arrived is now less prominent, there are still tensions, not only between me and others, but among the different racial groups. I can sense this tension in the air every day.

But the many things I have learned in college have made me see things differently from the way I used to. My years in college have taught me to see viewpoints I did not even know existed. My perspective on life has been widened. I have learned more about myself as a Hmong as well as a person. At the same time, I have learned to fit much better into my surroundings. I now know how to see below the surface of things in order to gain a deeper understanding of the world around me. I have learned to understand and gradually to accept the American way of life.

The Tcha Family of Fresno

Xer Lo (*far right*) with her husband and his other wife in Laos.
Courtesy of Xer Lo.

The Tcha family in Fresno, 1992. *Back row:* Tchue Vue (*far left*), Vu Pao Tcha (*second from left*), Chou Nou Tcha (*third from left*) *Middle row:* Zer Lo (*second from left*). *Courtesy of Chou Nou Tcha, Tchue Vue, and Vu Pao Tcha.*

Zer Lo's Life Story

as told to her grandson, Vu Pao Tcha

My name is Zer Lo. My mother's name was Me Cha, and my father's Lu Chai. I am the youngest child in my family. My parents lived in a very poor place in Laos, where I grew up. When I was old enough to get an education, I could not go to school because the country was very poor and the government could not afford to give us an education. There were not enough teachers. So we decided to move to find a better place to live—a place where we could grow crops more easily. The soil in the place where I was born was very infertile.

I was still quite young when we moved. My parents and the older children worked in the fields while I stayed at home because I was not yet old enough to work. My parents grew such crops as rice, corn, vegetables, and sugarcane. When I was little, I was very ignorant. No one in our village knew how to read or write. My parents were uneducated and had nothing to teach us except how to take care of ourselves. They taught us not to be lazy, to work hard, to wake up very early in the morning to work in the fields. This way we would not be hungry when we became old enough to take care of ourselves.

When I was old enough to work, my parents gave me hoes, axes, and knives and showed me how to use them. I helped my parents cut down trees, bushes, and grass, using very big and heavy knives.

At first I did not know how to do any of this, but they showed me everything I needed to know. They taught me all the tricks—the ways of farming. When I was tired, my parents let me rest. But I did not really rest: I had to watch children. In those days, anything that was not related to farming was "rest." I also learned to do other things—to feed the pigs, chickens, and other animals, to get water far from the village, to cook, to do housework, and to get wood for making fire. I carried water in large bamboo buckets. It was not an easy job. Water was very scarce. It's not like here in the United States where you have electricity and water at home and can use as much as you want. After getting wood and water for cooking, I also had to get food for the animals. I went into the jungle and gathered plants that could be mixed with corn to feed the pigs. If I didn't do it right, the pigs wouldn't eat it and I would have to make a new batch of vegetables and corn. Then I had to feed the chickens and make sure they had plenty of water. It was a lot of work, a lot of work. The work was done mostly by women. Life in the fields was very hard, but life at home was not any easier. Life as a Hmong was very hard.

When my parents died, I was left with my older brothers and sisters. I had four brothers and two sisters. Two of my brothers died. One died of sickness, while the other was captured and killed when he was in the army.

When I became fifteen and could take care of myself, I got married and went to live with my husband in another place. I was my husband's second wife. We worked hard and our crops were very good. But at that time there was a big lake where demons lived who caused people to get sick and die. They did a lot of evil in our village, where many people died. So we had to go live in the jungle. We suffered because we had no food. We had left all of our harvest in the village. We ate whatever we could find in the jungle: bananas, other fruits, leaves, and wild plants. Life was very hard in the jungle. We had nothing to cover us from the rain. Water was very scarce. We lived there for more than a year before we went elsewhere to build a new village, where we could grow crops again and raise animals such as pigs, chickens, cows, and horses. Life was better for a while until my children came.

I had my first child after I had been married for three years. I had six children in all. Since I had poor health, I got very sick at childbirth. To feed my children, I had to work hard under the hot sun. There was very little time for rest. Only when my children became old enough to work did I get some help in the fields. But that did not make life any easier: the land near our new village was poor and it was hard to grow a good crop there. Life was not easy at all. We had to go far away to find fertile land. Sometimes we slept in the fields because the plot we cultivated was far from our home. We did not come home until our work was done.

Then war came and my husband had to go to war. He left us alone and it became even harder to feed ourselves. We went hungry often and had to eat corn [which we normally fed to the animals]. My two brothers-in-law said they would not feed us. But I did not care whether or not they were willing to help us. I told myself that once my children grew up, they would take care of me. My husband came back only once in a while to visit us. My husband did not seem to care about us. He did not come back to help us. He did not love us. It was not until my two older sons became men that we stopped going hungry. Only then did we grow enough food to feed ourselves. Later, two of my daughters got married.

My eldest son's name is Chia Chao, my second son is Tong Zea, and the third, Seng. They took care of me and did not allow me to go hungry and I finally felt happy. My husband was still in the army. He was a military commander. In time, when the war got worse, he came home. But by then, we were no longer hungry or worried about food. But such a state did not last long.

When the Communists got close to our village, my two older sons suggested that we go to Thailand where we would be safer. We had to leave everything behind—everything that had taken us a whole lifetime to acquire. Five years after we escaped to Thailand, we came to the United States. But our new life in America is not easy, either. My sons who are uneducated, because they never had a chance to go to school, have to work hard to earn a living. I did not get any support from the government such as social security when I first arrived. I was told I had to work to support myself even though I was already very old. I am tired of working and suffering. My husband died five years ago; three years after his death, I finally started receiving social security as his widow. It was not until last year that my youngest son found a really good job. Since then, my life has been better. We now have everything we need: food, clothes, a house, a car. We no longer suffer.

Now I will tell you some more about my past—other things that I had left out earlier. When we were little, boys and girls could play together. But when we got older, we could no longer do so. The only times we could play and joke was during lunch in the fields or in the evenings, after the girls had finished their chores. It is not like here in America where boys and girls can be together every day at school. In those days, we traded labor with other Hmong. We would go, our whole family, to work for another family for a day or two; then that family would come and help us. Sometimes several families would come and help us and then we would help them in return. When other families came, they brought their children. So there was a lot of excitement. Boys and girls only saw each other if their families traded labor. Everyone worked hard because no one wanted other people to think he or she was lazy. So when a boy noticed a girl or vice versa, he or she worked harder. Neither wanted the other to think he or she was lazy. Only after our work was done could we feel comfortable talking to each other. It was not acceptable to socialize while working, so boys and girls never exchanged words except during lunch and in the evenings. The girls were not allowed to play even among themselves until they had finished their house chores. The boys did not have much to do in the evenings because their sisters took care of everything.

When girls reach a certain age, they are expected to behave like good girls. They can no longer be around any boys. It is acceptable for a boy to be around several girls but not for a girl to be around several boys, especially in public. Girls are expected to have better manners than boys. It is more disgraceful for a family to have a bad girl than a bad boy. But boys are valued more than girls, no matter how bad they are.

Even when their families trade labor, boys and girls are not very talkative with each other. They are not like Americans who are very good at socializing. Hmong boys and girls feel shy talking to each other because they are being watched by their parents and they cannot say what they want to say. This silence exists mainly among younger youth. The older ones are less shy and interact more with each other, especially when they are attracted to each other. But then, more manners are expected from these older boys and girls, especially when other people are around.

In Hmong society, young lovers are not allowed to hold hands in public, nor can they sit together. They can do so only when they are alone. In public, they can talk and joke all they want but can never show their love for each other. It is all right for a son's parents to see him take a girl's hand or hold her, but that would be an insult to *her* parents. So, whenever a boy is with a girl at her parents' house, he can never sit next to her or hold her hand. However, some parents will allow it if they like the boy and know he plans to marry her. If they think he is not serious about her, the young lovers can only talk. But even though holding hands may be allowed under certain conditions, few young people do so because they do not wish other people to see their love. So it often happens that they have never even touched each other before their marriage.

Girls begin to take care of their looks when they start feeling attracted to boys. Sometimes they can start at a very young age— around nine or ten years old. A girl is not allowed to talk to a boy first; it is considered poor manners for her to do so. She is not allowed to offer him any help or to carry his things. A boy, however, can chase after any girl he likes. He can offer to help her, wait for her on a road, or walk with her alone. A girl can never show her feelings for a boy unless he comes to look for her. She cannot ask his name or invite him to visit her, but it is all right for the boy to ask for her whereabouts or what she is doing. A boy can have as many girls as he desires. If he tells his parents about these various girls, they will be happy to know that they have a handsome son who is admired by girls. This gives them pride, whereas a girl can give very little pride or none at all to her parents, no matter how polite or hardworking she is. The only pride she can bring them is to marry a respected and rich boy and have a stable and good marriage.

When girls have fully matured and are ready to become brides, boys come to visit them more often. When a girl sees a boy she likes, she will work some distance from her parents so that the boy can get close to her. She tells him when he could come back, usually at night when everyone is asleep. He whispers her name through a hole in the wall. If she wishes to see him also, she will get up. Houses in Laos are made of slats that can be easily removed. So a girl can remove a slat from the wall of her room and go outside to talk to her lover. The boy usually covers himself with a piece of cloth so that he cannot be recognized. If he is seen by the girl's parents and they recognize him, they will call him and make him uncomfortable or ashamed. After the lovers finish talking, she can come back through the hole and cover it up again with the slat. A girl can never open the house door to see her lover. She will be harshly punished if she does so. This is how romances were carried on in my time—not like now when your girlfriend can follow you anywhere she wants to in public. It was never like that in Laos.

When a young girl has a lover, she is usually faithful to him. She does not try to cheat on him. If by chance other boys who do not know she already has a lover come to meet her, she will not open her heart to them. She can still talk or joke with them so long as she keeps her distance, but she will usually avoid other boys. If she is caught by her lover talking to another male, the result will be a quarrel.

Girls will usually avoid falling in love with the same boy. They know it is not good for them to dispute over boys. If a girl knows that a boy is in love with such and such a girl, then no matter how handsome he is, she will not try to steal him from the other girl. Even if the boy comes to her, she will refuse to see him.

When a boy really likes a girl and wants to marry her, he will give her an engagement present. He will say to her, "I love you. I want to marry you. I want you to be my wife. Please accept this gift as an engagement present. Don't see anyone else." If the girl accepts the gift, she will be completely faithful to her future husband. No one else can claim her as his. If, however, she does not accept his present, it means that she does not like him or has someone else who has already given her a present. If the boy really likes her and wants to marry her, he will offer her better gifts or win her parents' favor by giving them gifts or doing them favors. The parents may then try to change their daughter's mind and push her to marry the desperate boy. Usually, an obedient daughter will not refuse her parents' wish. She will marry the boy as a duty to her parents, even though she does not like him.

Even after she is married, however, a former lover can still come to try to claim her, if she had accepted presents from him. Trouble will arise and it will take weeks, even months, to resolve the problem. The husband has to either give up his wife or fight for her. He may lose a lot of money because he has to repair the damage that his wife has caused her former lover. The more difficult the former lover is, the more money the husband will lose. He usually has to repay the former lover double what the latter had given his wife. A dispute like this usually involves a very pretty girl who the husband feels is worth his money. Of course, if the husband is poor, he may indeed lose his wife, unless he can borrow money to keep her. If he loses her, then the former lover has to pay to the husband double what the latter had given the woman.

[Although Hmong parents may exert a great deal of influence on their children's choice of partners,] in our customs we do not force our children to marry someone they do not like. We do not have arranged marriages without the consent of the children. We usually let our children choose whomever they want. But we are sometimes pushy and try to manipulate our children to get them to change their minds. When we do so, we think it is in their best interests.

Strictly speaking, however, parents have the right to give their daughters to whomever they wish. So, some parents who are driven by the desire for money will give their daughters to young men who offer them valuable presents or a large sum of money. But the parents cannot initiate the marriage arrangement. It is the boy who must go to the girl's parents' home to ask for her. The proposal will be discussed in the presence of both young people. After an agreement has been reached, a dutiful daughter has to go with her new husband. The only instance when the two sets of parents negotiate directly with each other is when a girl marries a boy of her own choosing without her parents' consent. Her parents can then try to reclaim her and take her home.

A wife who is liked by her husband and his parents and other relatives is usually someone who was already liked by them before the marriage. They say of her: "She is a good young girl. We consent to your marrying her."

When a girl becomes a wife, she has to act like one. When friends and relatives come to visit, she must invite them in, even though her husband may be away. When her guests leave, she must walk them to the door and say goodbye. When she cooks something that her neighbors or relatives do not have, she has to give them some. If her husband brings home game from hunting, she has to give a little of it to those neighbors whose husbands have been less fortunate. Because we [Hmong] are very poor, in a family that has more than others—for example, more salt, more oil—the wife has to give some to those who do not have as much and who come ask for some. She must not ask for money or anything in return. The worth of a woman is measured by the good deeds she does. People will say, "That woman is very kind hearted. She is a good wife."

To be called a good wife and to be liked by her friends and relatives, she has to be not only kind but also hardworking. She must work hard at everything: in the fields, providing for the children, and taking care of them. When everybody says, "She is kind *and* hardworking," it means she is well liked.

A good wife has to like and respect the elderly people who are related to her husband. When she cooks something delicious, she should always think of her husband's father and other elderly relatives first. Also, when these relatives have no more rice left and are eating only corn, if she has cooked some rice, she must take some to them. The elderly people get top priority—meaning they get to eat the best things that a family has.

When she makes new clothes, she should give the old ones to those less fortunate. When there is a special occasion, she has to invite all the family's friends and relatives. Even if they bring all their children, she has to feed them. Even if her guests are full, she must insist they eat and drink some more. In addition, she cannot be angry at the children if they spill drinks or waste food and mess up the house. She must be tolerant always. This is how she proves she is a good wife and is worthy of her relatives' respect. In return, the clan takes pride in her because she brings them honor and is an example to other wives.

Some wives are not so good. A bad wife is not hardworking and does not treat her husband's family well. She does not take good care of the children, does not respect and like the elderly people, and despises them instead. Such a woman is disliked by the clan. She is not trusted but is not mistreated. The clan members treat her like everyone else out of politeness, but show her no favor or respect. Even when a wife becomes really unacceptable, the husband cannot divorce her. He has to live with her for the sake of the children.

To the Hmong, divorce is a disgrace to the family and clan. If a man divorces his wife, he will lose face and gain a bad reputation. He can only divorce his wife if she leaves him, if she commits adultery, or has done him wrong and evil. When a bad wife is divorced by her husband, she gets nothing. All the property stays with the husband. All the children also belong to the husband. However, if the divorce is due to the husband's fault (adultery, beating his wife, neglecting his children, constantly being away from home), then the wife has the right to keep some of the children. Women have more rights here in the United States, where wives and husbands have the same rights. Back in Laos, women have fewer rights than men. In fact, they have few rights at all. They must submit to their husbands. [Here in the United States] wives have too many rights. Their rights are protected, so they do not have to listen to their husbands. If husbands mistreat their wives, they can call the police. In Laos, wives have nobody to call when their husbands mistreat them.

You asked me whether it is good to be a wife in Hmong society. If a husband and wife know how to love each other, the answer is yes—if they help each other at home and in the fields, if they help each other to bring up the children. Whether the work is light or heavy, whether it is easy or hard, if a husband helps his wife, then the marriage is good. But if the husband does not help and lets his wife do everything while he goes away from home or just stays home doing nothing except smoking opium, then it is bad and really difficult for the wife.

If a husband does not love his wife, it is not worth being a wife in this world. Even if a wife has worked very hard to get something, the husband can take it away and say it is his. That was how your grandfather treated me. Your grandpa never listened to anybody. We had an opium field. After he and I gathered the opium, I asked him to sell it, but he would not listen. He kept every ounce for himself. He would not let me sell a little to buy cloth for making clothing, even when our clothes were torn. He would say, "Don't sell it. Give it to me. I'll sell it myself and buy you some cloth." But when he sold it, he used the money for his own pleasures and never brought anything home. So your aunt and I had to sell whatever we could— vegetables, fruit—in order to live. But after your grandpa smoked all of our own opium, he would take our money to buy some more. That is why we were very poor. One day, your other grandma and I had just finished collecting our opium when she saw a Chinese dealer and went up to him to sell it. Your grandpa stopped her and took the opium back. We had collected quite a bit of opium, but your grandpa took it all. He even invited his friends to share it with him. Yes, your grandpa was not good to us.

After we got to America, he never gave me a dollar of what he received from the government. I never knew how much money he had. He received five hundred dollars, the same amount as your aunt got, but he made us pay a larger share of the rent than he did. He only paid fifty dollars while we paid the rest. He spent all his money to treat his friends or spent it on useless things. When I criticized him, he would say, "It's only a little. It's nothing. Why do you make such a big fuss?" When your uncle Seng moved in with us, he had no job. Your grandpa would not help us buy food. I told him, "They are your children. You would let them starve?" He said, "They are *your* children, not mine. There are three of you. I'm alone. You pay your share and I pay mine." That's how your grandpa was. I never saw his money, even when I asked to see and count it. He said, "I have only a little," and would not let me see it.

Your grandpa never loved me. He never helped feed the children nor clothe them. When he died, he was penniless. We even had to use our money to buy him opium when he was dying because smoking eased his pain. When he died, we used all our money for his funeral. We had nothing left of our savings. He was always unjust to me. If this is the life that every woman in this world has to live, then it's not worth it to be a wife.

Chou Nou Tcha's Life Story

as told to his son, Vu Pao Tcha

My name is Chou Nou Tcha. My mother and father brought me into this world on the afternoon of May 15, 1950, when the sun was high in the sky. I was born in a village called Tula on the outskirts of the town of Sin Ung in Luang Prabang Province. My parents raised me for two years in Tula, then moved to a village called Kasat, which soon grew to be a small town. When I was five years old, I was constantly sick. I had a lot of ailments, including a kidney stone. My father took me to a doctor who removed it by surgery. After the surgery, my health got better.

My parents did not obtain food the way that people do here in America. They had to grow everything themselves. They cleared jungles, burned the brush and the stumps of trees, and then planted rice and corn. They themselves had to make the knives and hoes used to work the land and weed the fields. When the crops ripened, they gathered the harvest and put the grain into baskets and sacks. They used horses to bring these containers to the house. They unloaded these heavy containers and carried them on their backs to the storage shed. After that, they made rice pounders with which they pounded the paddy to get the husks off.

We lived in Kasat from 1952 to 1961, when the Americans came to fight a war in our country. I was only ten or eleven years old then. The Americans brought guns, grenades, cannon, and other weapons. My father, Tcha Chong Xiong, was made a commander in the Hmong guerrilla army. He became an American [mercenary] soldier. When I was fifteen, the war got closer to where we were and we could no longer live there in safety. I, too, had to become a soldier. I fought in the war when the Vietnamese Communists came to attack our villages. They destroyed our homes and we fled into the jungle. We lived in the jungle until the Communist soldiers left, because we were afraid of dying. In 1973, the Royal Lao Government and the Communists agreed not to fight any more, so we were able to live in relative safety for a few years after that.

However, when our leader, General Vang Pao, fled to the United States [in 1975], we knew we could not continue to live in Laos for long without being persecuted. The Pathet Lao were looking for former army and community leaders, whom they intended to kill. They lied to us when they said they wanted to find these individuals only to learn from them. Instead, when they took these men, they tortured them. They made them pull plows to break up the earth and then they made them carry the dirt to fill up the large holes made by the bombs that the Americans had dropped. The prisoners also had to carry earth from the mountains to fill up these bomb craters. A lot of the Hmong leaders died while doing such strenuous work. That was why we decided we could not stay in Laos any longer and began to look for a way to escape.

I decided to go to Sin Neua Bac, where we had some relatives. When I found out that these relatives also wanted to leave, I went home to fetch my family, but when I got back, your aunt was about to have a baby. Thus we could not leave then. We felt very desperate and were very afraid people would find out about our plans and tell the Communists. We waited until your aunt's baby was born and then we fled. By then, the Communists had already closed all the roads. By the time we got papers to go to Thailand, it was already August 1975. Then your grandfather decided he did not want to leave. Only after long discussions did he agree to go with us. I had only two children then. One was four years old, the other was one. We did not have time to sell any of our property, so we had to leave everything behind. Since the loads we initially carried were too heavy, we had to throw some things away while we were walking through the jungle. But we carried all our papers with us, including my military documents.

Soon the Communists caught up with us. We were afraid they would kill us all if they found our papers. We hid them under some bushes. We ran as fast as we could until we reached the road that connects Luang Prabang and Sin Neua Bac. We hired a taxi to take us to the banks of the Mekong River. We boarded a boat and got to the other side. We stayed in Nam Hia for about ten days before we headed into the mountains near the Thai border. Long ago, a trail had been made in this region for people to transport salt. The Laotians did not know how to make salt, therefore they had to get it from Thailand. There is a village called Bukua, meaning "salt hole," where the people came to get salt. We followed the same trail that these people had used.

Since a lot of our relatives were still in Kasat, I went back to get them and to lead them out of Laos. I traveled for two days and two nights on foot and by taxi. One of my cousins did not want to come along, so we left him in a village inhabited by Iu Mien [another mountain tribe]. The rest of us went ahead and looked for a way to cross the Mekong River. We walked for a whole day before we found some Lao boatmen, but the boatmen told us it was too dangerous to cross at that time because Vietnamese soldiers were in the village on the other shore. So we had to wait. I told my relatives that having taken them this far, I could not endanger them. We waited until nightfall and walked along a trail to a Hmong village called Pamhom. The people in that village also wanted to leave, so they decided to join us. I told them that I had to find the rest of my family; I bought two sacks of rice for them to eat until I could return. The group had swelled to about two hundred people by then.

I hired a Lao to take me downstream. Then I took a taxi to Nam Hiem, where I bought various kinds of medicine as well as batteries for our flashlights. I walked for a whole day before I found my family. My mother, father, and everyone else in my family were ill. They had fever and stomachaches. Since I had been a medic when I was in the army, I knew how to give them all shots. It took five days for them to get well.

A group had already left, so we followed them. Even those who were very sick had to walk. A lot of people died along the way. Some people stepped on mines along the trail and were either killed or badly injured. That made us very worried and scared. In the jungle we caught up with another group that was also fleeing. But soon the Communists captured us all. They told us to go back to our villages. We asked the people who lived closest to where we were to take all our pack ponies carrying our belongings with them. After they departed, the rest of us fled into the jungle.

There were a lot of flies in the jungle and, strangely, they laid their eggs only on the bags of my family but not on the belongings of others. This made me very superstitious, so I brushed off the eggs. When we got to a river, suddenly a flashlight shone in our faces. We had run into Vietnamese soldiers! We turned around and ran back into the jungle. We walked in a big circle to evade them. By then, it was daylight and raining heavily. We decided to stop and cook some food to eat. We had barely started the fire when a bear appeared. It growled and started coming toward us. We were very scared, but the bear, though still growling, moved to the side of the trail. I thought the bear was an omen indicating either that our ancestral spirits did not want us to leave or that they wanted us to follow that path. I told everyone to pack up so we could keep going.

We walked all afternoon till we got to some houses with banana trees in their yards. Other refugees were already camped there. We stopped and cooked a meal. Then we went to the river and cut down some trees so we could walk on the logs to the other side. We followed an old trail to a village, but when we got there, we discovered it was occupied by soldiers. They captured us. Their leader's name was Boon Chai. He was a Thai. He would not let us cross the Thai–Laotian border. We offered him some money, but he would not accept the bribe. Instead, he made us go back the same way we had come. He sent two soldiers along with us to make sure we did so. After walking two days and two nights, we finally got back to Nam Hiem. We stayed there for twenty-eight days. By then it was December 1975.

Then your uncle, who was with the first group of relatives I had led to Thailand, came back to look for us. As soon as he found us, we left that very night. I called upon all our ancestral spirits to guide and protect us. It was raining heavily as we departed. There was a thunderstorm and the wind was so strong that it broke and felled many coconut palms and banana trees. We continued walking as the thunder rolled and lightning struck. Soon we were wading through water that came up to our knees. When we got to a river, its currents were so strong that I had to help each and every one of the two hundred people I was leading—including carrying some of them on my back—across the river. By the time everyone had crossed, it was morning.

We were at a Lao village but we did not dare stop. We walked all day until it got dark and then used our flashlights to show us the way as we continued walking through the night. We could not afford to rest. We paused only long enough to cook our meals and, as soon as we had finished eating, we continued on our way. We crossed another river and reached the base of a mountain. I had never seen such a high mountain before in my entire life. I paid a Lao five silver coins to carry my eldest son all the way up the mountain.

The next morning, we descended the other side of the mountain. When we got to the Thai–Laotian border, we collapsed on the ground and slept. [When we awoke,] soldiers belonging to the Thai border patrol were searching through all our belongings. We had two handguns that we had hidden. Fortunately, they did not find them. We also had two combines loaded with ammunition. We gave those to the Thai soldiers. They also took our knives. My father had two medals, and they demanded we hand them over. Then they let us go.

We tried to buy food, but it was very expensive. We could buy only a little. We arrived at a place called Pumniovai, where we slept one night. The next morning, after eating breakfast we walked toward another river, where we encountered robbers. They jumped out from the bushes and tried to seize our belongings. I whispered to my father that these men were robbers and he told me to take out our guns. I took one and ran across the river as he aimed the second gun at our attackers. With me and him pointing our guns at the robbers from the two banks of the river, the rest of our party managed to get across the river. We shouted to the robbers, "Don't come near our bags or we'll shoot you!" The robbers had only knives, so they were afraid to do anything to us. But they ran ahead of us all the way to a town where they reported us to the authorities. To reach this town, we had to walk across a bridge made, not of wood, but of rope. Those of us who had never crossed such a swaying bridge were terrified and had a very difficult time walking across it. As soon as we got across, the Thai police searched all our belongings. We had hidden our guns in the waists of two women, and since they did not search the women, they did not find the guns.

By this time, we were so hungry we thought we would starve to death. Some people cried while others groaned. Those who could still walk went and bought food for us to eat. As soon as we ate, we felt better. We got out our papers and went to see the Thai authorities. We applied for permission to enter Thailand as refugees. While we were waiting for them to process our papers, they gave us food to eat and clothes to wear. We bought some bamboo to build sheds for shelter.

We lived in this makeshift refugee camp for about a year. Your brother was born there. Then we moved to another refugee camp, where we lived for almost three years. During that period, some Americans came to tell us about their refugee program, but when they saw how many of us there were, they told us they did not have room for so many people. We worried constantly that we would never be able to leave Thailand. We lived in filth in the refugee camp and wanted desperately to leave. When some French officials appeared, we applied for refugee status and they granted us permission to go to France. We were moved to Bangkok, where we waited for a month before departing for France.

It took a whole day for the plane to fly us to Israel, where we stopped and had our papers examined once again. Then we boarded another plane and flew to France. We landed at Charles de Gaulle Airport on August 16, 1979. Fortunately, all our papers were in order. We were taken to a building, where we stayed for two weeks. Then we were moved to a small town called St. Martin de Crow near the city of Marseilles. There, after attending classes for several months, I was told I had to find work.

I got a job helping a jeweler make gold jewelry. I did that for two months. Then I got a job planting grapes for a man named Staver. He made me work seven days a week, but paid me only five days' wages each week. I worked in that vineyard for four months before the government found out that he had been cheating me. The officials told me they would make sure I got paid for all the work I had done. They filed a suit against him. He got angry and beat me. I reported it to the police, and they came and took him to jail. We went to court, where he signed papers to release me from his employ.

My family and I then moved to Argent-sur-Sauldre, near the city of Bourges. The government found me a job developing photographs. I worked there for almost a year until the company went bankrupt. Then I received unemployment insurance for a month until I got another job in Tours repairing antique furniture like dressers, tables, and so forth. It was a good job and was not hard on the body. I worked there for four years.

Meanwhile, my father had been admitted as a refugee into the United States. When he died, I came to attend his funeral. While here, I applied for permission for our family to enter the United States as refugees. But when we finally got here on May 15, 1985, we discovered life was very hard. We had spent all except three thousand dollars of our savings to buy our eight plane tickets. I had to find a way as soon as possible to earn a living. I decided to become a grower and borrowed money from the bank to get started. I first planted sugar peas and squash but later decided to grow strawberries. I have been in the United States now for seven years.

In comparing my life in Laos, France, and the United States, it was easier to make a living in Laos because we had a lot of land and water that we could use for free. We could use the land any way we wished. We did not have to use fertilizers for our crops, nor did we need to irrigate them, due to the abundance of rain. Life was also easier because I could communicate in my own language. In France, life was hard because I could not get any land to farm and so had to find wage labor. France is a good country, a beautiful country, but it is almost impossible to make any money there. In the United States, making a living is also hard. If we want land to farm, we have to rent it. If we need water to irrigate the fields, we have to buy the water. If we want the crops to grow well, we have to use chemical fertilizers. Everything is so expensive here. We cannot cultivate only small plots as we did in Laos. Farming small plots in America would not allow us to make enough money to live on. Here we have to grow everything on a large scale. We have to use tractors, which I had to rent and learn to drive. It is so much harder to make a living as a grower in this country.

In the seven years since I have been in California, I have worked every day throughout the year. I have never taken any weekends off. I have never found time to go to the weddings, or cultural events, or big feasts that my relatives have held. Every day, I work until my ears are full of dust, until my skin burns from the sun. Yet I still do not make much money. Every month, I have to pay rent for my farm and my house, as well as for all the utilities. In Laos, we never had to pay for the water we drank. We simply got it from springs. But here, we have to pay even for our drinking water, and then we have to buy a machine to purify it. If anyone gets sick, we cannot afford to see the doctor and we worry about whether the sick person will recover. I feel really frustrated about my hard life in the United States.

Tchue Vue's Life Story

as told to her son, Vu Pao Tcha

When our mother and father brought us into the world, they tore up cloth and wrapped us in it. Our mother gave birth, not on a bed, but on the ground. Our parents had a bed but it was high and they were afraid the baby would fall off and get hurt. They put a blanket next to the bed, and my mother gave birth on it. We did not have any doctors then. When the baby came out, the women helping our mother would pick it up and wash it. Our mother would then get up to change her clothes, come back into the room, take the baby in her arms, and breast-feed it. We did not have any dairy milk where we lived. Three days after a baby was born, our parents would give him or her a name. Before naming the baby, however, they would kill some chickens and perhaps a pig and have a feast.

I was my mother's last child. She breast-fed me until I was five years old. When she went to help our father work in the fields, she strapped me on her back with a piece of cloth. At the age of six, children start helping their parents by carrying water from the well to the village—a distance of about a quarter-mile. The river is much farther away, but our elders had built an aqueduct to bring water to the village. We carried water in hollow lengths of bamboo. We children also helped to bring chopped firewood as well as dead twigs that we picked back to the house.

When we got a little older—around the age of eight—we began to help feed the animals and work in the fields. When our parents fed the pigs, we used a stick to chase away other people's pigs. When we fed corn to our chickens, we children would chase away other people's chickens that tried to eat our corn. After we fed the animals, we would go work in the fields. Our job was to pull up the weeds among the crops that our parents planted to feed our family. When we were little we used only our hands, but as we got older we started using tools.

Our meals consisted of rice with a little meat and vegetables. Sometimes we also ate fish, rats, and birds. We grew corn, rice, and opium. The first crop we grew each season was rice. We used the slash-and-burn method to prepare the fields. After we burned the woods, we used knives to dig and cut up the roots and whatever else that had not burned. We put these in piles and burned them. When the field had been completely cleared, we used a special tool to dig holes about five inches apart in the ground. We dug these holes all over a ten-*rai* plot. As the men dug the holes, the women followed with bags of seeds strapped to their waist, dropping several seeds in each hole. They usually finished a section of the field before beginning another. By the time they finished the last section, the seedlings in the first section would already be about two inches high. In the fields belonging to people who worked slowly, the seedlings in the first section would be knee-high by the time they finished planting the last section. Meanwhile, the children were busy pulling up the weeds. We went home only after we had finished planting the whole field.

Our village was not close to our fields. During planting season, we slept out in the fields in a small shed. We had to walk about two hours to get home. Whenever we went home, we would stay two to three weeks, but sometimes we had to plant another crop, such as corn, right after finishing the rice. As soon as we finished planting the corn, we had to go back to the rice field to weed it. We ourselves ate the rice; the corn we fed to our chickens and hogs.

In addition, we grew opium as a cash crop. To prepare the opium field for planting, we used a hoe about a foot long to dig small trenches. Then we raked and pulled up all the weeds. After clearing the field of all weeds, we loosened up the top soil to sow the small opium poppy seeds. As the plants grew, we had to keep weeding the area around each plant until the poppy flowers bloomed. We used a small knife to make incisions into the bulb and used pieces of cloth to gather the latex that dripped out. We put the opium in a container and wrapped it in newspaper. Then we sold the opium by the pound to buyers—either for money or silver bars. With the money, we bought cloth to making clothing for everyone. We used the silver to make jewelry. We usually worked ten *rai* of rice, ten *rai* of corn, and ten *rai* of opium. Our lives were filled with work. We have worked as long as we can remember.

When your father came to marry me, he had to walk two days from his village to mine. In all, it took ten days for your father to pay for me, marry me, and bring me home to his village, where I immediately went to work alongside him in his fields. Before he came to marry me, he had already slashed and burned ten *rai,* but when we got to his house, we discovered the field had not burned completely, so the two of us had to dig up and then cut up the roots and stumps, place them into piles, and burn them again. We used our hands to rake leaves from the ground. When the field was all black, we started planting.

When we finished planting the rice, we came home for a few days. Then we had to go weed your father's cornfield. After we were done with that, we went back to take care of the rice, pulling up weeds with our bare hands. Then it was time to dig trenches for the opium. When we finished doing that, we returned to the rice field to cut the stalks with a sickle. We placed the stalks in piles on the ground to dry. We then had to go weed the opium field again. After that, we carried the rice to a big container and beat the stalks so the grain would fall into the container. We climbed up a ladder carrying bags of grain and poured it into another container so that the wind could blow away the husks and stalks. We kept winnowing this until there was only "pure" rice left in the container. We placed the grain in a cart pulled by oxen and took it to a storage room that we had built earlier. By then, the opium was ripening and we had to go gather the resin, wrap it up, and sell it so that we could get money to buy clothes and food. During the off season, we made new knives, hoes, sickles, and other farming tools. Soon it would be time to slash and burn another field, and the cycle would start all over again.

Chapter Four

As our children were born, we took them everywhere with us. I breast-fed them and strapped the youngest on my back, even when I chopped wood. Your father took care of the rice field while I took care of the opium because it was closer to the house. I also cared for the vegetable plots and the animals and did the chores around the house. Whenever I had to carry a bundle of plants on my back to the house to feed the pigs, I strapped you to my chest. When your father came home from the field, he helped me pound the rice in the mortar to remove the husks. Dinner involved breast-feeding you first, next we fed the animals, and last your father and me. I had to make one fire for boiling the rice and another for cooking the vegetables. We used kerosene lanterns for light. We went to sleep only after we had finished all the chores. We got up early every day and ate breakfast before sunrise. We fed the animals before there was light in the sky. Such was my life as a wife and mother. There was so much to do.

Sometimes when your father came home early, he would cut up the plants and grind the corn for feeding the hogs. The corn grinder was some distance away in the village. He had to carry the corn to the grinder and back. We fed the piglets only cooked corn and leftover rice. The adult pigs got a mixture of plants and corn. Those pigs we intended to butcher for a feast were fed only corn and rice, so that their meat would be good to eat. This is what our life was like in the old country.

When we heard from Hmong leaders that General Vang Pao, who had fought on the side of the Americans, had fled, we decided to leave Laos for Thailand. Your father went to get passports so we could leave. He went to the city of Luang Prabang to get the papers, because we heard that the Communists were going to close all roads to Thailand. Your father got passports, not only for us, but also for all his cousins. We had to leave all our belongings behind. Some people were reluctant to leave their money and their animals, so they tarried. Our papers expired before anyone was ready to go, which meant your father had to go get new papers. While he was away, you became ill. When he returned, we began a ritual to heal you, during which the new set of papers expired again. This time, your father went to Sayaboury to get the required documents. We sold our house and all our belongings, including a new mattress we had just bought, as well as our chickens, pigs, horses, and cows.

We brought along only a pot for cooking rice. Each person left with only two changes of clothing, wearing one and carrying the other. Your father carried our money and a sack of rice on his back. He held your brother's hand while I had you strapped on my back. Several of our cousins came with us. Your uncle and grandfather had left the day before. Uncle Va, Aunt Va, and Aunt Neng followed us until we crossed the big river. Uncle Chong asked us to take along three of his children. We paid a man to take us to the highway—a big road that would be easier to walk on. It took an hour and a half to reach the highway. There we said goodbye to our guide and went on our way. We walked for an hour until we got to a place where we could hire a car. We also bought a flashlight and a few other things.

We drove a whole day until we reached a town where we had planned to stay. But we found a lot of Vietnamese soldiers there, so your father took us to a small village to spend the night. He himself went back to the town to look for your grandfather and uncle, who were supposed to be staying there, so that we could all go to Thailand together. (We were still in Laotian territory.) But he soon discovered that the Vietnamese soldiers had tried to capture your grandfather and uncle, so they had apparently fled on foot to another town. Your father slept in the town that night. In the morning he came back and told us that we were going to take a different route. We were very afraid because we were refugees.

When the Americans pulled out of Laos, the Laotian and Vietnamese leaders told the people that the war was over, that everyone was united now and that we should stop killing each other. The various political factions did unite for one year, but General Vang Pao did not agree with the terms of the union. The Laotian and Vietnamese leaders decided to kill General Vang Pao. General Vang Pao told all the Hmong that he was going to leave and said that whoever wanted to follow him should do so. That was why the Communists blockaded all roads. When your father went to get our passports, he first said we wanted to cross the Mekong River only to visit relatives. The second time he said we wanted to go to Thailand for a vacation. We decided to flee because we knew anyone who had been involved with General Vang Pao or had fought in the guerrilla war was going to be captured, tortured, and killed. That is why the Hmong fled and still harbor great fear [in Laos] today.

Getting back to how we fled, your father bought a mule to carry the rice, but he himself carried the money and held your hand while I carried your brother. We crossed one river after another. It was raining and the ground was very slippery. We covered ourselves with plastic sheets and were bitten by countless mosquitoes. We were in total misery. We walked for two days until we got to a village, where your father left us. We bought some food to eat.

Your father went back to our village to fetch the rest of our cousins. It took him a whole month to return to us. Their trip was far worse than ours, because they could find no cars or boats. They walked and ran and had to be in hiding most of the time. They could not stop in any villages, because there were so many people in the group that they would attract notice. When your father found us again, we split up. His cousins went their way and we went ours. The Communists did not find the first group, so they reached Thailand safely. We ourselves, on the other hand, had walked only half an hour before we got intercepted by Communist soldiers who ordered us to go back the way we had come.

We ran back, not to the village, however, but into the jungle. We abandoned all our belongings except for one sack of rice and our children. There were no roads, only jungle and more jungle. I had your brother strapped to my back while swarms of mosquitoes bit you and us. Our legs were swollen and we could barely walk anymore. We did not have anything to eat. Although we had a bag of rice and sugar and salt, it was raining so hard that it was very difficult to build a fire. When we did try to cook some rice, [it did not cook properly, but] we ate it even though it was still half raw. We walked blindly for five days and nights until we reached a big river. Those who reached the river first had already cut down some trees and tried to lay them across the river. Your father made us walk across the logs, but the current was wild, the water was deep, and we were terrified. What we did not know was that there were Thai soldiers waiting for us on the other side. As soon as we waded ashore, they forced us to go back across the river.

Some Communists began following us. When we sensed their presence we ran, but they caught us. They said, "If you want to stay here with us, that's fine, but we don't have any food for you. If you want to go back to Laos, we'll take you back." We told them we were going to see our cousins who were in the next town across the border in Thailand. The soldiers told us that was too far for us to walk. We told them we would go back to Laos. It took us five days to get back to the town we had left ten days earlier. We were completely worn out. We bought some food and cooked rice in the dark, but it took seemingly forever to cook. We had eaten virtually nothing during the ten days of our flight.

Your father soon left to look for another escape route. He did not dare stay anywhere for more than a night. After walking one whole day, he found an Iu Mien who agreed to take us across the border. We paid him several silver bars, worth about a thousand dollars. We also managed to send a message to your Uncle Chong, who had already reached Thailand. He feared for the safety of his children whom he had left with us, so he came back to look for them. When Uncle Chong arrived, he threw stones at us to catch our attention. We went to see who it was, and when we discovered it was he, we told the Iu Mien to keep the money, while we fled in the midst of a big storm. We walked as fast as we could so that the Communists would not find us. Even though all of us were utterly exhausted, we walked nonstop for five days and nights without resting at all. There were about thirty persons in our group.

The Communists were right behind us. Your father and I decided to divide our money and rice and to separate. He told me before he left, "If they capture me, they'll kill me; take the children and go back to Laos if they catch you." I had you and your brother with me. I did not want to go back to where we had come from because we had already lost everything there, and we were so close to freedom. Though I had no strength left, I covered you with a blanket and a piece of plastic and walked behind you with a flashlight. We kept going with your brother strapped on my back. Your grandparents walked behind me. We met some Hmong soldiers who had come back from Thailand to lead people out of Laos. They asked us if we wanted to hire them. We said no. We told them, "If you want to be hired, the people with gold and silver are at the back." So, the soldiers ran to the back of the line and protected the people there. We walked for another five days until we got to a city in Thailand.

The Thai authorities came up to us and checked us for diseases and questioned us. We did not know whether they would let us stay.

Whatever money we had, they wanted to see it. Finally, they put us in a refugee camp. We felt so miserable. You had been bitten by so many mosquitoes that your whole body was swollen. We had arrived at night. The next day, we were given some food. We took you to the camp doctor—a white American woman. She gave you some shots and medication for your mosquito bites. She also gave us some canned chicken to eat. It took you a week to get better.

We stayed in that refugee camp for a year. We applied to go to the United States, but our names did not appear on the list of persons chosen to go there. Instead, the officials told us we would be eligible to go to France and asked us if we wanted to go there. Since we were afraid we would never get accepted into the United States, we decided to fill out the application forms for France. However, they did not accept your grandparents and your uncle for France. We did not want to go without them, so we waited almost three more years to see if our names would appear on the U.S. list, but they never did. Finally, we decided we had better go to France. Once again, what few things we had accumulated had to be left behind.

The authorities rented a bus to take us to the airport in the capital city of Thailand. Our ride was free. Our airline tickets were not ready yet, so we had to stay in Bangkok for a while. The living conditions there were very bad. There were a lot of mosquitoes. By then, I had already given birth to your younger brother. We ran out of money, so we had to eat whatever the authorities gave us. After one month's waiting, our tickets arrived and we left for France.

When we landed in France, the authorities took us to a big building and told us we could stay there for five months. They fed us and gave us a little money. After the five months were up, we were told we had to leave the building and your father had to go find a job. I was not required to look for a job because I had to look after you and your two brothers. We were supposed to receive family support payments (like welfare here) but they did not come immediately. We lived on the little bit of money that we had saved from what the government had given us. We managed to pay our own rent for four months. We did not have any relatives whom we could call on for help. After two months, our family support payment finally came, but it was not enough to pay for our rent, food, and clothing. Fortunately, your father found work and soon was able to buy a small car. I decided to leave you children at home and also looked for a job.

We were living in a town called Argent-sur-Sauldre, near the city of Bourges. I worked for two months, after which my employer did not have enough work for me to do, but I received unemployment insurance for a while.

Your father moved us to another city, where he worked for five months. When that job ran out, we moved once again, this time to Tours, where your father worked for four years. He and I decided I should also look for a job so that we could save up enough money to buy airplane tickets to the United States. That is why I left you and your brothers in the house by yourselves. We had a hard time in France.

After we arrived in America, we once again worked in the fields. We settled in Fresno, California, where we have grown sugar peas and strawberries. One summer we grew tomatoes, then we switched back to strawberries. That is what we have been doing ever since we came to the United States.

Life is very difficult for us adults in the United States. We now live in a place that is strange to us. We do not know the language, nor are we educated. It is not easy to make a living here. We do not have much money, so it is impossible to start a business. Since we cannot speak English, others will not hire us. Farming in the United States takes so much investment that we even have difficulty growing crops. It takes a great deal of money to lease the land and buy the water. When we were in Laos, we had land, we had water. We could farm as much as we wanted to. One thing we did not have, though, was tractors or any other kind of power equipment. All we had were our own strength and our bare hands.

In our old country, we worked very hard, we were always very tired, and we got very little profit. The government in Laos was poor, so it could not help us. There were no roads, so we could not use any tractors or automobiles. Our land was in the mountains, so we had to haul our crops on our own backs or by mules and pack ponies. But there, it was easy to get as much land as we could work. We lived in a poor country, but we grew enough food to feed ourselves. The United States is a big and very wealthy country, but it is difficult to find enough to eat and drink here. Since we have no education, we do not know what else we can do.

You have asked me, son, to tell you about my life in Laos, France, and the United States, and that is what I have done today.

A New American

by Vu Pao Tcha

Every morning at eight-thirty, my alarm clock rings to tell me that sleeping time is over and that I should get up if I want to be in school on time. As usual, my hand reaches out from under the warm blanket to turn it off. Then I cover my head up to get some more sleep. A few minutes later, the clock rings again. This time, I tell myself that I *have* to get up if I do not want to be late for my nine o'clock class. I have less than twenty minutes to get there. Quickly I jump out of bed and rush to the bathroom to wash my face. Then I pick up my jeans, which I had left lying on the floor the night before, and search in the laundry basket for one of my wrinkled shirts that does not smell too bad yet. After I am dressed, I take a quick look at myself in the mirror to see if I will look presentable enough in public. Oops! My hair needs some major fixing. "No problem," I mumble to myself, "my hat will take care of that."

Next, I grab my backpack, run out the door, unlock my bike, and rush to school. Still, I am late for class. "Stupid me," I always say to myself. "Why do I always rush to class even though I know that I'll be late anyway?" When classes are finally over, I hurry home to find something to satisfy my empty stomach. Fried eggs and instant noodles usually do the trick. After such a delicious meal, I call my friends for a basketball or volleyball game. Later, we crash at someone's place to study together or sometimes just to talk and share jokes and laughs. We stay up very late—that's why I always have a hard time getting up early in the morning.

Finally comes Friday—my liberation day. Friday nights are the craziest and wildest nights of the week when all my friends and I party like animals. Friday is my best time of the week, but it's Saturday and Sunday that I look forward to the most. They allow me to catch up on the sleep lost during the school week. I can finally cook myself some decent meals and maybe do the laundry that lies long overdue in the closet. On weekdays I hardly have any time for myself. So, during weekends, I try as much as I can to relax, think, and do the things that I enjoy doing. Good God, what a life college is! Sometimes, I wonder what my purpose is here at the university. "What am I doing here?" I often ask myself. "Who am I and how did I get to where I am now? How did I become what I am today?" I am so much involved with my new life in college that I often don't remember who I really am and where I've come from.

When I was a little child looking over the vast horizon from the mountaintops of Laos, I never imagined that I would one day live in a country so great and complicated as the United States of America and go to one of its most prestigious universities. I vaguely remember watching my parents, hoes in their hands, working vigorously on a small plot of unlevel land. I saw them do the same thing day after day, and I realized that it would be what I would be doing when I grew up. I never imagined that, one day, I would go to college far away from home and friends and that I would have to cook for myself and wash my own clothes. It never occurred to me that there could be another life or another world, other than the one in the mountains. Even the thought of living somewhere else never crossed my mind. And why would I want to live in some other place? The mountains were my home, and I felt safe and happy there.

Thinking that life in the mountains would be the only life for me, I grew to accept it. I learned to love and appreciate it mainly from observing my parents. Each day, my parents got up before dawn to go to the fields. They worked all day long under the hot sun and returned home only after dark, tired and exhausted. That was their daily life but they never complained.

As a little child, I never saw my parents. When they left for work, I was still sleeping. When they came back, I was already in bed. It was not until I was able to walk that my parents began to take me with them to the fields to show and teach me all the things that I would need to learn. It was very important that parents teach their children the necessary knowledge and skills so that they could support themselves when they became adults.

Life in the mountains is difficult, but it is not an unhappy one. Our people (we call ourselves the Hmong) live peacefully with nature. Although considered one of the most backward people on earth, we are very organized. We hate to think of ourselves as backward, but rather as a civilized people of a different civilization. We have rules that are respected by everyone. We live in equality. Because everybody is poor, there are no social classes. Of course, there are certain social positions that can be attained by individuals, but most Hmong are peasants. The theft and murder rates in Hmong communities in Laos are very low. Homeless people and beggars are almost nonexistent. We all help each other to make sure that no one is in need. Indeed, the Hmong are poor, but they live a modest and proud life.

As I grew up, I learned to appreciate Hmong values. In time, I became proud of my own heritage, for I thought there could be no greater pride than being a Hmong. I was only four years old then, but I already had a very good vision of how my future life would be. The hope for a happy life was promising. But it soon faded.

One day, we heard the news: "We've lost the war! General Vang Pao has fled the country."

"What are they talking about?" I asked myself. "What is war? Who is this general Vang Pao? Why has he fled the country? Where to?"

I did not get any answers, but for weeks the news was the talk of the village. Children were still playing and people were still going about their everyday routine, but every night, village leaders would secretly hold meetings. Apparently, something was awfully wrong. Once, I overheard a conversation between my father and other relatives. They were whispering instead of talking. I heard them talk about the Communists.

"Who are the Communists?" I wondered. But I did not need to ask: I knew they must be the enemy. I shivered at the sound of the word: *niala*. Its sound was more terrifying than the English word, *Communists*. No one dared say it aloud.

One night, while I was sleeping, my father woke me up. He whispered in my ears: "Wake up, son. We're going to Thailand." I did not need to ask why. I knew we were leaving our village for very frightening reasons. Father loaded his back with heavy things. So did Mom. Very quickly, we started to walk into the dark. Soon, we were joined by other families, all of them our cousins and relatives.

I had no idea where we were going. All I knew was that we were headed toward the unknown. Even Father, who was never frightened, seemed afraid for the first time. To relieve myself of my fear, I pretended that our journey was an exciting and pleasant experience. I enjoyed the game at first, but as the trip began to seem long and as I began to feel pain in my sore legs and feet, which were full of cuts and bruises, I started to worry. I began to ask my father questions.

"When will we get to Thailand, Dad?"

"Soon."

Each passing day, I would ask him the same question and hear the same reply, "Soon."

As we continued our walk, I began to realize that it would be a very long time before we reached Thailand. Suddenly the trip became a frightening experience. Soon, we were short of food. All the rice we had brought had run out, and we went hungry. To satisfy our hunger, we had to feed on roots, leaves, fruits, and other edible plants we found in the jungle. With no sturdy clothes on, our bodies were left unprotected as we walked through thick grasses and woods. Mosquitoes never let us alone, even when our bodies were swollen from their bites. Although some of us suffered severely from hunger and sickness, we never stopped to rest or sleep. We continued walking even when it rained. We did not want to be caught by soldiers and taken back to Laos.

We were constantly on the alert for nearby soldiers. Sometimes, when we heard gunshots, we hid under bushes where we wouldn't be seen. There was no talking among us, except the leaders of our small group who exchanged a few words from time to time. The children never said a word. We knew we were to stay quiet. We were too scared to make any noise, anyway. Even the babies were quiet.

As hard as we tried to keep ourselves from being seen and heard, it did not stop soldiers from finding us. One day, we ran into a few soldiers. It was a frightening scene. I had never seen soldiers before, and the sight of their uniforms terrified me. We could have panicked, tried to run away, and risked being killed. But we stayed calm. I heard someone say to my father that we should fight them if we did not want to be taken back to the mountains. My father, who was the youngest but the wisest of the leaders, disagreed.

"We don't have enough guns," he said. "It would be stupid to try to resist the soldiers. Who will take care of our wives and children if we are killed?" He said we should talk with the soldiers and try to persuade them to let us go. "It doesn't matter if they take us back," Father said. "What matters is that we stay alive."

There was a long talk between my father and the leader of the soldiers. We were all ready to run if the soldiers opened fire. Then Father came back and told us that we were to follow the soldiers. There was no objection. We did what we were told. The soldiers forced us to walk back to where we had come from. We stopped at a town where we were to stay for a couple of days before we were taken back to the mountains. We were told that we could go wherever we wished as long as we did not try to leave the town.

I never asked my father how, but he must have contacted some friends there for help, because one night, two of my uncles who had gone to Thailand with another group showed up and talked with Father. We started to make preparations immediately. The next night, we left the town without anybody knowing it.

We walked quickly and quietly without stopping because we were frightened that the soldiers would try to catch us again. Some of us got very sick and had to be carried. A few died of fatigue, some of hunger, and others of accidents. Sometimes we passed tombstones of dead people from groups that had fled earlier. The sight was horrifying. The smell was unbearable. There were no graves. The corpses were just covered with stones, dirt, leaves, and whatever could be found. There was no time to dig any graves, even if there were shovels. Neither was there time for rituals. Crying and mourning were not even suggested.

One day, after many days of nonstop walking through thick jungles and grasslands, often under heavy rain, and after having lost more than ten people, we reached a big, flat, open space. We realized we had finally reached Thailand. Many shelters and newly constructed bamboo huts appeared before our eyes. What joy we felt when we got close to the place! Our relatives and cousins recognized us and ran to welcome us with tears in their eyes. It was a moment of happiness as well as of sadness, because not everyone who had left with us survived.

I did not understand what all the crying was about, but I did not care. I was just happy that everything was going to be all right. I would finally be able to rest, sleep, play, and talk with my friends again. Yes, I thought that all the suffering and horror were over, and that life would soon be back to normal. I did not know that life would never be the same again and that our arrival at the refugee camp was just the beginning of many long struggles that I would later face in life.

Life in Thailand was unlike life in the mountains of Laos. We had no food that was our own except what the Thai gave us. I was not used to being hungry in Laos. But hunger was so common in the refugee camp that I got used to it. However, I would sometimes find myself staring at some kids who were fortunate enough to have a piece of bread or doughnut in their hands. The thought of stealing crossed my mind many times. Eventually, I did steal.

One day, I saw one of my neighbors come back to his shelter. He carried a box of milk powder in his hands. My mother had once bought one like it for my little brother. She had let me taste a little of it. I found the taste very appealing. So when our neighbor took the box inside, I and other kids followed him. We wanted to taste the powder and hoped he would open the box. He did not and put it on a shelf, instead.

"That's for the baby?" someone asked.

"Yes," our neighbor said, after which we ran outside, because he obviously had no intention of letting us taste the powder.

In the following days, I kept going inside this neighbor's shelter to check if the box had been opened. Days went by. The box was still on the shelf. The thought of stealing it came to my mind, and the thought of having it all for myself was very tempting. But I did not have the guts to do it. I had never stolen before and did not know how to steal.

One day, when I went back to check again, the box was gone. I thought our neighbor must have fed the milk to his baby. Later that day, two other kids came to meet me and asked if I wanted to eat some milk powder. How could I refuse such an offer? They took me to an isolated spot and handed me a box. It was almost empty, but I took it anyway. Then the two kids disappeared. Quickly, I dipped my wet hand into the box and began to scrape what little was left inside. It tasted so good. I was very happy.

Suddenly, the two kids reappeared, but not by themselves. They brought our neighbor with them. I immediately realized what I had got myself into. I wanted to throw the box away and hide, but I had no time to run. I knew I was caught and there was no escape. One of the kids opened his mouth:

"It's him. We saw him take the box."

Their lie was an outrage. I could not believe that the two real thieves were accusing me of their own crime, but I did not know what to say or do to defend myself.

"It's a lie!" I wanted to shout. "They used me. They are the ones who stole the box."

But I knew my situation. Where was my proof? I was the one holding the box. My mouth and fingers were sticky with milk powder. I knew that no matter what I said, I was lost.

The real thieves got away scot-free, while the news of my shameful deed quickly spread among the people who knew me. Father flogged me until I fainted. So much did my behind hurt that I could not sit for weeks. But the scars that my father inflicted on me were less deep than the shame that I faced as a thief in everyone's eye. Although I found it unfair that the real thieves got away, I accepted my punishment. I was set up, but I also knew I was guilty, nevertheless, because I did eat some of the milk powder. It was the same as stealing, so I couldn't deny my guilt. I realized later that the humiliation and shame I endured were not in vain, because this incident taught me a very important lesson—never to steal again.

Life was very hard for the children living in the refugee camp. Many hungry children would do whatever they could to satisfy their stomachs. Some would resort to barbaric methods such as cheating or stealing. Others would eat anything they could find, such as fruit, plants, and leaves. A lot of them suffered from sickness caused by what they ate. Malnutrition was very common in the camp.

The conditions in Camp Ban Nam Yao, where we were, were terrible, especially when it was first opened. There were no toilets.

People had no water to wash themselves. There was no clinic for the sick. There were no jobs, no land to grow food, and virtually no way of getting money to buy food.

There was also no school for the children. I remember spending most of my early days in the camp playing in the dirt and wandering around the ever-growing village. I had no shoes on and wore the same clothes every day. I didn't take any baths and never washed my clothes. There was nothing that wasn't unsanitary in our surroundings. It wasn't until two years later that schools were built. It was a big blow for all of us kids. Our days of freedom were at an end. Instead of doing the things we wanted to do, we now had to go to school.

My father was very happy, however, and bought me a notebook and a pencil. He was very anxious to see me go to school. He had always said that education was the only key to a good life. He used to tell me:

"Son, there are only two kinds of life in this world: that of the body and the hoe, and that of the brain and the pen."

I never understood him. I saw no need for education in a society such as ours. Life in the camp did not require any skills in writing or reading. Because I only knew the life of the "body and hoe," I told myself:

"It's no use for us to learn how to read and write. Our ancestors never had any need for an education. Why should we suddenly need it now?"

I did not have an answer to this question until long after we had left Thailand and settled in France, our next host country. Three years had passed since we got to Thailand. The Americans and French started to accept refugees into their countries. We applied to go to both countries. The French accepted us before the Americans did, so we went to France.

Going to France was a big shock to me, because when I arrived in Thailand, I never thought that I would have to leave for another country. I assumed that I would be living in the camp for the rest of my life.

"Where is France?" I asked. I had never seen any French people before. I had only heard that the French and Americans have white skin and that they're very tall. But one day, while we were still in Camp

Ban Nam Yao, I saw a very tall white man surrounded by children. I wondered if he was French or American. The children were playing around him. He was smiling and laughing. He had a camera and was taking pictures of the kids. The desire to be in a picture drew me close to him. I saw that he had a long nose and his teeth were shiny. His hair was blond and well combed.

"He is so clean," I thought. "Are all French and Americans like him? Whoever he is, he sure smells good."

For a second, I felt shy as I got near him, out of fear that he would see how dirty and smelly I was. But he did not seem to care and seemed to enjoy our company. He let us touch his clothes and bags, even his golden hair that we were all very anxious to feel.

"It'll be great to live with people like that," I thought.

Finally, the big day came. A bus took us to the airport, where all kinds of planes were constantly coming and going. I was amazed. I had never seen anything like that before. I was in awe when we walked toward the big plane that was to take us to France. The sight of the tricolored metallic bird was fantastic. I could not wait to get in. The long line of passengers made me more anxious. There were more than a hundred people waiting to climb into the plane. I noticed a few black people, and the sight of them struck me because I had never seen any blacks before.

"How did they become so black?" I asked myself.

I suddenly remembered tales about black people eating humans, and I was terrified when one black man looked toward me with a smile. I thought he was going to eat me. There were other Asians like us, too. But they were dressed in elegant suits. All of them carried shiny leather briefcases.

"They are probably Chinese or Japanese," I told myself. "They look so important. They must be very rich and powerful people—maybe princes and emperors."

The rest of the people were mostly white. Some had blond hair, some dark hair. Some had whiter skins than others. They were all very tall and spoke strange languages. The diversity of the passengers struck me a lot, but already I was getting used to the sight. I knew that I had no choice but get used to it, because where I was going, I wouldn't see many people who looked like me.

Finally, we climbed the stairs of the plane. Very beautiful women were waiting for us at the door. We sat in very comfortable seats. Before I knew it, we were rolling. From the window, I could see that we were moving very fast. Then suddenly, I felt the plane lifting into the air. I was scared at first because I did not think that such a big and heavy plane could stay in the air. But as I saw the plane climb higher and higher, I felt more relaxed.

It was just awesome to look down at the earth and see everything so small. I used to look at the clouds and wonder how I could ever touch them. Now I was flying over them. It was a dream come true. I felt as if I was flying toward paradise. I did not know much about that paradise, but I knew I was leaving the poverty-stricken and hungry life of the camp forever.

Two days later, we arrived in France. We stayed in Paris for a week before we were sent to a rehabilitation home in another city. My parents were soon put in some job-training program, while I was sent to school. Before long, we were living by ourselves. It was hard at first to get adjusted to the urban life, especially for us mountain people. It was almost like living a couple of centuries into the future. We were born at the heart of nature and never knew the life of the city. Now, everything was new and had to be learned in order to survive.

At the time, I was only nine years old and learning was still an exciting part of my life. For my parents, however, it was almost like starting another life again. They had to learn how to buy food, read prices, and use money. They had to learn how to use an oven, a washing machine, an iron, and apply all the safety rules, and the like. My parents were very fast learners, though. Very soon, they found jobs. Before we knew it, we were living a life just as normal as that of our French neighbors.

My new life in France tremendously changed my values, the way I see things and the way I think. When I was in Laos, I thought that my life would be no different from that of my parents. I had no ambitions, no hope, but just the desire to stay alive and have a long and happy life. France opened a new door for me and gave me hope and inspiration and a strong desire to achieve many things I had never dreamed of. It gave me new visions and dreams. I found out that there are a lot of things I could do and have in this new life. I realized that I could acquire important knowledge and skills that would enable me to help and influence other people. I would also be able to use the knowledge and skills to make a lot of money so that I could buy many good things. I understood, too, that this new life was not so simple as that of the mountains. I knew it was much more complicated, but I also knew it was better.

Although my knowledge of the new world was still very rudimentary, I knew that the only key to the things that I wanted to do and have is education. Never before did my father's words resound so loudly in my head. I remembered what he had always told me:

"Son, I am your father, but there is only one thing in this life which I can provide you with. It is a hoe. If you want a better life than what we have, you're going to have to give it to yourself, and the way you can get it is with a pen."

In Laos, anyone who knew how to use a pen—that is to say, how to read and write—was considered very educated and was treated with respect. These individuals were also the most important people in the community and had direct relations with the government. Accordingly, they were very wealthy and powerful. My father always wanted his children to go to school so that they could one day become rich and live a better life than his. I never understood him until I was flooded with dreams and ambitions, which can only be realized through education.

I was still very young, but I took school more seriously than most of my peers. I was inspired and determined to do my best and to succeed in everything. Being a newcomer, school was not an easy challenge for me. But I struggled and fought with devotion and a seriousness of purpose against all the obstacles that were in my way. Before long, I won the admiration of my teachers and friends. I excelled in almost everything and was among the top students. I was happy about my accomplishments.

My new life in France may have been a success, but it was not very exciting. Because I devoted all my time to school work, I had little time for a social life. I never had any real friends. I didn't participate in any social activities, didn't date, didn't play any sports, didn't go to church, and didn't go anywhere interesting. In fact, during the whole time I was in France, I never once went outside my city except during field trips. A lot of times I have wondered why I was so different from the other students. Why didn't I have any interest in the things that they did? Why did I always study so much? What did I really want? Did I have a life?

Then I remembered the times when I was still in Laos and Thailand. There was nothing then that worried me. All I cared about was to have fun and enjoy life. I was happy just to be alive. I never thought that one day I would be so busy with books that I would forget to enjoy the pleasures of life.

I somehow knew that my devotion to getting an education was depriving me of a lot of things in life. I did not like it because I did not want to miss anything in life. But I stayed strong and stuck to my books, because I thought that if I wanted a good life, I would have to sacrifice my youth in order to secure a better life for the future.

Six years passed. A lot of things happened. My grandparents went to the United States. So did our other relatives. Father had applied to emigrate to the United States several times but with no success. After my grandfather's death in 1984, Father decided that we would go to the United States. He and Mom got us visas to visit the United States as tourists, but once we were here, we did not return. We managed to become permanent residents later.

I did not really want to come to the United States because I knew that by coming, I would have to give up all the goals that I had so carefully planned for my life in France. I was only a couple of years from finishing my education there. Going to the United States would ruin everything. Father disagreed. He said that there would be more opportunities for me in the United States, even if I have to start all over again.

He was right. I had to start all over again and live a totally different life. We went to live in Fresno, California, where most of our relatives lived and where there is a very large concentration of Hmong. Our relatives helped and supported us financially. They paid our rent and bought us food until my parents could find jobs to support our family. Soon my parents were working again as they had done in France. As for me, things went in a totally different direction.

After I arrived in Fresno, I found myself in a completely different world. First, the environment was new. I used to live in tall buildings of twenty or more stories, and now I was living in an apartment no higher than the second floor. There was not much traffic in France, while in Fresno, cars ran by all day long. Second, the people are different. Fresno is a city with people of diverse ethnic backgrounds, of whom the majority is Euro-American, though there are a lot of blacks, Chicanos, and Central Americans, too. There is also a large concentration of Asians, mostly Southeast Asians, a new group that has increased rapidly in recent years. Because of this large increase of minority groups in Fresno, especially of Southeast Asian refugees, a lot of tension arose between the old residents and the newcomers. Prejudice can often be observed, whether at school, in hospitals and shopping centers, or on the street.

One day, while I was driving home from school, a group of white boys riding in a pickup truck tried to intimidate me. They yelled and cursed at me. They gave me the finger and screamed a four-letter word repeatedly. I heard them say, "Go back home! This is our country!"

Then they spat at me and laughed. One of them even pointed his finger at me as if he were shooting at me. I could hear him laugh and say, "Bang! Bang! You're dead, you f——— Hmong."

I had witnessed similar violent actions toward other Asians before, so I knew they were just trying to intimidate me. Instead of reacting angrily, I took a turn and disappeared. Of course I was shocked and angry, and I wanted to get back at them, but I held my temper. I knew that if I tried to get revenge, I would be just as inhumane as they were. My father has always taught me to be tolerant. He said that revenge only makes things worse. I agree.

Many of my friends who could not tolerate the racism against our community in Fresno have become racists themselves. They have often provoked other groups, usually whites, into bloody fights. As a result, their actions not only heightened the reaction against us but have also brought a negative image to our community. Revenge is definitely not the answer to racism.

Indeed, racism was the first shocking thing I observed after my arrival in the United States. It was very common to witness racist actions against minority groups by Euro-Americans. However, it was also not unusual at all to observe the same kind of tension among different minority groups themselves. In Fresno, it was very rare to see minorities around whites, but it was even rarer to see minority groups interacting with each other.

Racism was probably the hardest challenge and most difficult obstacle that I've encountered in the United States. The other challenge that I had to face was school. When I got to the United States, I was already fifteen years old. In France, I would have been at the climax of my intellectual growth. But in the United States, it became the most difficult stage in my education. Things are much harder to learn at that age, especially a new language. As a result, my intellectual as well as my personal growth suffered, not because I was incapable of learning as much as I would have in France, but because in order to learn, I had first to learn the new language—English—and it was not an easy task. My personal growth was tremendously affected because the long interruption in my intellectual growth gave me a great sense of insecurity and low self-esteem. In France, I used be the top student in almost everything. But now I was suddenly behind everyone in every subject. I used to have all my teachers' admiration, but now I became a nobody. I was looked down on just because I did not speak English well. I could hardly carry on a conversation because I could not express my thoughts and opinions very clearly. I used to make fun of others. Now, I knew how they must have felt—being laughed at and humiliated.

Because I was picking up the new language very slowly, I started to lose hope. I was forever behind in my school work. I could never reach the level of my American peers. I thought that if I could graduate from high school, I would like to go to a university, but it looked as though I couldn't even reach my senior year. I even considered dropping out of school and getting married and living on welfare, as so many of my friends were doing.

I was at the point of giving up, but I did not. I was taught never to give up, even if it meant humiliation and dishonor. My father always said, "When you start something, you must finish it."

Yes, I wanted to finish high school and go to college. I could not accept being discriminated against, like some of my friends, just because I did not go beyond high school and could get only a very low-paying job or live on welfare. I would not allow that to happen to me.

So I decided to push really hard in school and do my best. But because of the language barrier, it took me four entire years to regain a sense of self-confidence. Even after four years of hard work, my English was not as good as I wanted it to be. My speech was still very poor and people said I had a strong French accent. These obstacles, however, did not stop me from taking the hardest courses in school. By my senior year, I was once again among the top students in my class. The fact that I was one of only a few Asians in that rank made me very proud. I had gone very far, indeed, in only a very short time.

However, I was not all that happy. I had sacrificed a lot of things in order to accomplish what I did. I have been so devoted to my education all my life that I forgot to have a social life. I've never invested my talents and time in things such as sports and other activities. As a result, I never made any real friends. In sum, I have wasted all my teenage years. I have deprived myself of a lot of good things that life has to offer. I did not realize that until I came here to the University of California, Santa Barbara.

Soon after I came to school at UCSB, my life began to change. I discovered new things, new people—a whole new world. Not all things are what I thought they are. Not all people are what I thought they are. Not all people are racists. Whether we're white, black, or yellow, we all hate racism. Before long, I started to pick up new values and perspectives on life.

During my first year in college, I made friends with many people of different backgrounds. I found everyone very open and friendly. I did a lot of things that I had never done before with them—fun things as well as crazy things. We partied, drank, joked, and laughed together. I became a brother to these new friends, and they, brothers to me. Education began to seem less important to me than the things I did with my friends. I began to realize that a social life was what I had missed all my life. As a result, I concentrated less on my studies while enjoying life more. I developed new interests. I got involved in sports, with girls, and in various activities. I wanted to enjoy the few remaining years of my youth. I thought, "It's time that I start enjoying life."

I felt that there is no good life if there is no good youth. Besides, I had already wasted much of my childhood. I did not want to waste the rest of my youth. For the first time in my life, I feel as if I belong somewhere. I am doing almost all the things that my American friends do. Although we are from diverse social and ethnic backgrounds, we are leading similar lives. We go to school together, we play sports, we date, we party and get drunk. We all hold similar values in life and share the same interests, goals, and dreams—to have a successful and happy life.

I believe I am living an American life with an American dream today. Yet it's still hard for me to consider myself an "American." Why? Is it because there is a part of me that is not American at all? Is it because I look different? Yes and no. I have no definite answer. But what is an American? What does it mean to be an American—especially an Asian American? I agree with what my Asian American peers tell me: although I am Asian and look Asian, I am not an Asian of Asia any more. I am no longer a Hmong of the mountains of Laos. I no longer hold strong Hmong cultural values. What I once treasured is no longer important to me. Now, could I ever live the mountain life again if I go back to Laos? It's very unlikely. Since I'm no longer totally Hmong, nor am I a real American, what am I?

I believe that being an American means being something different from what I used to be, having different values, and living a different life. People who choose to make the United States their home are Americans because they have chosen to live differently from their ancestors. They have become something different—something new. Of course, they can never be completely like other Americans because there are so many different Americans. There are different kinds of Euro-Americans just as there are different kinds of Asian Americans and Afro-Americans. In short, Americans can never be completely alike even if they are all Americans because America is a country of diverse people.

It is harder to deny my new identity than to accept it. I know I have become an American even though I am different from other Americans. Whether I like it or not, I am a new Asian American—a Hmong American. So why not make that my identity?

Hello, my fellow Americans!

CHAPTER FIVE

The Moua Family of Sanger

The Moua family in Santa Ana. *Middle row:* Thek Moua (*far right*), Buoa Neng Moua (*second from right*). *Front row:* Pang Yang (*seated, middle*). *Courtesy of Boua Neng Moua, Pang Yang, and Thek Moua.*

Boua Neng Moua's Life Story

as told to his son, Thek Moua

Today is a great day because I am going to tell my son Thek about Hmong life in Laos and how we escaped during the war in Vietnam. My grandfather's name was Moua Pang Yia. I never met my grandparents. They died long before I was born. According to what my parents told me, my grandparents had many children, but my father was the only son. Since there are so many Hmong named Moua, our clan is always called the Mouanoutoua clan. Moua Nou Toua was the name of my great-grandfather.

My father married and had several children, only two of whom were sons. I am the eldest. My mother gave birth to me on March 27, 1927, so I am now sixty-five years old. I was born in Pernao. We raised pigs, cows, horses, goats, chickens, and ducks and sold them for money. We also farmed and grew rice, corn, opium, and vegetables. I grew up as an obedient lad. I had no formal education because there were no schools in my village. I helped my family to farm our land. I raised cows and horses, herding them as they grazed. My brother's name is Moua Yee. I do not know if he is still alive in Laos. There is no communication between us anymore.

My parents lived a very hard life. Farming was the only means they had to get food. A lot of hard labor was involved in farming—cutting down trees, burning the land before planting, traveling by foot back and forth between our village and the fields. The distance between the two was quite great. Raising animals also took a lot of work. All those things had to be done, for they were essential for survival in the Hmong way of life. Those unwilling to work starved.

Though my parents worked hard, they had no fear of war. Unlike the years when I was an adult, there was peace and tranquility in their times. People could travel freely all over the country without any worries about being shot at or captured.

When the Hmong had migrated southward from China to Southeast Asia, they brought with them their animistic beliefs. We have many gods living on separate levels. The chief god resides on the first level. He is the master of all the gods and lives in the center of Heaven, which is held up by four gods, one at each corner. The second level belongs to the four gods holding up Heaven, who are kind and do not harm mankind. Humans look to them for spiritual guidance and assistance. The gods on the third level are wild spirits who roam the world freely. They are nature spirits who live in the mountains, trees, rivers, ponds, and valleys. They have little interest in mankind. The spirits on the fourth level, our ancestor spirits, are quite tame.

The Hmong believe everyone has three souls. The first stays with the body. The second wanders around while we sleep. The third protects the body from harm. In death, the first soul stays with the body, the second comes to live with the dead person's family, while the third goes to Heaven to be reborn. It can be reincarnated into anything—a human, an animal, or an object—depending on a person's past life. If the individual has lived a good life, then he or she will be reborn into a good family. Those who have lived bad lives will be reborn as animals or objects.

[Hmong communicate with the spirit world through shamans.] Shamans go into a trance to achieve ecstasy. They lose track of reality and enter into an altered state of consciousness. In this way, they can accompany good spirits to the spirit world. They perform rituals for many reasons—to honor the dead and to ask them for guidance, assistance, or prosperity. These rituals take place inside the house in front of an altar. Shamans also perform rituals when souls call out to them. When people get sick, we believe their souls are trapped or lost in the spirit world. A shaman needs to go there and bring them back to the sick person's body. While performing their rituals, shamans cover their heads with a black veil. This means they are no longer existing in the present reality. A lamp is lighted to guide them as they travel in the dark spirit world.

Shamans are important individuals in Hmong society. They give us guidance and advice. When Hmong people move, they ask a shaman to tell them where to go and how to get there safely. Shamans are very powerful individuals because they influence many people who act on the basis of what they say.

The Hmong way of life, especially marriage, is different from that of Americans. Americans usually do not have to pay a huge sum to the bride's parents. From what I have seen, all they do is hold a large party for the relatives and friends present at the wedding. In my youth in Laos, marriage was very complicated. It cost a lot of money. [An amount equal to] several thousands of dollars had to be given to the bride's parents as a token of appreciation for the effort they had made to raise her. Long bars of silver were spent for the wedding feast, for which cows, pigs, and chickens were butchered and served. The guests were also served corn whiskey. Many people, especially the groom, got drunk. Some people got seriously ill from their excessive eating and drinking at weddings.

Our marriages were usually arranged by the parents or close relatives of the prospective bride and groom. The parents of girls who were kidnapped by young men interested in marrying them usually resisted the marriage. Hmong with the same clan name were forbidden to marry. It did not matter whether one individual knew the other or not. So long as they had the same clan name, they could not marry. Only people with different clan names could marry.

One saying we have is that when children do not obey their parents, then *their* children will also disobey them. This saying is almost like a curse: those who refuse to listen to their elders will be punished. My father told me this long ago.

I was in my teens when the Japanese invaded our country. The imperial Japanese troops chased the French all over the place. The battles between them took place mostly in the northern part of Laos near the border with China. I served in the Hmong militia directed by the French. I and other Hmong soldiers were ordered to guard our villages from the Japanese. After a few years, the Japanese returned to their homeland.

In 1947, I joined the French [colonial] army and learned to use guns. I stayed in the army until around 1952. I guarded the airport, cooked, and cleaned. I also helped carry injured soldiers to the medical tent for treatment. I helped fill airplanes with gasoline. Then the French also went back to France.

I married my beautiful wife, Yang Pang, in 1952. I remember our wedding quite well. The Yang clan was cruel and harsh. They made my Moua clan pay a lot of money and animals for her. Two pigs and a cow were slaughtered for the wedding feast. Unlike most Hmong marriages, mine was not arranged. I met my wife at a well. She was fetching water to take to her village. I followed her home. We did not talk much, but a few days later, my relatives and I came to see her again. We waited for her by the road. On her way home from the well, I asked her to marry me. She refused. So we caught her by the arms and legs and brought her home with us. We then sent two messengers to her parents' house, telling them that their daughter had just been married to a young Moua man. At our wedding, there was a lot of drinking. Many of the relatives got drunk. I did, too. I think I passed out. I feel very lucky to have married my lovely wife.

In 1960, I became a guerrilla fighter when the Americans came. A lot of Hmong young men were recruited by General Vang Pao to serve in his army under the direct supervision of the Americans. General Vang Pao was our leader. All Hmong soldiers served under him. Wherever he went, we followed. If he stayed in a place, we also stayed there.

The Americans used airplanes to strike against the Communist forces, but the latter were not afraid. Though many Vietnamese died, those who were injured but could still stand kept on fighting till they could stand no more. The Vietnamese had good long-range cannon, which they used to strike at the Americans and at our villages. When we searched for the enemy, we did so on foot—no cars, no airplanes. People walked through the jungles. Many got sick and never recovered. Their comrades had to leave them behind to die a slow death. We were afraid of the Communist troops. There were too many of them. Fearful of dying, we moved from one place to another. But the Communists followed us and chased us all the way to the border of Thailand. The Vietnamese were engaged in a war that devastated, not only their own country, but ours as well because we were in the way of the Vietnamese forces moving south.

While I and other Hmong fought the Communists, our wives and children also suffered. We could not live in our villages any more and were forced to find shelter in caves in the jungles. Wild fruits and plants became our main diet. When I was seriously injured by a mine in 1962, I could no longer serve as a soldier, so I left the army and we moved to Long Cheng.

Those days were very frightening and stressful for all of us. I believe that many Hmong men, young and old, have died of the Sudden Unexplained Nocturnal Death Syndrome because they had flashbacks of their frightening experiences in Laos. Sometimes these flashbacks seem so real that the individuals having them believe them and their heartbeats increase very rapidly. Thus, these nightmares can have tragic consequences.

After General Vang Pao left the country, we went to Thailand and then came to the United States. When we first landed, we were astonished to see how remarkable and beautiful America is. Everything flourishes here. People have food and live in peace and freedom. America is great and prosperous. I like it here. I have no fear of war, so I am happy.

People say America is a country with golden opportunities, one filled with many cultures and traditions. There are many different faces in the United States, yet the people live close together. Since my family arrived, we have tasted the prosperity of this nation. If you want to understand how my family's life has changed in the United States, you must know the suffering, agony, and hardships we had experienced in Laos. In my old country, we were simple human beings. Farming was our way of life. We grew our own food. We lived peacefully in the highlands. Then war came. It brought destruction, suffering, and hatred. We were lucky we managed to get out of the chaos and reestablished our lives in the United States.

We arrived on January 21, 1979, in Rhode Island. It was a strange feeling. At the airport, white people stared at us as though we were the center of attention. Our sponsor, a very big, tall white man, was very nice. He provided us with financial assistance for the first few months, until we could receive federal aid for refugees. My brother-in-law drove me around Providence. I thought it was a big town, even though it is small compared to other American cities. The houses in Providence are very nice.

I found it very hard to adjust, but I like the land and its people. There are so many people with different traditions here. The hardest part of my adjustment was the language. We could not speak English. Everywhere we went, we had to depend on our relatives and friends who could. Now most of them are working, so this leads to complications. Whenever we need their help, they are not around. We have no car, but we do not want to walk because we are afraid we will get lost if we go to the stores by ourselves. As time passed, my children learned English and they began to take me places. They have been like my eyes and mouth. I speak through them. I no longer feel a handicap.

I like the life here because there are many different kinds of jobs— hard jobs, easy jobs. After a year, when our federal aid ran out, I had to go to work. I did various odd jobs, but it was very difficult. I did not know enough English to fill out the job application forms. Therefore, my sponsor suggested that I apply for public assistance while I went to adult education classes to learn English. Our public assistance application was approved. In my classes, they trained me to do various kinds of work. Most important of all, they taught me English. I tried very hard to learn the language, but since I was already an old man, it was very difficult for me. The teachers taught me and some other old Hmong men the basics: I can still remember saying, "a, b, c, d, e, . . ." after my teachers.

If given the chance, and if Laos becomes stable again, I would like to go back to live there, even though I am grateful that the United States has allowed us to settle here. This is a great country. But there is one thing I do not like: the country is too big. All my relatives live so far away, I have to ride a car for many days or fly on an airplane for hours to get to where they are. It is not like Laos, where everybody lived in one village or close enough so that we could walk to see them in a short time.

Another thing that has bothered me is that other children hate my children, and my children hate them back. I have seen black and Hispanic children fight. I have seen Hmong children fight with other people's children. My son told me that people discriminate against each other and that is why they fight. I do not like this. I see some black people hating us. I do not understand why they do. I do not hate them; why do they hate me and my family so much? They throw rocks and rotten eggs at my house. They call my children names. I do not understand why such things happen in such a wonderful country.

So far, however, my family life since I moved to California has been a success. We have many relatives here and we help each other. The weather in California is like that in Laos. I thank God for protecting my family for the last thirteen years that we have been in America.

The people in the United States are very industrious. I see people working all the time. I think this is good. I know there are many jobs available, so I am not worried about my children finding jobs. I know they will find good jobs to support themselves. I do not have to worry about them engaging in the same hard labor as I have done. I farmed and hunted in Laos. That was very hard. Now I see people working in large buildings in nice, cool, and quiet offices. They seldom sweat. I know my children will do just as well as these workers or even better.

Pang Yang's Life Story

as told to her son, Thek Moua

My ancestors originally came from China. Both my grandparents died before I was born. My parents told me very little about them. All I know is that my grandfather's name was Yang Mau Yee. My mother gave birth to Ah, Nou Tou, Txee, me, Cha Neng, and another daughter who passed away at the age of five. Today, Ah, Txee, Cha Neng, and I are still alive. Ah and Txee live in Rhode Island. Cha Neng lives in France. I lived in Santa Ana, California, until a year ago, when we moved to Sanger [a town in the San Joaquin Valley], because my husband got tired of living in the city and wanted to live in a small town. I, however, prefer living in the city.

From the age of seven onward, I was trained by my parents to run errands and do chores around the house. I began helping them farm when I was twelve. The planting season usually began in January, when trees were cut down and burned. Clearing the land took nearly two months. The ashes helped to soften the soil. We planted rice, corn, opium, and all kinds of vegetables like cabbage, green beans, squash, cucumbers, tomatoes, and lettuce. As they grew, we had to keep pulling out the weeds around each plant.

Each family grew only enough food to feed itself. If there was a surplus, we either sold it locally or took it to the lowlands and sold it in the market. Opium was our main trade item—we sold it for money, with which we bought food, fabric, thread, and farm tools. The cloth we used was made from a plant called *mang,* which was planted in April and harvested in July. The skin of the plant is peeled off and boiled so it becomes soft and white. The fabric is dried and made into dresses.

When I was thirteen, I married Moua Boua Neng. Our life was hard because farming was difficult. When my first two babies came, I had a hard time because there was no one to help me. While I worked in the fields, I strapped the younger one on my back. In Laos, each Hmong family was usually large. I myself had thirteen children, four of whom died before they reached maturity. The reason for having such large families is that we needed many hands to help with farming. The more children, the faster we could do our farmwork, especially at harvest time. One child fed the animals, another helped with the cooking, a third carried water from the well, while a fourth brought in the firewood, and so forth. Chores were divided and each was done very efficiently. My life became a little easier as soon as my first child, Ying, was old enough to look after the younger ones. He started babysitting his sister, Xay, when he was only two years old. Then, Ying and Xay learned to look after Thai, Thek, and Mai. Also, the more children—especially male children—a family has, the better chances the clan has to survive and to preserve our clan name.

On a typical day, I got up early in the morning, made breakfast for the family, and fed the animals. I packed lunch and placed it in a bamboo bucket, into which I also placed the hoes, axes, and knives. I carried the bucket on my back and tied the baby with a piece of cloth to my front. Once we reached our field, I untied the baby from my front and retied him on my back. Then farming began. Around noon—we judged the time by the position of the sun as we had no watches—we ate lunch while I breast-fed the baby. After lunch, we resumed farming. Around sunset, we gathered firewood and packed it to be carried home. Once again, I tied my baby to my front while carrying the firewood and tools on my back as we headed home. The walk was very tiring, but we had nothing to fear except bobcats or tigers. Our country had lots of tigers, but there were no thieves or robbers like you have in America. I prepared dinner as soon as we got home. I ground the rice and corn and also fed the animals. After dinner, I put the baby to sleep. Older children and adults went to bed around midnight. We got up again before dawn, as soon as the roosters crowed.

Our lives were difficult, but we were not endangered until the Vietnamese invaded our country. Until then, there was peace in our village. There was no stealing or acts of immorality. We had no worries when the harvests were good and our food lasted us through the year. After I married your father, we lived quietly in Pasa for two or three years. Then we moved to Hamongni, where I gave birth to Xay. We lived there for two years before moving to Pernong, where we remained for two harvests.

When our country was invaded by outsiders, fear gripped everyone in the villages. In Pernong, news of the invasion spread like wildfire. Everyone was scared. When the enemy got closer, we began to think of the options we had. People sold their animals—pigs, cows, horses, chickens—as well as their stored grain for cash, in preparation for departure. People also called on the shamans and sought the spirits' guidance in making their decisions about where to move. They offered sacrificial chickens to the spirits. Those who were Christians sang hymns and prayed.

When the Vietnamese soldiers came to Pernong, we fled to the Plain of Long Chao. The Vietnamese soldiers, however, were hot on our trail. When they caught up with us, we surrendered to them because there were so many of them and they threatened our lives. But we managed to escape and moved to Padong. Your father went off to serve in the army, while your grandmother, your aunt, and I were left behind to do the farming. We harvested only one crop at Padong. At the beginning of our second year there, just as we started to burn the land for planting, the Vietnamese soldiers reached Padong. So, once again we had to flee. We walked twenty days and nights to reach Long Cheng.

Meanwhile, your father was injured by a mine. His friends carried him for several days until they reached Taling, where they sent for a helicopter and flew him to Vientiane. His treatment took about six to ten months—I no longer remember how long. His legs got better and he was sent to Paka. When I heard the news, I carried Xay on my back and took Ying's hand and we walked for a whole day to get to Paka. I also carried about twenty-five pounds of rice and our blankets with me. After staying in Paka for a month, we all went back to Long Cheng, where we lived in a large house for about two years. Your father designed the house himself. It had two living rooms and two bedrooms.

Throughout this period, many people, including us, were very fearful. Though we continued to cultivate our fields by day, we did not dare sleep in our villages at night. Instead, we slept in the jungle. We were afraid that the Vietnamese soldiers might come to kill us all in the middle of the night. Very early in the morning, we would return to our village to see if any soldiers had passed through in the night. We quickly made breakfast and ate it before going to our fields. We came back earlier in the afternoon than we normally would have, hurriedly cooked and ate dinner and went off to hide in the jungle. When it rained, the night was unbearable. We had no roof over our heads. We slept under banana leaves. Our babies caught colds and pneumonia. Those who were lucky found caves to sleep in, but we could not build fires inside these cold, dark caves. The only light we had came from flashlights. It was a very frightening time.

From Long Cheng we moved to Sam Thong, where we stayed for two years. Our first harvest there was good, so we were able to carry the second harvest with us when we moved, once again, to Moua-ping. At that time, you, Thek, were still a baby, so I carried you. Thai, who was two, had to walk part of the way and was carried part of the way. Men carried our possessions, while women carried their children, one tied to their chest and another to their back. Our horses and oxen carried the heavier loads containing our food and utensils. There was no transportation, that's why we had to walk. My children, who were still young, had a very difficult time. Their feet were swollen with blisters. We were poor, so we could not afford shoes, which were very expensive. We walked from Sam Thong through the Nianue Valley to Nongpern and finally to Mouaping.

We never held our traditional New Year's celebrations during those long, hard years when we were constantly on the run. We were afraid that holding the celebrations would enable the Vietnamese soldiers to find us. Only after we settled into a refugee camp in Thailand could we have a celebration without fear.

We stayed at Mouaping for only two months. Then we went to Persanai, where we remained for three years. Next we moved to Vientiane and then to Napong. As Hmong civilians fled toward Thailand, they were sometimes escorted and protected by Hmong soldiers, some of whom walked in front of the group and some at the back. Soldiers also stayed behind to prevent the enemy from reaching us. The terrain was rough and the jungles were thick with shrubs, bamboo groves, and trees. The growth was so thick that it was very dark as very little sunlight shone through. Through this jungle, the Vietnamese troops chased us. The noise of gunshots and cannon fire was unbearable. It seemed to come from everywhere. We could hear the hissing sound of bullets flying over our heads. Night-time was especially difficult. It is only by God's grace that we are still alive today.

After living in Napong for one year, we crossed the Mekong River to Thailand. Many people lost their lives in that river. They were either shot by Communist troops or the Thai shore patrol or drowned while trying to swim across when the current was too strong. Some people bought rubber tubes from Lao or Thai merchants to help them swim across the river safely. But some were unlucky: they were caught between the bullets flying from both shores.

Our family was able to get a boat through the help of your uncle, Moua Yee. He paid our fare and the boatmen delivered us to the other side safely. The fare for each person was five hundred *baht* in Thai currency. We crossed the Mekong at 2 or 3 A.M.—the hour when most people tried to cross—because in the middle of the night there was less danger of encountering Thai patrol boats. In Thailand we stayed at the refugee camp in Ban Vinai, where we had to cut down trees and bamboo to build our own shelter when we first arrived. When the Thai government built wooden apartment complexes in the camp, we moved into one of those buildings.

Now I shall tell you about my life in the United States. I am very happy that my son Thek is working for his professor to produce a book on the Hmong, because my family and I have gone through so much, and most people don't even know about our suffering. I remember the exact date we arrived in the United States: January 21, 1979. What looked to me like salt was snow—the first amazing thing I saw when I landed in Rhode Island. Life at first was hard. We stayed with my husband's sister and her husband for the first three months. Our American sponsor helped us find a house and brought us many

American clothes. I am very happy they helped us so that we did not suffer much. They gave us food and money until the American government was able to issue refugee cash assistance to us. Later, our sponsor helped us to apply for public assistance until we could learn the American language and find jobs.

The American language is very hard to learn. Even today, I do not know it well. I still cannot read or write. I am so glad my sons and daughters have learned the language. I use them as my interpreters when I talk to Americans.

In September 1979, my children enrolled in a public school for the first time. I watched them quickly learn the American ways. They began to dress like American boys and girls. They soon talked like them and cut their hair like them. They made many friends, most of whom were black. I went to the parents–teachers conference and found out how the teachers were educating my children. I saw my children's report cards and was very proud that they got A's and B's. America has been good to us. We do not have to pay for my children's education, as I had to do for my eldest son Ying's schooling in Laos.

I am thankful that the American people let us stay in their country. They are very nice, and I am honored to have them as my neighbors. My neighbors bring my children cake and candy, and I cook many Hmong snacks and offer them to my neighbors in return. They like *na vanh* (a sweet, cold liquid soup) the best.

The first house we lived in in America was very nice and I liked it very much. It was yellow on the outside and light blue on the inside. It was very spacious. We had four bedrooms, two bathrooms, a kitchen, a living room, and a dining room. American houses are huge compared to our homes in Laos. Cooking food here is very fast and efficient. We do not have to gather wood, we do not have to stoke the fire, we only need to turn on a switch and the stove is on! This is very easy and requires very little labor. I have grown to like the American stove so much that I cook a lot.

My children often spoke of the hamburger, so I tried it. I like American food, but my body is not used to it. Often I get indigestion and other illnesses when I eat American food. My children prefer American food, so I have learned to cook them spaghetti, pizza, and hamburgers. They never seem to get tired of these foods. I also cook

Hmong food, but most of the time, my husband and I are the only ones eating it. If my stomach could tolerate any kind of food, I would eat more varieties.

My eldest son quickly learned the language and how to drive. He passed the test and helped us buy our first car. I was very scared to ride in it, but he took me shopping and the family to the park to play and relax. Having a car is very good: we do not have to walk everywhere. But I am scared of the roads because there are so many cars on them. I am afraid they might crash into each other and people get killed.

The longer we have lived in the United States, the better our lives have become. We attend a nice American church for Sunday worship and put our faith in Jesus Christ. Pastors are very respectable leaders in American communities. They help us understand the Bible and counsel my family about spiritual problems. Sometimes they bring us food and clothing.

My sons often speak of this country as the land of opportunity. At first, I did not understand why they called it that, but now I do. Not only are there public schools, but there are lots of jobs, friendly neighbors, and a rich environment. All these contribute to the greatness of the country.

Rhode Island has weather that changes from season to season. But in California, especially in Santa Ana, the weather is similar to that in Laos. The temperatures are not drastically cold in the winter; in the summer, the heat is not too intense. It is the kind of weather that Hmong are used to. Yet, I liked Rhode Island better. While we were living there, I noticed that our skins changed colors with the seasons: whiter in the winter and more tan in the summer.

My family has gone through many experiences. As a mother of thirteen children, I have faced sorrow and losses when some of my children passed away. One of my sons and three of my daughters died in Laos. My eldest son, Ying, died here suddenly one night in July 1990. I felt very sad that God had taken him away. I felt cheated. I cried for a very long time. But I am also thankful that I still have five sons and three daughters. One daughter is married and lives in Thailand. The rest are here in California. I feel very lucky to have them close to me. Any time I need to go anywhere, one of them takes me. My husband and I are now old. We are happy that our children are near us. They cook for us and take care of us, unlike Americans who put their aging parents in old folks' homes. I know those old people must be lonely. I do not understand why Americans would do that to their own parents. If my children did that to me, I would be very sad.

Nowadays, I see many Hmong children who have become Americanized. In the town of Sanger in Fresno County, where I now live, there are many bad Hmong children. Some of the teenagers become thieves, join gangs, party till very late at night, smoke, drink alcohol, take drugs, and have sex before marriage. Some who are married get divorced. There are many other bad things they do. I hope my children will never associate with such bad children. I do not want them to be influenced by the bad Hmong children when they meet them in school. I pray that they do not befriend such bad people, as I would fear for their safety.

In Fresno County, there are a lot of reports of gang shootings. Some of my relatives' children have become gang members in Fresno. They steal stereos and cars and demand money from old folks. They rob people's houses and minimarkets. I do not like these bad children. I wish the police would catch them and put all of them in jail.

I feel that the Americanized Hmong are too liberal. They let their children who want to be independent move out of the house when they turn nineteen or twenty. I think it is all right for some of the children to move out of the house so long as their old parents are taken care of in terms of cooking, doing the laundry, and in other ways. As long as someone remains to take care of the elders, then the rest can move out, if they wish.

Taking care of our old parents and grandparents is our tradition, our way of life. Even those Hmong who have become Americanized still keep this tradition. [I am not opposed to] Americanization [because it] helps us assimilate into American society better. But, at the same time, I feel Hmong culture should not be abandoned. Many children I have talked to deny their Hmong heritage. I feel ashamed of them. It is good to be Americanized, but we Hmong should never forget our heritage, our traditions, our way of life. We should always remember where we came from.

Surviving the Storms

by Thek Moua

According to my great-grandparents, the surname Moua originated in Mongolia during the sixteenth century. Moua means "to
conquer." It was a popular and well-known name. It is said that
many of the powerful leaders in Mongolia were named Moua. As
wars broke out, members of the Moua clan scattered to other parts
of China and carried their name with them. My great-grandparents
and grandparents said that the surname of the Communist leader,
Mao Zedong, may possibly have come from the name, Moua. They
said that as people moved, the pronunciation may have changed from
Moua to Mao.

My ancestors also told me that as a result of warfare, different clans
of Hmong moved into Southeast Asia, bringing their traditions and
customs with them. My people settled in Xieng Khouang Province,
Laos, where they lived in small villages. Most of my ancestors were
farmers, but several of them were blacksmiths. Among their progeny
were my father, Moua Boua Neng, and his younger brother, Moua
Yee. Since the Moua clan is so large, my own family is always identified as the Mouanoutoua family—Moua Nou Toua being the name
of my great, great-grandfather.

My parents grew up in two nearby villages in Xieng Khouang
Province. My parents told me that they enjoyed their childhood
enormously. They helped their parents with the work in the fields

while their older brothers went to school in Vientiane. At home, all the siblings shared chores. Sometimes they had an opportunity to travel with their parents to a town, where they went shopping and played with other children. My parents met and fell in love at first sight when they were teenagers. Although their families did not know each other well, my father did not allow this problem to stop him from loving and marrying my mother. Their wedding was a beautiful day, filled with happy singing and joyous shouting.

Some years after their wedding, my father was drafted into the Hmong army to serve under General Vang Pao, whose soldiers were fighting against the Communist forces from North Vietnam. My father had a hard time during the battles because he had never received any concrete military training. He managed to stay alive by using the skills he had learned as a hunter. Rather than fight according to the way he was told, he used hunting techniques, which he found to be more appropriate in the heart of the jungle.

Though his years in the military were very difficult, my father survived. But disaster struck at the beginning of 1962. During an ambush by the enemy, my father accidentally stepped on a mine. Both of his legs were seriously injured. He tried to get up but could not. He recalls that, before he lost consciousness, he was thinking he would be a cripple for the rest of his life. His friends abandoned him because they thought he was dead. But miraculously he did not die. His brother and some of our relatives carried him to an airstrip where they put him on a helicopter to be flown to a hospital in Vientiane. A few hours later, he woke up in the hospital. At first, he did not know where he was or why he was there, but after he talked to a nurse, he remembered what had happened.

After extensive treatment, my father was released from the hospital. The doctor considered him a handicapped person and recommended that he be discharged from military service. The doctor thought that if my father had to rejoin the army, he might very well become a cripple for the rest of his life. He refused to listen to the doctor: he wanted to remain in the military to defend his country from Communism. But many of his relatives and friends persuaded him to leave the army, so he returned home. He and my mother lived as farmers in a small village and had two children—my two older sisters. But my father never gave up his desire to fight for freedom.

My parents farmed by the slash-and-burn method. They cleared the field by cutting down trees and burning them. In those days, in Laos, they had no farm machinery, so they made a plow with sticks that had been sharpened at one end. They used this plow and a hoe to loosen up the earth before planting the seeds. When it was time to sow the seeds, they sharpened both ends of a stick, which one person used to poke holes in the ground while the other person dropped the grains of rice into the holes and covered them with dirt. Planting crops this way took a long time, but neighbors and relatives all helped each other. During the harvests, they used scythes as well as their bare hands to gather the crop. Like other farmers, my parents used methods that were very ancient. Farming in those days was very difficult and required a lot of labor under the hot sun.

Around 1973, the situation in Laos got worse and many people got killed. Our relatives in the military sent us news that the entire country was falling into the hands of the Pathet Lao. They told us that if we hoped to survive, we had to make plans to leave. Without any hesitation, my parents sold all their livestock and started making preparations for the journey.

Our trip to freedom was extremely difficult. We walked mainly during the night. People rarely traveled during the day because the chances that they would be spotted by the Pathet Lao troops were much greater in the daytime. We encountered many hardships along the way. Food was scarce. When we ran out of food, my parents fed us the tender shoots of bamboo. Also, my father shot and killed animals that we ate. This was the only way we had to keep up our strength in order to continue on our journey.

One of the terrible things we witnessed was that people whose children would not stop crying gave them opium. If the children got an overdose, they had very little chance of survival. Some died within a few hours. These poor children looked as though the blood in their arteries and veins had became clotted. Their hearts began to beat more and more slowly until they stopped. Some of the children vomited blood and within seconds, their bodies became as cold as ice. Young babies, especially, died instantaneously. Those parents with crying children who refused to give them some opium to keep them quiet were cast out of the group. People felt this had to be done to ensure everybody else's survival.

People who were too weak to walk were left behind to wither and die. They were given rifles with which to defend themselves, while the rest of the group continued on its journey. Those who had been shot or were injured in some other way received very little help. Their wounds did not heal because there was no medicine and no one to aid them. Individuals with no families especially suffered tremendously. Later, as I learned about Charles Darwin's theory about the survival of the fittest, I could not help recalling what I had seen on our journey to Thailand.

Life in Thailand was not easy either. When my family and I arrived at the refugee camp in Ban Vinai, I was about six years old. When my father discovered that the Thai government provided public education for everyone, he immediately enrolled me in school. I was initially placed in the first grade, but later that year I was promoted to the second grade. Due to my eagerness to learn and to be the best student in my class, my teacher often gave me rewards. Among these rewards, the one I have treasured most to this day was the privilege of helping my teacher teach the various subjects to the other students. My being chosen as the teacher's aide made my parents very proud of me. They were so happy that I was given this honor after our long, hard journey.

Most of my classmates were very nice to me. I remember one instance when some of the kids who disliked me tried to bully me, but in the end, they pretended nothing had happened because they knew quite well that if they mistreated me, they would have to face the wrath of our teacher, who was very strict and who showed very little mercy to those who crossed his path. Most of the time, he treated me kindly since I was his assistant and was one of the most popular students at school. However, he did punish me sometimes. I am grateful that he did because had he not done so, I would have become an arrogant brat and used my authority over the other kids to my own advantage.

The rules and regulations we had to follow in that school in Thailand were extremely strict. If we broke any of those rules, we were punished severely not only by the teacher but also by the principal. Unlike the United States, where all a student who breaks a rule gets is a referral or a phone call to the parents, students in Thailand who disobeyed rules were swatted by the principal. If these students continued to break the rules, they were expelled from school permanently. Parents approved of such discipline. I was swatted by the principal several times with a tiny, flat bamboo stick, and it was quite painful. I could hardly sit down afterwards.

In addition to the strict discipline, the school day seemed very long. Classes began at eight in the morning and ended at three in the afternoon. We had an hour for lunch, during which I played with my friends. Sometimes we played marbles; at other times we played soccer. I had classes in math, English, social studies, and art. Throughout my years of schooling in Thailand, I enjoyed those subjects tremendously. Although I found them all quite difficult, especially English, I looked upon them as challenges.

As far as other aspects of camp life were concerned, the housing, food, and sanitation were actually better than those in some Third World countries like India and Ethiopia. When we first arrived there was no housing, but sensing that many more refugees would be coming, the Thai government built huge apartment complexes at Ban Vinai to house them. Ten to fifteen families occupied each of these buildings. Although these structures were not well built compared to houses in the United States, they were certainly better than tents. During the years that my family and I were at Ban Vinai, conditions were not so bad as they became later. Food, however, was often scarce. The food was provided by the United States, the United Nations, and the Thai government. Realizing that there was insufficient food, the Thai government assigned each family a plot of ground to grow their own vegetables and other crops. Since all the Hmong knew how to farm, we did not suffer from starvation. Only those people who depended entirely on the food handouts sometimes starved.

After living in Ban Vinai for three years, my family decided to move to the United States. At first, there were many arguments among the family members. My father did not want to emigrate to the United States due to the various rumors he had heard. He was told that the United States was a wild, horrible, and corrupt country. In spite of my father's negative feelings, my older brother had made up his mind to leave for America, regardless of whether or not my father approved. After much discussion, we finally decided to take the risk and go to the United States.

In August 1978, the American Immigration Committee moved us to Bangkok. A few days before we boarded the bus for Bangkok, my oldest sister, Xay, got married. My parents opposed her decision very strongly but she was determined to get married, so all my family could do was to have the wedding ceremony several days before our departure. We were all very sad to leave my sister behind and to know that she would be separated from the rest of us by a great distance. I learned to accept our separation only years after I got here.

Bangkok is a beautiful city. While there, we were immunized against many illnesses. After several weeks, we flew to Hong Kong, where the plane refueled and where we stayed for a night. Then we flew over the Pacific Ocean to California and landed at LAX [Los Angeles International Airport], where we changed planes and flew on to New York. Finally, on January 21, 1979, we reached Providence, Rhode Island, at seven o'clock in the evening. All our relatives came to welcome us at the airport. Then they drove us to my uncle's house where our family spent our first night in America.

When I woke up the next morning, I saw snow for the first time. I didn't know what all the white powder on the ground was. I thought it was sugar provided by God. I went outside to take a closer look. I grabbed a handful and tasted it. I was surprised that it did not taste like sugar at all but more like cold water. Then I went back into the house and asked my uncle what the white powder was. It took him ten minutes to explain to me what snow is.

Life in America was hard in the beginning. For the first few weeks, my family and I lived with my uncle and aunt until we could find a decent place of our own. One very special moment that I still treasure was the first time I got lost in the big, bright city. We were visiting one of our relatives who lived only about half a mile from my uncle's house. Being a wise guy, I thought I could get back to my uncle's house without any problem. Instead of waiting for my uncle to drive us home, I decided to make the trip home on foot. For a while, everything seemed fine, but as I kept walking, I suddenly realized that the streets, intersections, and buildings all looked unfamiliar. That was when I knew for sure I was lost. I walked back and forth along the street so many times that my legs got really tired. I nearly collapsed on the sidewalk. Knowing that I was lost, I began to cry. Suddenly, as though by a miracle, I saw my uncle's car stop at a traffic light. I ran as fast as I could to the car, forgetting the ache in my legs. Hoping to catch his attention, I yelled extremely loudly.

Chapter Five

By the time I caught up with the car, I had nearly lost my voice. I was so relieved to ride home with the rest of my family. They asked me many questions, but I refused to admit that I had been lost in the big, bright city. Had I admitted that I was lost, my reputation as a smart kid and a wise guy would have been ruined!

It didn't take us long to find a perfect place to live. The house had three stories and each story was very spacious. Around the same time that we moved into our new home, I started school. I entered the third grade in an ESL [English as a Second Language] class. Although we were in the same classroom the whole day, we studied many different subjects. I did not have a hard time adjusting to class because I had already been exposed to education in Thailand. My greatest trial was learning the American culture so that I could befriend American students. I found it very hard to make friends at the beginning because some of the American students, especially the boys, discriminated against Asian students. They called us names, imitated our talk, and shoved us around. Their actions made me really mad. I wanted to fight them, but instead, I watched closely how those Asian students who were more Americanized behaved so that I could learn from them. By following their example, I soon made more friends than I needed. Having these friends made it easier for me to learn English. To this day, I still keep in touch with some of the friends I made in Rhode Island.

The person who influenced me the most and whom I admire very much was my fourth grade teacher, Angie Solitro. She had a way of helping her students learn easily and effectively. Through her, I was able to succeed in my educational career. I shall continue to admire her for the rest of my life.

Among my friends, the one I became closest to was Chee Lee. We did everything together during our childhood. The best times were when we spent the night at each other's house. With my parents' permission, we camped out in the backyard in a tent. Dressed up as cowboys and Indians, we played games similar to the scenes we saw in Westerns on television. Sometimes we got dressed up in our Boy Scout uniforms and reviewed what we had learned from our Scout masters at the Youth Missionary Catholic Association. In school, Chee Lee and I competed with each other in all the subjects because we were trying to prove to the girls we liked that one of us was better. At the end of the year, two Asian students were given awards for their academic achievement. I was one of the two. The principal announced at a school assembly that I was one of the smartest students at the school, and I received a two-dollar silver coin and a certificate with three gold seals on it, which I have kept to this day to remind me of my excellence in grade school.

Before I started intermediate school, my parents decided that it would be better for us to move to California. I could not understand why, but I sensed they thought such a move would be best for our family. Later, I found out from my grandmother that we had more relatives in California, and so my parents thought that if we went there, we could perhaps help one another more easily in times of difficulty. My mother also told me that the main reason we came to California was to help my uncle manage his grocery business. So during the summer of 1981, we moved to California, the Golden State. My grandmother and two of my sisters did it the easy way. They flew by plane while the rest of our family traveled by Greyhound bus in order to save money. Besides, we wanted an opportunity to see what the United States looked like. Initially, my parents had wanted to drive our white station wagon across the country, but my uncle advised them against doing so because they had not been in the United States long enough to familiarize themselves with the highways and driving laws of the different states. So we sold our car and took the bus.

Riding the bus across America was a great experience. I saw new places I had never dreamed of seeing. Some of the places and things I saw were absolutely gorgeous. The Grand Canyon is the loveliest sight I have ever seen in my entire life. As we rode past the Grand Canyon one evening, the setting sun made it look truly astonishing. The sunlight sparkled, the sky was ablaze with beautiful colors, and the Grand Canyon looked like a serene paradise. We arrived in California after an exciting and adventurous weeklong journey across the United States.

At summer's end, I enrolled in the sixth grade at Carr Intermediate School in Santa Ana. There, I spent three years of my life as a junior high school student. I became involved in a lot of school activities. Among the many clubs I joined, the Honor Society was the best; I really enjoyed being a member and an officer. The members of the club did various things together. One memorable activity was making Easter baskets, filling them with all kinds of candy and decorated eggs, and distributing them to the senior citizens in hospitals during Easter vacation. This was our way of telling the elderly people that others still cared about them.

After three years at Carr Intermediate School, I graduated with honors. My peers in the Honor Society and I had the privilege of leading the procession during the graduation ceremony. It was a day filled with joy and happiness. Then, in September 1984, I entered Los Amigos High School and remained there until my graduation in 1988. During my four years of high school, I went through a lot of spiritual, emotional, psychological, and political changes. I was in good standing academically; my grade-point average never fell below 3.3, which made me happy, given all the honors courses I was taking. Perhaps the best part of my high school years was my participation in the Orange County Academic Decathlon. As a member of the team, I enjoyed competing against students from various schools in the county. We had a tough time, especially during our preparation for the competition, but there were happy and joyful moments as well. Seeing my team's scores as we placed among the top-ten schools for three consecutive years made me feel really proud.

I was also on the tennis team. Although tennis is the only sport I can play decently, I nevertheless learned to enjoy athletics. But socially, I found it quite difficult to associate with some American students, especially those who were officers in the Associated Student Body. For some reason, I never got along with them. However, I became friends with some other Americans and we had the best times. Now that I understand how the lives of Asian Americans can be very hard at times, I shall not give up the fight for equality and acceptance. There were many times when I lost my battles, but I have also tasted the sweetness of victory.

As I look back at my high school career, those years were hard, stressful, and sometimes painful. In spite of the hardships, I have tried to do the best I was capable of. I am now a student at the University of California, Santa Barbara. I want to study pharmacology after I graduate, so in addition to the courses I am taking, I am doing an internship at Rivera Professional Pharmacy in Santa Barbara. I have also worked as a research assistant in the Biological Sciences department. I am proud of my accomplishments, which at times seemed impossible to achieve.

Over the years, the lives of members of my family have changed dramatically. Making the long, hard journey to escape Communism, witnessing the death of one of my younger brothers, saying good-bye to loved ones were the most painful moments for both me and my family. On the other hand, we feel our decision to come to the United States to live in a free country gave us some of the most joyful days of our lives. Now that the Moua family is surrounded by cousins, uncles, aunts, and other relatives and friends who have also immigrated to the United States from Laos and Thailand, all of us are thankful that God has carried each and every one of us through the terrible storm.

Epilogue
October, 1992

Of all my activities in college, the one that has been most inspiring and worthwhile is working as a research assistant for Professor Sucheng Chan to help her collect an anthology of life stories from several Hmong families in Isla Vista and Goleta,* in addition to the stories of my own family. Reaching out to these families has helped me learn better public relations skills. People have received me gladly into their homes to converse with them and often they have invited me to stay for dinner. They really made me feel welcome so that I was no longer a stranger in their midst.

Working on this research project has helped me to capture the beauty of my heritage. I have learned so much about my tradition and culture that I was unaware of before. I now realize that Hmong culture is quite unique, and I appreciate it even more than I used to. Perhaps this collection of Hmong life stories will help other people get a better sense of what Hmong tradition is like and how the Hmong have suffered so much to gain so little. Despite their suffering, these older people I have talked to gave me the sense that they are happy to have the privilege of living in a free country, knowing that their children and grandchildren will never experience the same kind of suffering, agony, and fear that they themselves have experienced.

---

*Only two of the interviews that Thek Moua did are included in this book. [*Ed.*]

Notes to the Introduction

1. Louisa Schein, "The Miao in Contemporary China: A Preliminary Overview," in *The Hmong in Transition*, ed. Glenn L. Hendricks, Bruce T. Downing, and Amos S. Deinard (Staten Island, N.Y.: Center for Migration Studies, 1986), 77.

2. Guy Morechand, "The Many Languages and Cultures of Laos," in *Laos: War and Revolution*, ed. Nina S. Adams and Alfred W. McCoy (New York: Harper Colophon Books, 1970), 33.

3. For brief histories of Laos before French colonization, see Arthur J. Dommen, *Laos: Keystone of Indochina* (Boulder, Colo.: Westview Press, 1985), 9–23; John K. Whitmore, "The Thai–Vietnamese Struggle for Laos in the Nineteenth Century," in *Laos: War and Revolution*, ed. Adams and McCoy, 53–66; and Martin Stuart-Fox, *Laos: Politics, Economics and Society* (London: Frances Pinter Publishers, 1986), 3–11.

4. Brief discussions of Laos's complex ethnic divisions may be found in Frank M. LeBar and Adrienne Suddard, *Laos: Its People, Its Society, Its Culture* (New Haven: Human Relations Area Files, 1960), 35–43; G. Linwood Barney, "The Meo of Xieng Khouang Province, Laos," in *Southeast Asian Tribes, Minorities and Nations*, ed. Peter Kunstadter (Princeton: Princeton University Press, 1967), 271–94; Stuart-Fox, *Laos: Politics, Economics and Society*, 44–51; and Morechand, "The Many Languages and Cultures of Laos," 29–34.

5. The following account of how France colonized Indochina is based on John F. Cady, *The Roots of French Imperialism in Eastern Asia*, rev. ed. (Ithaca, N.Y.: Cornell University Press, 1967); Alfred W. McCoy, "French Colonialism in Laos, 1893–1945," in *Laos: War and Revolution*, ed. Adams and McCoy, 67–99; Stuart-Fox, *Laos: Politics, Economics and Society*, 11–21; Dommen, *Laos: Keystone of Indochina*, 25–47; and Geoffrey C. Gunn, *Rebellion in Laos: Peasants and Politics in a Colonial Backwater* (Boulder, Colo.: Westview Press, 1990).

6. McCoy, "French Colonialism," 74–75.

7. Ibid., 82.

8. Gunn, *Rebellion in Laos*, 51.

9. McCoy, "French Colonialism," 85.

10. Gunn, *Rebellion in Laos*, 101–67, provides the most detailed analysis of these revolts, while McCoy, "French Colonialism," 87–92, provides a succinct summary of the events.

11. See Gunn, *Rebellion in Laos*, 109–12 and 114–26, for details. Gunn's account is based mainly on F. Moppert, "Le Révolte des Bolovens (1901–1936)," in *Histoire de l'Asie du Sud-est: Révoltes, Réformes, Révolutions*, ed. P. Brocheux (Lille, France: Universitaires de Lilles, 1981).

12. Gunn, *Rebellion in Laos*, 142–44.

13. Ibid., 149–60.

14. Gary Y. Lee, "Minority Policies and the Hmong," in *Contemporary Laos: Studies in the Politics and Society of the Lao People's Democratic Republic*, ed. Martin Stuart-Fox (New York: St. Martin's Press, 1982), 200–201. In an endnote, Lee states that the claim in M. Dasse, *Montagnards, Révoltes et Guerres Révolutionnaires en l'Asia du Sud-Est Continentale* (Bangkok: DK Book House, 1976), 124, "that Nong Het was allocated two *tasseng*, one for the Lo clan under Song Tou and one for the Lee under Lyfoung's [Ly Fong's] oldest son" is incorrect. Lee's own account is based on personal communication with Nhia Long Lee, "who was closely involved in the political events of the times." Ibid., 217.

15. McCoy, "French Colonialism," 97–98; Gunn, *Rebellion in Laos*, 160–62; and Alfred W. McCoy, with Cathleen B. Reed and Leonard P. Adams II, *The Politics of Heroin in Southeast Asia* (New York: Harper Colophon Books, 1972), 81–85.

16. Arthur J. Dommen, *Conflict in Laos: The Politics of Neutralization*, rev. ed. (New York: Praeger Publishers, 1971), 75.

17. David Feingold, "Opium and Politics in Laos," in *Laos: War and Revolution*, ed. Adams and McCoy, 325.

18. Joseph Westermeyer, *Poppies, Pipes, and People: Opium and Its Uses in Laos* (Berkeley and Los Angeles: University of California Press, 1982), provides the most detailed discussions of opium and its medical and addictive qualities. See also McCoy, *Politics of Heroin*, for an account of the contemporary opium and heroin traffic.

19. Gunn, *Rebellion in Laos*, 162.

20. This account of cultivation is based on Westermeyer, *Poppies, Pipes, and People*, 37–42, and Feingold, "Opium and Politics," 327–32.

21. Westermeyer, *Poppies, Pipes, and People*, 44.

22. Feingold, "Opium and Politics," 335.

23. McCoy, *Politics of Heroin*, 2–5.

24. For details, see ibid., 15–57.

25. Feingold, "Opium and Politics," 335–36. Feingold's evidence comes from a series of articles in the French newspaper, *Le Monde*, November 22 and 23, 1953, and from John T. McAlister, *Vietnam: The Origins of a Revolution* (New York: Alfred A. Knopf, 1969), 240; Joseph Buttinger, *Vietnam: A Dragon Embattled* (New York: Praeger Publishers, 1967), 792; and Hugh Toye, *Laos: Buffer State or Battleground* (New York: Oxford University Press, 1968), 130.

26. Dommen, *Laos: Keystone of Indochina*, 29–30.

27. McCoy, "French Colonialism," 92–95.

28. Ibid., 96.

29. Dommen, *Laos: Keystone of Indochina*, 30.

30. Ibid., 32; and Nina S. Adams, "Patrons, Clients, and Revolutionaries: The Lao Search for Independence, 1945–1954," in *Laos: War and Revolution*, ed. Adams and McCoy, 103–4.

31. Dommen, *Laos: Keystone of Indochina*, 33–35; and Adams, "Patrons, Clients, and Revolutionaries," 107–8.

32. Dommen, *Laos: Keystone of Indochina*, 33–38; and Adams, "Patrons, Clients, and Revolutionaries," 108.

33. Dommen, *Laos: Keystone of Indochina*, 36.

34. Ibid., 38–39.

35. Bernard B. Fall, *Anatomy of a Crisis: The Laotian Crisis of 1960–1961*, ed. by Roger M. Smith (Garden City, N.Y.: Doubleday, 1969), 43. For detailed histories of the Pathet Lao, see Paul F. Langer and Joseph J. Zasloff, *North Vietnam and the Pathet Lao: Partners in the Struggle for Laos* (Cambridge, Mass.: Harvard University Press, 1970); Joseph J. Zasloff, *The Pathet Lao: Leadership and Organization* (Lexington, Mass.: Lexington Books, 1973); MacAlister Brown and Joseph J. Zasloff, *Apprentice Revolutionaries: The Communist Movement in Laos, 1930–1985* (Stanford, Calif.: Hoover Institution Press, 1986); and C. J. Christie, "Nationalism and the Pathet Lao," in *Contemporary Laos*, ed. Stuart-Fox, 62–75. For accounts by two of the Pathet Lao's key leaders, Prince Souphanouvong and Kaysone Phomvihane, see *A Quarter Century of Grim and Victorious Struggle* (Khang Khay [?], Laos: Central Committee of the Neo Lao Haksat, 1970).

36. Fall, *Anatomy of a Crisis*, 46–57, and Dommen, *Conflict in Laos*, 40–45.

37. Adams, "Patrons, Clients, and Revolutionaries," 117.

38. Jane Hamilton-Merritt, *Tragic Mountains: The Hmong, the Americans, and the Secret Wars for Laos, 1942–1992* (Bloomington: Indiana University Press, 1993), 48, 56, and Fall, *Anatomy of a Crisis*, 49.

39. Fall, *Anatomy of a Crisis*, 52.

40. Ibid., 53–54.

41. Dommen, *Conflict in Laos*, 42–43. For a classic account of Dien Bien Phu, see Bernard B. Fall, *Hell in a Very Small Place: The Siege of Dien Bien Phu* (New York: Vintage Books, 1968). See also Jules Roy, *Battle of Dienbienphu*, 2nd. printing of English trans. (New York: Carroll and Graf, 1984).

42. Charles A. Stevenson, *The End of Nowhere: American Policy toward Laos since 1954* (Boston: Beacon, 1972), 20.

43. Ibid., 28.

44. Detailed discussions of postindependence politics in Laos include Roger Smith, "Laos," in *Governments and Politics of Southeast Asia*, ed. George McTurnan Kahin (Ithaca, N.Y.: Cornell University Press, 1964), 527–92; Roger Hilsman, *To Move a Nation* (Garden City, N.Y.: Doubleday, 1967), 91–155; Toye, *Laos: Buffer State or Battleground;* Fall, *Anatomy of a Crisis;* Dommen, *Conflict in Laos;* Stevenson, *End of Nowhere;* Marek Thee, *Notes of a Witness: Laos and the Second Indochina War* (New York: Vintage, 1973); Perala Ratnam, *Laos and the Superpowers* (New Delhi, India: Tulsi Publishing House, 1980); and Dommen, *Laos: Keystone of Indochina*, 49–103. On the Pathet Lao, see the citations in note 35.

45. Stevenson, *End of Nowhere*, 39; Charles M. Simpson III, *Inside the Green Berets, The First Thirty Years: A History of the U.S. Army Special Forces* (Novato, Calif.: Presidio Press, 1983), 88; and Shelby L. Stanton, *Green Berets at War: U.S. Special Forces in Southeast Asia, 1956–1975* (Novato, Calif.: Presidio Press, 1985), 16.

46. Len E. Ackland, "No Place for Neutralism: The Eisenhower Administration and Laos," in *Laos: War and Revolution*, ed. Adams and McCoy, 143.

47. Stevenson, *End of Nowhere*, 35.

48. Ibid., 46–47.

49. Ibid., 47–48; Ackland, "No Place for Neutralism," 148–49; and Fall, *Anatomy of a Crisis*, 109.

50. Stevenson, *End of Nowhere*, 58–59; Stuart-Fox, *Laos: Politics, Economics and Society*, 22; and Brown and Zasloff, *Apprentice Revolutionaries*, 63–64.

51. Stevenson, *End of Nowhere*, 66, and Dommen, *Conflict in Laos*, 110.

52. Brown and MacAlister, *Apprentice Revolutionaries*, 68, 70, and Dommen, *Conflict in Laos*, 137–39.

53. Dommen, *Laos: Keystone of Indochina*, 62–63; Ackland, "No Place for Neutralism," 152; Stevenson, *End of Nowhere*, 85–87; Dommen, *Conflict in Laos*, 133–34; and Toye, *Laos: Buffer State or Battleground*, 133–35.

54. Dommen, *Conflict in Laos*, 129–33.

55. Ibid., 140–46, and Toye, *Laos: Buffer State or Battleground*, 141–45.

56. Dommen, *Conflict in Laos*, 147–51, 154, 160. Air America was originally established by General Claire Chennault during World War II as the

Flying Tigers to supply Chiang Kai-shek's government in Chungking, China. For more information, see Scott, "Air America," in *Laos: War and Revolution,* ed. Adams and McCoy, 301–21. The *New York Times* published an article on October 10, 1961, claiming that General Phoumi Nosavan had been "persuaded to spurn his post in the Government and to rebel against it by agents of the C.I.A. and the U.S. military officers stationed in Laos." Quoted in Toye, *Laos: Buffer State or Battleground,* 149.

57. Dommen, *Conflict in Laos,* 152.

58. Fall, *Anatomy of a Crisis,* 171–72, and Dommen, *Conflict in Laos,* 155–56.

59. Dommen, *Conflict in Laos,* 166–67; Fall, *Anatomy of a Crisis,* 195–97; and Toye, *Laos: Buffer State or Battleground,* 157–59.

60. Dommen, *Conflict in Laos,* 167–69, and Stevenson, *End of Nowhere,* 150.

61. Simpson III, *Inside the Green Berets,* 88–89.

62. This is the only name given in Hamilton-Merritt, *Tragic Mountains,* which contains the only account of how the CIA actually made contact with Vang Pao. At the time, "Colonel Billy" had his headquarters at the American air base in Udon, Thailand, where he trained the Thai Police Aerial Reinforcement Units, made up of experts in communications, intelligence, and weaponry, each of whom spoke several languages and was an experienced parachutist. His title, "Colonel," had been conferred on him by the Thai. Ibid., 78–79.

63. Ibid., 54–66.

64. Ibid., 89.

65. Ibid., 92.

66. D. Gareth Porter, "After Geneva: Subverting Laotian Neutrality," in *Laos: War and Revolution,* ed. Adams and McCoy, 183. Porter's assertions are based on an interview with a Special Forces officer who was sent to train the Hmong in 1959, and on Fall, *Anatomy of a Crisis,* 189, and Barney, "Meo of Xieng Khouang Province," 275.

67. Stanton, *Green Berets at War,* 23–24, and Porter, "After Geneva," 184. According to Stevenson, *End of Nowhere,* 153, not only did Kennedy decide to use the U.S. Special Forces to train the Hmong, he also authorized covert operations against the North Vietnamese—by sending infiltrating agents into North Vietnam for sabotage purposes and South Vietnamese forces into Laos on intelligence and harassment missions.

68. Stanton, *Green Berets at War,* 23.

69. Fall, *Anatomy of a Crisis,* 207, and Dommen, *Conflict in Laos,* 207–8.

70. Dommen, *Conflict in Laos,* 204–5; Toye, *Laos: Buffer State or Battleground,* 192; and Stevenson, *End of Nowhere,* 154.

71. Dommen, *Laos: Keystone of Indochina*, 72–73; Toye, *Laos: Buffer State or Battleground*, 182–84; and Jonathan Mirsky and Stephen E. Stonefield, "The Nam Tha Crisis: Kennedy and the New Frontier on the Brink," in *Laos: War and Revolution*, ed. Adams and McCoy, 155–78.

72. Toye, *Laos: Buffer State or Battleground*, 186–88, and Dommen, *Conflict in Laos*, 223.

73. Stevenson, *End of Nowhere*, 182.

74. Ibid., 185–87. According to Stevenson, the code name for this CIA effort was Operation Hardnose. Stevenson cites a *New York Times* article dated October 26, 1969, that stated: "The Central Intelligence Agency then took over the functions [of organizing, training, and equippping the Meo], sometimes using officers who had resigned from the Army so they could continue their tasks."

75. Hamilton-Merritt, *Tragic Mountains*, 134.

76. Stevenson, *End of Nowhere*, 233.

77. Hamilton-Merritt, *Tragic Mountains*, 138.

78. Stevenson, *End of Nowhere*, 187.

79. Toye, *Laos: Buffer State or Battleground*, 190–91.

80. Dommen, *Conflict in Laos*, 247–54.

81. Stevenson, *End of Nowhere*, 198. The most detailed account of what happened to the Hmong during this period is found in Hamilton-Merritt, *Tragic Mountains*, 113–54.

82. Stevenson, *End of Nowhere*, 251–60, and Toye, *Laos: Buffer State or Battleground*, 192.

83. Stevenson, *End of Nowhere*, 196.

84. Dommen, *Conflict in Laos*, 291, 287.

85. Stevenson, *End of Nowhere*, 216.

86. Ibid., 201–8.

87. Ibid., 213.

88. Hamilton-Merritt, *Tragic Mountains*, 147, 172–74.

89. Ibid., 178–87.

90. Stevenson, *End of Nowhere*, 210.

91. Ibid., 212–14.

92. Hamilton-Merritt, *Tragic Mountains*, 213.

93. Stevenson, *End of Nowhere*, 212.

94. Hamilton-Merritt, *Tragic Mountains*, 334.

95. Ibid., 222.

96. Fred Branfman, *Voices from the Plain of Jars: Life under an Air War* (New York: Harper Colophon Books, 1972), provides the most details (including oral histories taken from dozens of refugees) about the destruction of the Plain of Jars.

97. Hamilton-Merritt, *Tragic Mountains,* 242.

98. Ibid., 277–90.

99. Stevenson, *End of Nowhere,* 224–26 and 230.

100. Lee, "Minority Policies and the Hmong," 204.

101. Stuart-Fox, *Laos: Politics, Economics and Society,* 30–31.

102. MacAlister Brown, "The Communist Seizure of Power in Laos," in *Contemporary Laos,* ed. Stuart-Fox, 22, and *Far Eastern Economic Review 1976 Yearbook,* 200–203.

103. Lee, "Minority Policies and the Hmong," 204, and Hamilton-Merritt, *Tragic Mountains,* 340.

104. Hamilton-Merritt, *Tragic Mountains,* 341.

105. Brown, "Communist Seizure of Power," 36, note 10.

106. Hamilton-Merritt, *Tragic Mountains,* 342–46.

107. Lee, "Minority Policies and the Hmong," 206–7.

108. Ibid., 213, and *Far Eastern Economic Review 1977 Yearbook,* 214–15.

109. Lee, "Minority Policies and the Hmong," 207, and Gary D. Wekkin, "The Rewards of Revolution: Pathet Lao Policy towards the Hill Tribes since 1975," in *Contemporary Laos,* ed. Stuart-Fox, 189.

110. Wekkin, "Rewards of Revolution," 192; Lee, "Minority Policies and the Hmong," 213–14; *Far Eastern Economic Review 1979 Yearbook,* 227; John McBeth, "Tracing Gas Leak," *Far Eastern Economic Review,* August 24, 1979; J. Hamilton-Merritt, "Poison-Gas War in Laos," *Reader's Digest,* October 1980, 36; Grant Evans, *The Yellow Rainmakers: Are Chemical Weapons Being Used in Southeast Asia?* (London: Verso, 1983); Frank Viviano, "Strangers in the Promised Land," *San Francisco Examiner Image Magazine,* August 31, 1986; and Hamilton-Merritt, *Tragic Mountains,* 390–460.

111. Hamilton-Merritt, *Tragic Mountains,* 393–99.

112. The issue of whether or not chemical weapons were used in Laos has never been settled. C. Dennison Lane, a former U.S. Army officer who served long years in Indochina, stated in a review of Jane Hamilton-Merritt's book in the *Wall Street Journal,* May 14, 1993, that while "no canister for dispensing the poison was ever found," the U.S. government did collect about eighty environmental samples from Laos and Cambodia between 1979 and 1986. Due to bureaucratic infighting in Washington, only six of these were analyzed. "All six tested positive for the presence of trichothecenes." Douglas Pike, a leading expert on the political and military history of the Vietnam War, said, "It now seems indisputable that *someone* [emphasis added] has been engaged in chemical warfare in these two countries. Something more than bee defecation has been going on in the hills in Laos and Kampuchea backcountry in the 1980s. Quite probably it is third-generation chemical warfare agents—biodegradable mycotoxins—

being tested by Soviet research-and-development scientists, with the assistance of the PAVN [People's Army of Vietnam] Chemical Force, certainly not without its knowledge." Douglas Pike, *PAVN: People's Army of Vietnam* (Novato: Calif.: Presidio Press, 1986), 259. The "bee defecation" refers to a theory propounded by Matthew Meselson, a Harvard scientist, who claimed that the "yellow rain" must have been bee excrement, and not chemical poisons.

113. Wekkin, "Rewards of Revolution," 189.

114. *Far Eastern Economic Review 1990 Yearbook,* 163.

115. *Far Eastern Economic Review 1979 Yearbook,* 227, and *Far Eastern Economic Review 1982 Yearbook,* 186.

116. *Far Eastern Economic Review 1979 Yearbook,* 229.

117. *Far Eastern Economic Review 1982 Yearbook,* 186.

118. Keith B. Richburg, "Insurgency in Laos Seeking to Emerge from Anonymity," *Washington Post,* February 11, 1990.

119. Claudia Rosett, "A Lonely Lao Fight for Freedom," *Wall Street Journal,* June 13, 1990.

120. *Far Eastern Economic Review 1991 Yearbook,* 149–50.

121. Ruth E. Hammond, "Sad Suspicions of a Refugee Ripoff: The Hmong Are Paying to Free Laos," *Washington Post,* April 16, 1989, and Seth Mydans, "California Says Laos Refugee Group Is a Victim of Leadership's Extortion," *New York Times,* November 7, 1990.

122. Wekkin, "Rewards of Revolution," 191.

123. Lee, "Minority Policies and the Hmong," 211.

124. Gil Loescher and John A. Scanlan, *Calculated Kindness: Refugees and America's Half-Open Door, 1945–Present* (New York: Free Press, 1986), 119.

125. Ibid., 125, 127.

126. Timothy Dunnigan, "Segmentary Kinship in an Urban Society: The Hmong of St. Paul–Minneapolis," *Anthropological Quarterly* 55:3 (1982): 126–34; John Finck, "Clan Leadership in the Hmong Community of Providence, Rhode Island," in *The Hmong in the West: Observations and Reports,* ed. Bruce T. Downing and Douglas P. Olney (Minneapolis: University of Minnesota, Center for Urban and Regional Affairs, Southeast Asian Refugee Studies Project, 1982), 21–28; George M. Scott, Jr., "The Hmong Refugee Community in San Diego: Theoretical and Practical Implications of Its Continuing Ethnic Solidarity," *Anthropological Quarterly* 55:3 (1982): 146–60; Cheu Thao, "Hmong Migration and Leadership in Laos and in the United States," in *Hmong in the West,* ed. Downing and Olney, 99–121; Christopher L. Hayes, "A Study of the Older Hmong Refugees in the United States" (Ph.D. diss., Fielding Institute, 1984); Kent A. Bishop, "The Hmong of Central California: An Investigation and Analysis of the Changing Family Structure during

Liminality, Acculturation, and Transition" (Ed.D. diss., University of San Francisco, 1985); Catherine S. Gross, "The Hmong in Isla Vista: Obstacles and Enhancement to Adjustment," in *Hmong in Transition,* ed. Glenn L. Hendricks, Bruce T. Downing, and Amos S. Deinard (Staten Island, N.Y.: Center for Migration Studies, 1986), 145–57; William H. Meredith and George P. Rowe, "Changes in Lao Hmong Marital Attitudes after Immigrating to the United States," *Journal of Comparative Family Studies* 17 (1986): 117–26; George M. Scott, Jr., "Migrants without Mountains: The Politics of Sociocultural Adjustment among the Lao Hmong Refugees in San Diego" (Ph.D. diss., University of California, San Diego, 1986); Hisashi Hirayama and Kasumi K. Hirayama, "Stress, Social Supports, and Adaptational Patterns in Hmong Refugee Families," *Amerasia Journal* 14:1 (1988): 93–108; Kathryn Rick, "An Investigation of the Process of Biculturation with Hmong Refugees" (Ph.D. diss., University of Colorado, Boulder, 1988); Joan Strouse, "The Reformation of Culture: Hmong Refugees from Laos," *Journal of Refugee Studies* 1 (1988): 20–37; Nancy Dorelle Donnelly, "The Changing Lives of Refugee Hmong Women" (Ph.D. diss., University of Washington, 1989); Sally Nina Peterson, "From the Heart and the Mind: Creating *Paj Ntaub* in the Context of Community" (Ph.D. diss., University of Pennsylvania, 1990); and Kathryn Rick and John Forward, "Acculturation and Perceived Intergenerational Differences among Hmong Youth," *Journal of Cross-Cultural Psychology* 23 (1992): 85–94.

127. Donald R. Sonsala, "A Comparative Case Study of Secondary Programs for Hmong Refugee Students in the Minneapolis and St. Paul Public Schools" (Ph.D. diss., University of Minnesota, 1984); Beth L. Goldstein, "Schooling for Cultural Transitions: Hmong Girls and Boys in American High Schools" (Ph.D. diss., University of Wisconsin, Madison, 1985); Renee E. Lemieux, "A Study of the Adaptation of Hmong First, Second, and Third Graders to the Minneapolis Public Schools" (Ph.D. diss., University of Minnesota, 1985); Joan Strouse, "Continuing Themes in U.S. Educational Policy for Immigrants and Refugees: The Hmong Experience" (Ph.D. diss., University of Wisconsin, Madison, 1985); Gail Weinstein-Shr, "From Mountaintops to City Streets: An Ethnographic Investigation of Literacy and Social Process among the Hmong of Philadelphia" (Ph.D. diss., University of Pennsylvania, 1986); Lila Jacobs, "Differential Participation and Skill Levels in Four Hmong Third Grade Students: The Social and Cultural Context of Teaching and Learning" (Ph.D. diss., University of California, Santa Barbara, 1987); Luc G. Janssens, "The Integration of Hmong Adults into American Society through the Community College: A Participatory Study of the Possibilities of Cultural Preservation" (Ed.D. diss., University of San Francisco, 1987); Finian McGinn, "Hmong Literacy

among Hmong Adolescents and the Use of Hmong Literacy during Resettlement" (Ed.D. diss., University of San Francisco, 1989); Henry T. Trueba, Lila Jacobs, and Elizabeth Kirton, *Cultural Conflict and Adaptation: The Case of Hmong Children in American Society* (New York: Falmer Press, 1990); May Yang, "The Education of Hmong Women," *Vietnam Generation* 2:3 (1990): 62–87; Sylvia Silva Lopez-Romano, "Integration of Community and Learning among Southeast Asian Newcomer Hmong Parents and Children" (Ed. D. diss., University of San Francisco, 1991); Colette L. Miller, "Some Contextual Problems Relative to the Acquisition of Literacy by Hmong Refugees" (M.A. thesis, California State University, Long Beach, 1991); and Joan Caryl Ostergren, "Relationships among English Performance, Self-Efficacy, Anxiety, and Depression for Hmong Refugees" (Ph.D. diss., University of Minnesota, 1991).

128. Ronald Munger, "Sudden Adult Death in Asian Populations: The Case of the Hmong," in *Hmong in the West,* ed. Downing and Olney, 307–19; Joseph I. Tobin and Joan Friedman, "Spirits, Shamans, and Nightmare Death: Survival Stress in a Hmong Refugee," *American Journal of Orthopsychiatry* 53 (1983): 439–48; Elizabeth Stewart Kirton, "The Locked Medicine Cabinet: Hmong Health Care in America" (Ph.D. diss., University of California, Santa Barbara, 1985); Bruce Thowpaou Bliatout, "Guidelines for Mental Health Professionals to Help Hmong Clients Seek Traditional Healing Treatment," in *Hmong in Transition,* ed. Hendricks, Downing, and Deinard, 349–63; Charles C. Irby and Ernest Pon, "Confronting New Mountains: Mental Health Problems among Male Hmong and Mien Refugees," *Amerasia Journal* 14:1 (1988): 109–18; Cerhan Ju, "The Hmong in the United States: An Overview for Mental Health Professionals," *Journal of Counseling and Development* 69 (1990): 88–92; Shelley R. Adler, "The Role of the Nightmare in Hmong Sudden Unexpected Nocturnal Death Syndrome: A Folkloristic Study of Belief and Health" (Ph.D. diss., University of California, Los Angeles, 1991); idem, "Sudden Unexpected Nocturnal Death Syndrome among Hmong Immigrants: Examining the Role of the Nightmare," *Journal of American Folklore* 104 (1991): 54–71; Pao Lee, "Health Care System Utilized by the Hmong in California: A Case Study in Stanislaus County" (M.A. thesis, California State University, Stanislaus, 1991); and B. Rairdan and Z. R. Higgs, "When Your Patient Is a Hmong Refugee," *American Journal of Nursing* 92 (1992): 52–55.

129. Glenn L. Hendricks and Brad Richardson, "Hmong in the Workplace," in *Hmong in the West,* ed. Downing and Olney, 387–401; William Hugh Meredith, "Level and Correlates of Perceived Quality of Life for Lao Hmong Refugees in Nebraska" (Ph.D. diss., University of Nebraska, Lincoln, 1983); Banjerd Bill Ukapatayasakul, "Hmong Refugee Economic

Adjustment in a California Community" (Ph.D. diss., United States International University, 1983); Sarah R. Mason, "Training Hmong Women for Marginal Work or Entry into the Mainstream," in *Hmong in Transition*, ed. Hendricks, Downing, and Deinard, 101–20; and George M. Scott, Jr., "The Advent of a Cottage Industry of Hmong *Paj Ntaub* Textiles in Southern California: The Roles of an Entrepreneur-Patron, an Applied Anthropologist-Broker, and a Shopping Mall Sale," *Human Organization* 51 (1992): 284–98.

130. Scott, "Migrants without Mountains," 12.

131. Ibid., 23–26.

132. Ibid., 119–22.

133. Ibid., 123–34.

134. Ibid., 149–50, 154, 162.

135. Ibid., 151, 208.

136. Ibid., 163.

137. Ibid., 235–39, 245, 247.

138. Nancy Dorelle Donnelly, "The Changing Lives of Refugee Hmong Women" (Ph.D. diss., University of Washington, 1989), 148.

139. Scott, "Migrants without Mountains," 291–319; Hayes, "A Study of the Older Hmong Refugees in the United States," 135–40; and Weinstein-Shr, "From Mountaintops to City Streets," 98–119.

140. Goldstein, "Schooling for Cultural Transitions," 100–102.

141. Donnelly, "Changing Lives of Hmong Women," 156.

142. Hayes, "A Study of the Older Hmong Refugees," 161; Weinstein-Shr, "From Mountaintops to City Streets," 51–67, 120–132; and Peterson, "From the Heart and the Mind," passim.

143. Donnelly, "Changing Lives of Hmong Women," 157.

144. Goldstein, "Schooling for Cultural Transitions," 213.

145. Trueba, Jacobs, and Kirton, *Cultural Conflict and Adaptation,* 67.

146. Strouse, "Continuing Themes in U.S. Educational Policy for Immigrants and Refugees," 65–66; Goldstein, "Schooling for Cultural Transitions," 29–32; and Trueba, Jacobs, and Kirton, *Cultural Conflict and Adaptation,* 2, 15–16.

147. Miller, "Some Contextual Problems Relative to the Acquisition of Literacy by Hmong Refugees," 60–71.

148. Lemieux, "A Study of the Adaptation of Hmong First, Second, and Third Graders," 71 and 73.

149. Goldstein, "Schooling for Cultural Transitions," 104–6.

150. P. Silverman and R. Maxwell, "How Do I Respect Thee? Let Me Count the Ways: Deference towards Elderly Men and Women," *Behavioral Science Research* 13 (1978), as cited in Hayes, "A Study of the Older Hmong Refugees," 63–64.

151. Hayes, "A Study of the Older Hmong Refugees," 73, 83.

152. J. Jackson, "Aged Negroes: Their Cultural Departures from Statistical Stereotypes and Rural-Urban Differences," *Gerontologist* 10 (1970): 140–45, as cited in Hayes, "A Study of the Older Hmong Refugees," 34.

153. Hayes, "A Study of the Older Hmong Refugees," 97.

154. Ibid., 107.

155. Ibid., 133.

156. Ibid., 172, 213–14.

157. Bishop, "Hmong of Central California," 98.

158. Ibid., 144–45.

159. Ibid., 137.

160. Goldstein, "Schooling for Cultural Transitions," 116–17.

161. Trueba, Jacobs, and Kirton, *Cultural Conflict and Adaptation,* xiii.

162. Cheu Thao, "Hmong Migration and Leadership," 114–19.

Selected Bibliography

This bibliography contains only writings in English. There is a sizable literature on the Hmong (also called Miao and Meo) in Chinese and French and, to a lesser extent, in Hmong and German. The listings in the section on Laos are relatively selective, while the listings in the two sections on the Hmong are more extensive. Two kinds of studies, however, are not included in this bibliography. The first category is technical linguistic studies of the Hmong language and studies of methods for teaching English to the Hmong (exceptions are those items that contain some discussion of the social context of language learning). Scientific reports on the medical, health, and mental health conditions of the Hmong, with the exception of a few that make more general observations about the Hmong's overall well-being, have also been excluded.

Many, but not all, of the individual chapters in the anthologies edited by Nina S. Adams and Alfred W. McCoy (1970); Bruce T. Downing and Douglas P. Olney (1982); and Glenn L. Hendricks, Bruce T. Downing, and Amos S. Deinard (1986) are listed separately in this bibliography. Readers interested in knowing what other topics are discussed in these three volumes should consult the books themselves. All of the chapters in the anthologies edited by Martin Stuart-Fox (1982) and by Joseph J. Zasloff and Leonard Unger (1991) are shown individually below.

For journal articles, issue numbers are given only when a journal does not use continuous pagination in the successive issues of each volume. With a handful of exceptions, articles less than ten pages long in periodicals or journals are not included in this bibliography.

Laos

Ackland, Len E. "No Place for Neutralism: The Eisenhower Administration and Laos," in *Laos: War and Revolution,* ed. Nina S. Adams and Alfred W. McCoy. New York: Harper Colophon Books, 1970, 139–54.

Adams, Nina S., and Alfred W. McCoy, eds. *Laos: War and Revolution.* New York: Harper Colophon Books, 1970.

Adams, Nina S. "Patrons, Clients, and Revolutionaries: The Lao Search for Independence, 1945–1954," in *Laos: War and Revolution,* ed. Nina S. Adams and Alfred W. McCoy. New York: Harper Colophon Books, 1970, 100–20.

Amnesty International. *Political Prisoners in the People's Democratic Republic of Laos.* London: Amnesty International, 1980.

Batson, Wendy. "After the Revolution: Ethnic Minorities and the New Lao State," in *Laos: Beyond the Revolution,* ed. Joseph J. Zasloff and Leonard Unger. New York: St. Martin's Press, 1991, 133–58.

Branfman, Fred. "Presidential War in Laos, 1964–1970," in *Laos: War and Revolution,* ed. Nina S. Adams and Alfred W. McCoy. New York: Harper Colophon Books, 1970, 213–82.

——— . *Voices from the Plain of Jars: Life under an Air War.* New York: Harper Colophon Books, 1972.

Brown, MacAlister. "Communists in Coalition Government: Lessons from Laos," in *Laos: Beyond the Revolution,* ed. Joseph J. Zasloff and Leonard Unger. New York: St. Martin's Press, 1991, 41–63.

——— . "The Communist Seizure of Power in Laos," in *Contemporary Laos: Studies in the Politics and Society of the Lao People's Democratic Republic,* ed. Martin Stuart-Fox. New York: St. Martin's Press, 1982, 17–38.

Brown, MacAlister, and Joseph J. Zasloff. *Apprentice Revolutionaries: The Communist Movement in Laos, 1930–1985.* Stanford, Calif.: Hoover Institution Press, 1986.

Burchett, Wilfred G. "Pawns and Patriots: The U. S. Fight for Laos," in *Laos: War and Revolution,* ed. Nina S. Adams and Alfred W. McCoy. New York: Harper Colophon Books, 1970, 283–300.

——— . *The Furtive War: The United States in Vietnam and Laos.* New York: International Publishers, 1963.

——— . *The Second Indochina War: Cambodia and Laos* New York: International Publishers, 1970.

Burley, T. M. "Foreign Aid to the Lao People's Democratic Republic," in *Contemporary Laos: Studies in the Politics and Society of the Lao People's Demo-*

cratic Republic, ed. Martin Stuart-Fox. New York: St. Martin's Press, 1982, 129–47.

Cady, John F. *The Roots of French Imperialism in Eastern Asia.* Rev. ed. Ithaca, N.Y.: Cornell University Press, 1967.

Castle, Timothy. *At War in the Shadow of Vietnam: The United States' Military Aids to the Royal Lao Government, 1955–1975.* New York: Columbia University Press, 1993.

Chagnon, Jacqui, and Roger Rumpf. "Education: The Prerequisite to Change in Laos," in *Contemporary Laos: Studies in the Politics and Society of the Lao People's Democratic Republic,* ed. Martin Stuart-Fox. New York: St. Martin's Press, 1982, 163–80.

Champassak, Sisouk Na. *Storm over Laos: A Contemporary History.* New York: Praeger Publishers, 1961.

Chanda, Nayan. "Economic Changes in Laos, 1975–1980," in *Contemporary Laos: Studies in the Politics and Society of the Lao People's Democratic Republic,* ed. Martin Stuart-Fox. New York: St. Martin's Press, 1982, 116–28.

Chiou, C. L. "China's Policy towards Laos: Politics of Neutralization," in *Contemporary Laos: Studies in the Politics and Society of the Lao People's Democratic Republic,* ed. Martin Stuart-Fox. New York: St. Martin's Press, 1982, 291–305.

Christie, C. J. "Nationalism and the Pathet Lao," in *Contemporary Laos: Studies in the Politics and Society of the Lao People's Democratic Republic,* ed. Martin Stuart-Fox. New York: St. Martin's Press, 1982, 62–75.

Decornoy, Jacques. "Life in the Pathet Lao Liberated Zone," in *Laos: War and Revolution,* ed. Nina S. Adams and Alfred W. McCoy. New York: Harper Colophon Books, 1970, 411–23.

Devillers, Philippe. "The Laotian Crisis in Perspective," in *Laos: War and Revolution,* ed. Nina S. Adams and Alfred W. McCoy. New York: Harper Colophon Books, 1970, 37–52.

Dommen, Arthur J. *Conflict in Laos: The Politics of Neutralization.* New York: Praeger Publishers, 1971.

———. "Lao Nationalism and American Policy, 1954–59," in *Laos: Beyond the Revolution,* ed. Joseph J. Zasloff and Leonard Unger. New York: St. Martin's Press, 1991, 243–74.

———. "Laos between Thailand and Vietnam," in *Contemporary Laos: Studies in the Politics and Society of the Lao People's Democratic Republic,* ed. Martin Stuart-Fox. New York: St. Martin's Press, 1982, 306–12.

———. *Laos: Keystone of Indochina.* Boulder, Colo.: Westview Press, 1985.

Dore, Amphay. "The Three Revolutions in Laos," in *Contemporary Laos:*

Studies in the Politics and Society of the Lao People's Democratic Republic, ed. Martin Stuart-Fox. New York: St. Martin's Press, 1982, 101–15.

Duncanson, Dennis J. "The Dependence of Laos," in *Contemporary Laos: Studies in the Politics and Society of the Lao People's Democratic Republic,* ed. Martin Stuart-Fox. New York: St. Martin's Press, 1982, 313–23.

Evans, Grant. *Agrarian Change in Communist Laos.* Singapore: Institute of Southeast Asian Studies, 1988.

———. *Lao Peasants under Socialism.* New Haven: Yale University Press, 1990.

———. "Planning Problems in Peripheral Socialism: The Case of Laos," in *Laos: Beyond the Revolution,* ed. Joseph J. Zasloff and Leonard Unger. New York: St. Martin's Press, 1991, 84–130.

———. *The Yellow Rainmakers: Are Chemical Weapons Being Used in Southeast Asia?* London: Verso, 1983.

Fall, Bernard B. *Anatomy of a Crisis: The Laos Crisis of 1961.* Garden City, N.Y.: Doubleday Books, 1969.

Feingold, David. "Opium and Politics in Laos," in *Laos: War and Revolution,* ed. Nina S. Adams and Alfred W. McCoy. New York: Harper Colophon Books, 1970, 322–39.

Gettleman, Marvin, Susan Gettleman, Lawrence Kaplan, and Carol Kaplan. *Conflict in Indo-China: A Reader on the Widening War in Laos and Cambodia.* New York: Random House, 1970.

Godley, G. McMurtrie, and Jinny St. Goar. "The Chinese Road in Northwest Laos, 1961–73," in *Laos: Beyond the Revolution,* ed. Joseph J. Zasloff and Leonard Unger. New York: St. Martin's Press, 1991, 285–314.

Goldstein, Martin E. *American Policy toward Laos.* Rutherford, N. J.: Farleigh Dickinson University Press, 1973.

Gunn, Geoffrey C. *Rebellion in Laos: Peasant and Politics in a Colonial Backwater.* Boulder, Colo.: Westview Press, 1990.

———. "Theravadins and Commissars: The State and National Identity in Laos," in *Contemporary Laos: Studies in the Politics and Society of the Lao People's Democratic Republic,* ed. Martin Stuart-Fox. New York: St. Martin's Press, 1982, 76–100.

Halpern, Joel M. *Economy and Society of Laos: A Brief Survey.* Southeast Asian Studies Monograph Series, no. 5. New Haven: Yale University, Southeast Asian Studies Program, 1964.

———. *Government, Politics, and Social Structure in Laos: A Study of Tradition and Innovation.* New Haven: Yale University Press, 1964.

Handley, Paul. "Laos: Making Connections," *Far Eastern Economic Review,* November 4, 1993, 28–34.

Hilsman, Roger. *To Move a Nation.* Garden City, N.Y.: Doubleday, 1967, 91–155.

Isaacs, Arnold R., and the editors of Boston Publishing Co. *Pawns of War: Cambodia and Laos.* Boston: Boston Publishing Co., 1987.

Khamsy, Saly. "Relations between Laos and Thailand, 1988," in *Laos: Beyond the Revolution,* ed. Joseph J. Zasloff and Leonard Unger. New York: St. Martin's Press, 1991, 209–13.

Lafont, Pierre-Bernard. "Buddhism in Contemporary Laos," in *Contemporary Laos: Studies in the Politics and Society of the Lao People's Democratic Republic,* ed. Martin Stuart-Fox. New York: St. Martin's Press, 1982, 148–62.

Lambertson, David Floyd. "U.S.–Lao Relations, 1988," in *Laos: Beyond the Revolution,* ed. Joseph J. Zasloff and Leonard Unger. New York: St. Martin's Press, 1991, 315–17.

Langer, Paul F., and Joseph J. Zasloff. *North Vietnam and the Pathet Lao: Partners in the Struggle for Laos.* Cambridge, Mass.: Harvard University Press, 1970.

LeBar, Frank M., and Adrienne Suddard. *Laos: Its People, Its Society, Its Culture.* New Haven: Human Relations Area Files, 1960.

Lee, Gary Y. "Minority Policies and the Hmong," in *Contemporary Laos: Studies in the Politics and Society of the Lao People's Democratic Republic,* ed. Martin Stuart-Fox. New York: St. Martin's Press, 1982, 199–219.

McCoy, Alfred W. "French Colonialism in Laos, 1893–1945," in *Laos: War and Revolution,* ed. Nina S. Adams and Alfred W. McCoy. New York: Harper Colophon Books, 1970, 67–99.

McCoy, Alfred W., with Cathleen B. Reed and Leonard P. Adams II. *The Politics of Heroin in Southeast Asia.* New York: Harper Colophon Books, 1972.

Morehead, Guy. "The Many Languages and Cultures of Laos," in *Laos: War and Revolution,* ed. Nina S. Adams and Alfred W. McCoy. New York: Harper Colophon Books, 1970, 29–34.

Neo Lao Haksat, Central Committee. *A Quarter Century of Grim and Victorious Struggle.* Khang Khay (?), Laos: Central Committee of the Neo Lao Haksat, 1970.

Ng, Shui Meng. "Social Development in the Lao People's Democratic Republic: Problems and Prospects," in *Laos: Beyond the Revolution,* ed. Joseph J. Zasloff and Leonard Unger. New York: St. Martin's Press, 1991, 159–83.

Nguyen, Duy Hinh. *Lam Son 719.* Washington, D. C.: U. S. Army Center of Military History, 1979.

Nolan, Keith William. *Into Laos: The Story of Dewey Canyon II/Lam Son 719.* Novato, Calif.: Presidio Press, 1986.

Pibulsonggram, Pradap. "Comment on the LPDR Statement," in *Laos: Beyond the Revolution,* ed. Joseph J. Zasloff and Leonard Unger. New York: St. Martin's Press, 1991, 213–14.

Porter, D. Gareth. "After Geneva: Subverting Laotian Neutrality," in *Laos: War and Revolution,* ed. Nina S. Adams and Afred W. McCoy. New York: Harper Colophon Books, 1970, 179–212.

Ratnam, Perala. *Laos and the Super Powers.* New Delhi: Tulsi Publishing House, 1980.

Robinson, W. Courtland. "Laotian Refugees in Thailand: The Thai and U.S. Response, 1975 to 1988," in *Laos: Beyond the Revolution,* ed. Joseph J. Zasloff and Leonard Unger. New York: St. Martin's Press, 1991, 215–40.

Sananikone, Oudone, *The Royal Lao Army and U.S. Army Advice and Support.* Washington, D.C.: U.S. Army Center of Military History, 1981.

Santoli, Al. *Forced Back and Forgotten: The Human Rights of Laotian Asylum Seekers.* New York: Lawyers' Committee for Human Rights, 1989.

SarDesai, D. R. *Indian Foreign Policy in Cambodia, Laos, and Vietnam, 1947–1964.* Berkeley and Los Angeles: University of California Press, 1968.

Scott, Peter Dale. "Air America: Flying the U. S. into Laos," in *Laos: War and Revolution,* ed. Nina S. Adams and Alfred W. McCoy. New York: Harper Colophon Books, 1970, 301–21.

Simpson, Charles M. III. *Inside the Green Berets, The First Thirty Years: A History of the U.S. Army Special Forces.* Novato, Calif: Presidio Press, 1983.

Smith, Roger. "Laos," in *Government and Politics of Southeast Asia,* ed. George McTurnan Kahin. Ithaca, N.Y.: Cornell University Press, 1964, 527–92.

Stanton, Shelby L. *Green Berets at War: U.S. Army Special Forces in Southeast Asia, 1956–1975.* Novato, Calif.: Presidio Press, 1985.

Stevens, Richard Lynn. "A History of the Ho Chi Minh Trail and the Role of Nature in the War in Vietnam." Ph.D. diss., University of Hawaii, 1990.

Stevenson, Charles A. *The End of Nowhere: American Policy toward Laos since 1954.* Boston: Beacon Press, 1972.

Stuart-Fox, Martin, ed. *Contemporary Laos: Studies in the Politics and Society of the Lao People's Democratic Republic.* New York: St. Martin's Press, 1982.

———. "Foreign Policy of the Lao People's Democratic Republic," in *Laos: Beyond the Revolution,* ed. Joseph J. Zasloff and Leonard Unger. New York: St. Martin's Press, 1991, 187–208.

————. "Laos at the Crossroads." *Indochina News,* March 1991.

————. *Laos: Politics, Economics and Society.* London: Frances Pinter (Publishers), 1986.

————. "National Defence and Internal Security in Laos," in *Contemporary Laos: Studies in the Politics and Society of the Lao People's Democratic Republic,* ed. Martin Stuart-Fox. New York: St. Martin's Press, 1982, 220–44.

Surachai, Sirikrai. "Thai–American Relations in the Laotian Crisis of 1960–1962." Ph.D. diss., State University of New York, Binghamton, 1980.

Thayer, Carlyle A. "Laos and Vietnam: The Anatomy of a 'Special Relationship,'" in *Contemporary Laos: Studies in the Politics and Society of the Lao People's Democratic Republic,* ed. Martin Stuart-Fox. New York: St. Martin's Press, 1982, 245–73.

Thee, Marek. *Notes of a Witness: Laos and the Second Indochinese War.* New York: Vintage Books, 1973.

Toye, Hugh, *Laos: Buffer State or Battleground.* London: Oxford University Press, 1968.

Tran, Van Dinh. "The Birth of the Pathet Lao Army," in *Laos: War and Revolution,* ed. Nina S. Adams and Alfred W. McCoy. New York: Harper Colophon Books, 1970, 424–38.

Unger, Leonard. "The United States and Laos, 1962–65," in *Laos: Beyond the Revolution,* ed. Joseph J. Zasloff and Leonard Unger. New York: St. Martin's Press, 1991, 275–84.

United Nations Development Program. "The Economy of Laos: An Overview," in *Laos: Beyond the Revolution,* ed. Joseph J. Zasloff and Leonard Unger. New York: St. Martin's Press, 1991, 67–83.

van der Kroef, Justus M. "Laos and Thailand: The Balancing of Conflict and Accommodation," in *Contemporary Laos: Studies in the Politics and Society of the Lao People's Democratic Republic,* ed. Martin Stuart-Fox. New York: St. Martin's Press, 1982, 274–90.

Van-es-Beeck, Bernard J. "Refugees from Laos, 1975–1979," in *Contemporary Laos: Studies in the Politics and Society of the Lao People's Democratic Republic,* ed. Martin Stuart-Fox. New York: St. Martin's Press, 1982, 324–34.

Vongsavanh, Southchay. *RLG Military Operations and Activities in the Laotian Panhandle.* Washington, D.C.: U.S. Army Center of Military History, 1981.

Wekkin, Gary D. "The Rewards of Revolution: Pathet Lao Policy towards the Hill Tribes since 1975," in *Contemporary Laos: Studies in the Politics and Society of the Lao People's Democratic Republic.* New York: St. Martin's Press, 1982, 181–98.

Westermeyer, Joseph. *Poppies, Pipes, and People: Opium and Its Use in Laos.* Berkeley and Los Angeles: University of California Press, 1982.

Whitmore, John K. "The Thai-Vietnamese Struggle for Laos in the Nineteenth Century," in *Laos: War and Revolution,* ed. Nina S. Adams and Alfred W. McCoy. New York: Harper Colophon Books, 1970, 53–66.

Wyatt, David K., ed. *Lao Issara: The Memoirs of Oun Sananikone,* trans. John B. Murdoch and 3264, Southeast Asia Program Data Paper no. 100. Ithaca, N. Y.: Cornell University, Department of Asian Studies, 1975.

Zasloff, Joseph J. *The Pathet Lao: Leadership and Organization.* Lexington, Mass.: Lexington Books, 1973.

———. "Political Constraints on Development in Laos," in *Laos: Beyond the Revolution,* ed. Joseph J. Zasloff and Leonard Unger. New York: St. Martin's Press, 1991, 3–40.

———. "Politics in the New Laos, Part I: Leadership and Change," *American Universities Field Staff Report,* no. 33, 1981.

———. "Politics in the New Laos, Part II: The Party, Political 'Reeducation,' and Vietnamese Influence," *American Universities Field Staff Report,* no. 34, 1981.

———. "The Economy of the New Laos, Part I: The Political Context," *American Universities Field Staff Report,* no. 44, 1981.

———. "The Economy of the New Laos, Part II: Plans and Performance," *American Universities Field Staff Report,* no. 45, 1981.

Zasloff, Joseph J., and Leo Unger, eds. *Laos: Beyond the Revolution.* New York: St. Martin's Press, 1991.

The Hmong in Asia

Aran, Suwanbubpa. *Hill Tribe Development and Welfare Programme in Northern Thailand.* Singapore: Regional Institute of Higher Education and Development, 1976.

Barney, G. Linwood. "The Meo—An Incipient Church," in *Practical Anthropology* 4 (1957): 31–50.

———. "The Meo of Xieng Khouang Province, Laos," in *Southeast Asian Tribes, Minorities, and Nations,* ed. Peter Kunstadter. Princeton: Princeton University Press, 1967, 271–94.

Bernatzik, Hugo Adolf. *Akha and Miao: Problems of Applied Ethnography in Farther India,* trans. Alois Nagler. New Haven: Human Relations Area Files, 1970.

Binney, George A. "Social Structure and Shifting Agriculture of the White Meo: Final Technical Report." Washington, D. C.: Wildlife Management Institute, 1968.

Boyes, Jon, and S. Piraban, comps. *Hmong Voices: Hilltribes of Northern Thailand—A Collection of Interviews with the People of a White Hmong Village in Northern Thailand.* Chiangmai, Thailand: Paisal Printing Co., 1988.

Conquerwood, Dwight. "Health Theatre in a Hmong Refugee Camp: Performance, Communication, and Culture." *Drama Review* 32 (1988): 174–78.

Cooper, Robert G. "The Hmong of Laos: Economic Factors in the Refugee Exodus and Return," in *The Hmong in Transition,* ed. Glenn L. Hendricks, Bruce T. Downing, and Amos S. Deinard. Staten Island, N.Y.: Center for Migration Studies, 1986, 23–40.

———. *Patterns of Work Organization in a Situation of Agricultural Transition: Their Implications for Development Plans in Hmong Opium Producing Villages in Northern Thailand.* Singapore: Institute of Southeast Asian Studies, 1980.

———. *Resource Scarcity and the Hmong Response: Patterns of Settlement and Economy in Transition.* Singapore: Singapore University Press, 1984.

Dunnigan, Timothy. "Processes of Identity Maintenance in Hmong Society," in *The Hmong in Transition,* ed. Glenn L. Hendricks, Bruce T. Downing, and Amos S. Deinard. Staten Island, N.Y.: Center for Migration Studies, 1986, 41–53.

Garrett, W. E. "No Place to Run: The Hmong of Laos," *National Geographic Magazine,* January 1974, 78–111.

———. "Thailand: Refuge from Terror," *National Geographic Magazine,* May 1980, 633–42.

Geddes, William Robert. *Migrants of the Mountains: The Cultural Ecology of the Blue Miao.* Oxford: Clarendon Press, 1976.

Graham, David Crockett. *Songs and Stories of the Ch'uan Miao.* Washington, D.C.: Smithsonian Institution, 1954.

———. *The Tribal Songs and Tales of Ch'uan Miao.* Asian Folklore and Social Life Monographs, vol. 102. Taipei, Republic of China: Chinese Association for Folklore, 1978.

Hamilton-Merritt, Jane. *Tragic Mountains: The Hmong, the Americans, and the Secret Wars for Laos, 1942–1992.* Bloomington: Indiana University Press, 1993.

Keen, Francis G.B. "Ecological Relationships in a Hmong (Meo) Economy," in *Farmers in the Forest,* ed. Peter Kunstadter, E. C. Chapman, and E. C. Sabharsi. Honolulu: University of Hawaii Press, 1978, 210–21.

Kreiger, John. "Still Waging the Vietnam War." *U.S. News and World Report,* September 14, 1992, 48–49.

———. *The Meo of Northwest Thailand: A Southeast Asian Hill Tribe.* Wellington, New Zealand: Government Printing Office, 1966.

Lemoine, Jacques. "Shamanism in the Context of Hmong Settlement," in *The Hmong in Transition,* ed. Glenn L. Hendricks, Bruce T. Downing, and Amos S. Deinard. Staten Island, N.Y.: Center for Migration Studies, 1986, 337–48.

Livo, Norma J., and Dia Cha, comps., *Folk Stories of the Hmong: Peoples of Laos, Thailand, and Vietnam.* Englewood, Colo.: Libraries Unlimited, 1991.

Long, Lynellyn D. "The Floating World: Laotian Refugee Camp Life in Thailand." Ph.D. diss., Stanford University, 1988.

Mickey, Margaret Portia. *The Cowrie Shell Miao of Kweichow.* Papers of the Peabody Museum of American Archaeology and Ethnology, Harvard University, 32:1. Cambridge, Mass.: Peabody Museum, 1947.

Munger, Ronald G. "Sleep Disturbances and Sudden Death of Hmong Refugees: A Report on Fieldwork Conducted in the Ban Vinai Refugee Camp," in *The Hmong in Transition,* ed. Glenn L. Hendricks, Bruce T. Downing, and Amos S. Deinard. Staten Island, N.Y.: Center for Migration Studies, 1986, 379–98.

Olney, Douglas P. *A Bibliography of the Hmong (Miao) of Southeast Asia and the Hmong Refugees in the United States.* Minneapolis: University of Minnesota, Center for Urban and Regional Affairs, Southeast Asian Refugee Studies Project, 1983.

Quincey, Keith. *Hmong: History of a People.* Cheney: Eastern Washington University Press, 1988.

Richburg, Keith B. "Insurgency in Laos Seeking to Emerge from Anonymity." *Washington Post,* February 11, 1990.

Rosett, Claudia. "A Lonely Lao Fight for Freedom." *Wall Street Journal,* June 13, 1990.

Schein, Louisa. "The Miao in Contemporary China: A Preliminary Overview," in *The Hmong in Transition,* ed. Glenn L. Hendricks, Bruce T. Downing, and Amos S. Deinard. Staten Island, N.Y.: Center for Migration Studies, 1986, 73–85.

Smalley, William A. "Stages of Hmong Cultural Adaptation," in *The Hmong in Transition,* ed. Glenn L. Hendricks, Bruce T. Downing, and Amos S. Deinard. Staten Island, N.Y.: Center for Migration Studies, 1986, 7–22.

Symonds, Patricia Veronica. "Cosmology and the Cycle of Life: Hmong

Views of Birth, Death, and Gender in a Mountain Village in Northern Thailand." Ph.D. diss., Brown University, 1991.

Tapp, Nicholas. "Geomancy as an Aspect of Upland–Lowland Relationships," in *The Hmong in Transition,* ed. Glenn L. Henricks, Bruce T. Downing, and Amos S. Deinard. Staten Island, N.Y.: Center for Migration Studies, 1986, 87–95.

————. *The Hmong of Thailand: Opium People of the Golden Triangle.* London: Anti-Slavery Society; Cambridge, Mass.: Cultural Survival, Inc., 1986.

————. "Hmong Religion." *Asian Folklore Studies* 48 (1989): 59–94.

————. "The Impact of Missionary Christianity upon Marginalized Ethnic Minorities: The Case of the Hmong." *Journal of Southeast Asian Studies* 29 (1989): 70–95.

————. *Sovereignty and Rebellion: The White Hmong of Northern Thailand.* New York: Oxford University Press, 1989.

Thao, Xoua. "Hmong Perceptions of Illness and Traditional Ways of Health," in *The Hmong in Transition,* ed. Glenn L. Hendricks, Bruce T. Downing, and Amos S. Deinard. Staten Island, N.Y.: Center for Migration Studies, 1986, 365–78.

Vang, Pao. *Against All Odds: The Laotian Freedom Fighters.* Washington, D. C.: Heritage Foundation, 1987.

Yang, Dao. "Why Did the Hmong Leave Laos?" in *The Hmong in the West: Observations and Reports,* ed. Bruce T. Downing and Douglas P. Olney. Minneapolis: University of Minnesota, Center for Urban and Regional Affairs, Southeast Asian Refugee Studies Project, 1982, 3–18.

The Hmong in the United States

Adler, Shelley R. "The Role of the Nightmare in Hmong Sudden Unexpected Nocturnal Death Syndrome: A Folkloristic Study of Belief and Health." Ph.D. diss., University of California, Los Angeles, 1991.

————. "Sudden Unexpected Norturnal Death Syndrome among Hmong Immigrants: Examining the Role of the Nightmare." *Journal of American Folklore* 104 (1991): 54–71.

Bishop, Kent A. "The Hmong of Central California: An Investigation and Analysis of the Changing Family Structure during Liminality, Acculturation and Transition." Ed.D. diss., University of San Francisco, 1985.

Bliatout, Bruce Thowpaou. "Guidelines for Mental Health Professionals to Help Hmong Clients Seek Traditional Healing Treatment," in *The Hmong in Transition,* ed. Glenn L. Hendricks, Bruce T. Downing, and Amos S. Deinard. Staten Island, N.Y.: Center for Migration Studies, 1986, 349–63.

———. *Hmong Sudden Unexpected Nocturnal Death Syndrome: A Cultural Study.* Portland, Oreg.: Sparkle Publishing Enterprises, 1983.

Brigham Young University, Language Research Center. *The Indochinese: New Americans.* Provo, Utah: Brigham Young University, Language Research Center, in cooperation with Salt Lake City: Utah State Office of Education, Curriculum and Instruction Division, 1981.

Calderon, Eddie. "The Impact of Indochinese Resettlement on the Phillips and Elliot Park Neighborhoods in South Minneapolis," in *The Hmong in the West: Observations and Reports,* ed. Bruce T. Downing and Douglas P. Olney. Minneapolis: University of Minnesota, Center for Urban and Regional Affairs, Southeast Asian Refugee Studies Project, 1982, 367–86.

Cerquone, Joseph. *Refugees from Laos: In Harm's Way.* Washington, D.C.: U. S. Committee for Refugees, 1986.

Chan, Anthony. *Hmong Textile Designs.* Owings Mills, Md.: Stemmer House, ca. 1990.

Chan, Sucheng. "Hmong Voices," in *New Visions in Asian American Studies: Diversity, Community, Power,* ed. Franklin Ng. Pullman: Washington State University Press, forthcoming.

Dewhurst, C. Kurt, and Marsha MacDowell, eds. *Michigan Hmong Arts: Textiles in Transition.* Publications of the Museum Folk Arts Series, vol. 3, no. 2. East Lansing: Michigan State University, Folk Arts Division, 1984.

Donnelly, Nancy Dorelle. "The Changing Lives of Refugee Hmong Women." Ph.D. diss., University of Washington, 1989.

———. "Factors Contributing to a Split Within a Clientelistic Needlework Cooperative Engaged in Refugee Resettlement," in *The Hmong in Transition,* ed. Glenn L. Hendricks, Bruce T. Downing, and Amos S. Deinard. Staten Island, N.Y.: Center for Migration Studies, 1986, 159–73.

Downing, Bruce T., and Douglas P. Olney, eds. *The Hmong in the West: Observations and Reports.* Minneapolis: University of Minnesota, Center for Urban and Regional Affairs, Southeast Asian Refugee Studies Project, 1982.

Dunnigan, Timothy. "Segmentary Kinship in an Urban Society: The Hmong of St. Paul-Minneapolis." *Anthropological Quarterly* 55:3 (1982), 126–34.

Everingham, John. "One Family's Odyssey to America." *National Geographic Magazine,* May 1980, 643–60.

Fass, Simon. "Innovations in the Struggle for Self-Reliance: The Hmong Experience in the United States." *International Migration Review* 20 (1986), 351–80.

Finck, John. "Clan Leadership in the Hmong Community of Providence, Rhode Island," in *The Hmong in the West: Observations and Reports,* ed. Bruce T. Downing and Douglas P. Olney. Minneapolis: University of Minnesota, Center for Urban and Regional Affairs, Southeast Asian Refugee Studies Project, 1982, 21–28.

Goldfarb, Mace. *Fighters, Refugees, Immigrants: A Story of the Hmong.* Minneapolis: Carolrhoda Books, 1982.

Goldstein, Beth L. "Resolving Sexual Assault: Hmong and the American Legal System," in *The Hmong in Transition,* ed. Glenn L. Hendricks, Bruce T. Downing, and Amos S. Deinard. Staten Island, N.Y.: Center for Migration Studies, 1986, 135–43.

———. "Schooling for Cultural Transitions: Hmong Girls and Boys in American High Schools." Ph.D. diss., University of Wisconsin, Madison, 1985.

Gross, Catherine Stoumpos. "The Hmong in Isla Vista: Obstacles and Enhancements to Adjustment," in *The Hmong in Transition,* ed. Glenn L. Henricks, Bruce T. Downing, and Amos S. Deinard. Staten Island, N.Y.: Center for Migration Studies, 1986, 145–57.

Hayes, Christopher L. "A Study of the Older Hmong Refugees in the United States." Ph.D. diss., The Fielding Institute, Santa Barbara, 1984.

Hayes, Christopher L., and Richard A. Kalish, "Death-Related Experiences and Funerary Practices of the Hmong Refugees in the United States." *Omega: Journal of Death and Dying* 16 (1987–88): 63–70.

Hendricks, Glenn L., Robert T. Downing, and Amos S. Deinard, eds. *The Hmong in Transition.* Staten Island, N.Y.: Center for Migration Studies, 1986.

Hendricks, Glenn L., and Brad Richardson. "Hmong in the Workplace," in *The Hmong in the West: Observations and Reports,* ed. Bruce T. Downing and Douglas P. Olney. Minneapolis: University of Minnesota, Center for Urban and Regional Affairs, Southeast Asian Refugee Studies Project, 1982, 387–401.

Hirayama, Hisashi, and Kasumi K. Hirayama. "Stress, Social Supports, and Adaptational Patterns in Hmong Refugee Families." *Amerasia Journal* 14:1 (1988), 93–108.

Howard, Katsuyo K. *Passages: An Anthology of the Southeast Asian Refugee Experience.* Fresno: California State University, Fresno: Southeast Asian Student Services, 1990.

Hmong Art: Tradition and Change. Sheboygan, Wis.: John Michael Kohler Arts Center, 1986.

Hurlich, Marshall. "Rural Hmong Population in Western Washington State: The Consequences of Migration for Nutritional Status and Growth," in *The Hmong in the West: Observations and Reports,* ed. Bruce T. Downing and Douglas P. Olney. Minneapolis: University of Minnesota, Center for Urban and Regional Affairs, Southeast Asian Refugee Studies Project, 1982, 320–52.

Ikeda, J. P., et al. "Food Habits of the Hmong Living in Central California." *Journal of Nutritional Education* 23 (1991): 168–75.

Irby, Charles C., and Ernest Pon. "Confronting New Mountains: Mental Health Problems among Male Hmong and Mien Refugees." *Amerasia Journal* 14:1 (1988): 109–18.

Jacobs, Lila. "Differential Participation and Skill Levels in Four Hmong Third Grade Students: The Social and Cultural Context of Teaching and Learning." Ph.D. diss., University of California, Santa Barbara, 1987.

Janssens, Luc G. "The Integration of Hmong Adults into American Society through the Community College: A Participatory Study of the Possibilities of Cultural Preservation." Ed.D. diss., University of San Francisco, 1987.

Ju, Cerhan. "The Hmong in the United States: An Overview for Mental Health Professionals." *Journal of Counseling and Development* 69 (1990): 88–92.

Kirton, Elizabeth Stewart. "The Locked Medicine Cabinet: Hmong Health Care in America." Ph.D. diss., University of California, Santa Barbara, 1985.

LaRue, Michele. "Stress and Coping of the Indochinese Refugees in a California Community." Ph.D. diss., United States International University, San Diego, 1982.

Lee, Pao. "Health Care System Utilized by the Hmong in California: A Case Study in Stanislaus County." M.A. thesis, California State University, Stanislaus, 1991.

Lemieux, Renee E. "A Study of the Adaptation of Hmong First, Second, and Third Graders to the Minneapolis Public Schools." Ph.D. diss., University of Minnesota, 1985.

Loescher, Gil, and John A. Scanlan. *Calculated Kindness: Refugees and America's Half-Open Door, 1945–Present.* New York: Free Press, 1986.

Lopez-Romano, Sylvia Silva. "Integration of Community and Learning among Southeast Asian Newcomer Hmong Parents and Children." Ed.D. diss., University of San Francisco, 1991.

MacDowell, Marsha, ed. *Hmong Folk Arts: A Guide for Teachers*. East Lansing: Michigan State University Museum, 1988.

McGinn, Finian. "Hmong Literacy among Hmong Adolescents and the Use of Hmong Literacy during Resettlement." Ed.D. diss., University of San Francisco, 1989.

McInnis, Kathleen M. "Ethnic-Sensitive Work with Hmong Refugee Children." *Child Welfare* 70 (1991): 571–80.

McInnis, Kathleen M., Helen E. Petracchi, and Mel Morgenbesser. *The Hmong in America: Providing Ethnic-Sensitive Health, Education, and Human Services*. Dubuque, Iowa: Kendall/Hunt Publishing Co., 1990.

Mason, Sarah R. "Training Hmong Women for Marginal Work or Entry into the Mainstream," in *The Hmong in Transition*, ed. Glenn L. Hendricks, Bruce T. Downing, and Amos S. Deinard. Staten Island, N.Y.: Center for Migration Studies, 1986, 101–20.

Meredith, William Hugh. "Level and Correlates of Perceived Quality of Life for Lao Hmong Refugees in Nebraska." Ph.D. diss., University of Nebraska, Lincoln, 1983.

Meredith, William, and Sheran Cramer. "Hmong Refugees in Nebraska," in *The Hmong in the West: Observations and Reports*, ed. Bruce T. Downing and Dougals P. Olney. Minneapolis: University of Minnesota, Center for Urban and Regional Affairs, Southeast Asian Refugee Studies Project, 1982, 353–59.

Meredith, William Hugh, and George P. Rowe. "Changes in Lao Hmong Marital Attitudes after Immigrating to the United States." *Journal of Comparative Family Studies* 17 (1986): 117–26.

Meyers, C. "Hmong Children and Their Families: Consideration of Cultural Influences in Assessment." *American Journal of Occupational Therapy* 46 (1992): 737–44.

Miller, Collette L. "Some Contextual Problems Relative to the Acquisition of Literacy by Hmong Refugees." M.A. thesis, California State University, Long Beach, 1991.

Moore, David L. "Between Cultures: Oral History of Hmong Teenagers in Minneapolis." *Vietnam Generation* 2:3 (1990): 38–52.

———. *Dark Sky, Dark Land: Stories of the Hmong Boy Scouts of Troop 100*. Eden Prairie, Minn.: Tessera Publishers, 1989.

Munger, Ronald. "Sudden Adult Death in Asian Populations: The Case of the Hmong," in *The Hmong in the West: Observations and Reports*, ed. Bruce T. Downing and Douglas P. Olney. Minneapolis: University of Minnesota, Center for Urban and Regional Affairs, Southeast Asian Refugee Studies Project, 1982, 307–19.

Northwest Regional Educational Laboratory, Literacy and Language Program. *The Hmong Resettlement Study.* Washington, D.C.: U.S. Department of Health and Human Services, Office of Refugee Resettlement, 1984.

———. *The Hmong Resettlement Study: Final Report.* Washington, D.C.: U.S. Department of Health and Human Services, Office of Refugee Resettlement, 1985.

———. *The Hmong Resettlement Study: Site Report.* Washington, D.C.: U.S. Department of Health and Human Services, Office of Refugee Resettlement, 1984.

Numrich, Charles H. *Living Tapestries.* Lima, Ohio: Fairway Press, 1985.

Ostergren, Joan Caryl. "Relationship among English Performances, Self-Efficacy, Anxiety, and Depression for Hmong Refugees." Ph.D. diss., University of Minnesota, 1991.

Peterson, Sally Nina. "From the Heart and the Mind: Creating *Paj Ntaub* in the Context of Community." Ph.D. diss., University of Pennsylvania, 1990.

———. "Translating Experience and the Reading of a Story Cloth." *Journal of American Folklore* 101 (1988): 6–22.

Potter, Gayle S., and Alice Whiren. "Traditional Hmong Birth Customs: A Historical Study," in *The Hmong in the West: Observations and Reports,* ed. Bruce T. Downing and Douglas P. Olney. Minneapolis: University of Minnesota, Center for Urban and Regional Affairs, Southeast Asian Refugee Studies Project, 1982, 48–62.

Rairdan, B., and Z. R. Higgs. "When Your Patient Is a Hmong Refugee." *American Journal of Nursing* 92 (1992): 52–55.

Rick, Kathryn. "An Investigation of the Process of Biculturation with Hmong Refugees." Ph.D. diss., University of Colorado, 1988.

Rick, Kathryn, and John Forward. "Acculturation and Perceived Intergenerational Differences among Hmong Youth." *Journal of Cross-Cultural Psychology* 23 (1992): 85–94.

Schein, Louisa. "Control of Contrast: Lao-Hmong Refugees in American Contexts," in *People in Upheaval,* ed. Scott M. Morgan and Elizabeth Colson. Staten Island, N.Y.: Center for Migration Studies, 1987, 88–107.

Scott, George M., Jr. "The Advent of a Cottage Industry of Hmong Paj Ntaub Textiles in Southern California: The Roles of an Entrepreneur-Patron, an Applied Anthropologist-Broker, and a Shopping Mall Sale." *Human Organization* 51 (1992): 284–98.

———. "To Catch or Not to Catch a Thief: A Case of Bride Theft among the Lao Hmong Refugees in Southern California." *Ethnic Groups* 7 (1988): 137–51.

———. "The Hmong Refugee Community in San Diego: Theoretical and Practical Implications of Its Continuing Ethnic Solidarity." *Anthropological Quarterly* 55:3 (1982): 146–60.

———. "The Lao Hmong Refugees in San Diego: Their Religious Transformation and Its Implications for Geertz' Thesis." *Ethnic Studies Report* 5:2 (1987): 32–46.

———. "Migrants without Mountains: The Politics of Sociocultural Adjustment among the Lao Hmong Refugees in San Diego." Ph.D. diss., University of California, San Diego, 1986.

———. "A New Year in a New Land: Religious Change among the Hmong Refugees in San Diego," in *The Hmong in the West: Observations and Reports,* ed. Bruce T. Downing and Douglas P. Olney. Minneapolis: University of Minnesota, Center for Urban and Regional Affairs, Southeast Asian Refugee Studies Project, 1982, 63–85.

Sherman, Spencer. "The Hmong in America: Laotian Refugees in the 'Land of the Giants.'" *National Geographic Magazine,* October 1988, 586–610.

Simensen, Thordis. *Flower Cloth of the Hmong.* Denver: Denver Museum of Natural History, 1985.

Smith, J. Christina, comp. *The Hmong: An Annotated Bibliography, 1983–1987.* Minneapolis: University of Minnesota, Center for Urban and Regional Affairs, Southeast Asian Refugee Studies Project, 1987.

Sonsala, Donald Richard. "A Comparative Case Study of Secondary Programs for Hmong Refugee Students in the Minneapolis and St. Paul Public Schools." Ph.D. diss., University of Minnesota, 1984.

Spring, Marline A. "Ethnopharmacologic Analysis of Medicinal Plants Used by Laotian Hmong Refugees in Minnesota." *Journal of Ethnopharmacology* 26 (1989): 65–91.

Strouse, Joan. "Continuing Themes in U.S. Educational Policy for Immigrants and Refugees: The Hmong Experience." Ph.D. diss., University of Wisconsin, Madison, 1985.

———. "The Reformation of Culture: Hmong Refugees from Laos." *Journal of Refugee Studies* 1 (1988): 20–37.

Thao, Cheu. "Hmong Migration and Leadership in Laos and in the United States," in *The Hmong in the West: Observations and Reports,* ed. Bruce T. Downing and Douglas P. Olney. Minneapolis: University of Minnesota, Center for Urban and Regional Affairs, Southeast Asian Refugee Studies Project, 1982, 99–121.

Thao, Paja. *I Am a Shaman: A Hmong Life Story with Ethnographic Commentary.* Dwight Conquerwood, ethnographer; Paja Thao, shaman; Xa Thao, translator. Minneapolis: University of Minnesota, Center for Urban and Regional Affairs, Southeast Asian Refugee Studies Project, 1989.

Tobin, Joseph I., and Joan Friedman. "Spirits, Shamans, and Nightmare Death: Survival Stress in a Hmong Refugee." *American Journal of Orthopsychiatry* 53 (1983): 439–48.

Trueba, Henry T., Lila Jacobs, and Elizabeth Kirton. *Cultural Conflict and Adaptation: The Case of Hmong Children in American Society.* New York: Falmer Press, 1990.

Ukapatayasakul, Banjerd Bill. "Hmong Refugee Economic Adjustment in a California Community." Ph.D. diss., United States International University, San Diego, 1983.

Vang, Chia Koua, Gnia Yee Yang, and William A. Smalley. *The Life of Shong Lue Yang: Hmong "Mother of Writing."* Minneapolis: University of Minnesota, Center for Urban and Regional Affairs, Southeast Asian Refugee Studies Project, 1990.

Vang, Kao. "Hmong Marriage Customs: A Current Assessment," in *The Hmong in the West: Observations and Reports,* ed. Bruce T. Downing and Douglas P. Olney. Minneapolis: University of Minnesota, Center for Urban and Regional Affairs, Southeast Asian Refugee Studies Project, 1982, 29–45.

Vang, Pobzeb. *The Politics of Hmong Organizations in America.* Denver: Hmong Council Education Committee, 1990.

Viviano, Frank. "Strangers in the Promised Land." *San Francisco Examiner Image Magazine,* August 31, 1986, 13–21, 36.

Walker, Wendy Dianne. "The Challenges of the Hmong Culture: A Study of Teacher, Counselor and Administrator Training in a Time of Changing Demographics." Ed.D. diss., Harvard University, 1989.

Weinstein-Shr, Gail. "From Mountaintops to City Streets: An Ethnographic Investigation of Literacy and Social Process among the Hmong of Philadelphia." Ph.D. diss., University of Pennsylvania, 1986.

Westermeyer, Joseph, A. Callies, and J. Neider. "Welfare Status and Psychosocial Adjustment among 100 Hmong Refugees." *Journal of Nervous and Mental Disease* 178 (1990): 300–306.

Willcox, Donald J. *Hmong Folk Life.* Penland: Hmong Natural Association of North Carolina, 1986.

Yang, May. "The Education of Hmong Women." *Vietnam Generation* 2:3 (1990), 62–87.

Notes on the Editor and
Transcribers/Translators

The student transcribers, 1993 (*left to right*), Lee Fang, Vu Pao Tcha, Maijue Xiong, and Thek Moua.

SUCHENG CHAN is Professor and Chairperson of Asian American Studies at the University of California, Santa Barbara. She has published eight books and numerous articles. The recipient of a Distinguished Teaching Award from the University of California, Berkeley, in 1978, she has also won seven awards for her scholarly writings. She has held postdoctoral fellowships from the National Endowment for the Humanities, the Institute of American Cultures at UCLA, and the John Simon Guggenheim Memorial Foundation.

LEE FANG graduated in December 1993 with a degree in Law and Society from the University of California, Santa Barbara. He plans to go to law school after working for a few years. He was a member of the Asian Pacific American Student Union and the Asian American Law Club and was a cofounder of the Hmong Club at the University of California, Santa Barbara.

THEK MOUA graduated in June 1993 with a degree in biological sciences from the University of California, Santa Barbara. After working for a few years, he hopes to go to graduate school to study pharmacology. He was a cofounder of the Hmong Club at the University of California, Santa Barbara, and is treasurer of the Youth Board of the Lao Evangelical Church.

VU PAO TCHA is a senior majoring in French at the University of California, Santa Barbara. He plans to get a Master of Arts in Teaching degree and then teach high school French. A cofounder of the Hmong Club at the University of California, Santa Barbara, he is presently serving as its community representative.

MAIJUE XIONG is a junior majoring in sociology at the University of California, Santa Barbara. After graduation, she hopes to join the U.S. Peace Corps and teach English in a refugee camp in Thailand. She is a member of the Asian Culture Committee and a cofounder of the Hmong Club at the University of California, Santa Barbara.

Also in the series

Sucheng Chan, ed.,
*Entry Denied: Exclusion and the Chinese Community
in America, 1882–1943*

Gary Y. Okihiro,
Cane Fires: The Anti-Japanese Movement in Hawaii, 1865–1945

Karen Isaksen Leonard,
Making Ethnic Choices: California's Punjabi Mexican Americans

Yen Le Espiritu,
Asian American Panethnicity: Bridging Institutions and Identities

Shirley Geok-lin Lim and Amy Ling, eds.,
Reading the Literatures of Asian America

Velina Hasu Houston, ed.,
The Politics of Life: Four Plays by Asian American Women

Renqiu Yu,
*To Save China, To Save Ourselves:
The Chinese Hand Laundry Alliance of New York*

William Wei,
The Asian American Movement

Timothy P. Fong,
*The First Suburban Chinatown:
The Remaking of Monterey Park, California*

Chris Friday,
*Organizing Asian American Labor:
The Pacific Coast Canned-Salmon Industry, 1870–1942*